The Nature of Biblical Criticism

The Nature of Biblical Criticism

John Barton

Westminster John Knox Press
LOUISVILLE • LONDON

Book design by Sharon Adams
Cover design by Night & Day Design

First edition
Published by Westminster John Knox Press
Louisville, Kentucky

This book is printed on acid-free paper that meets the American National Standards Institute Z39.48 standard. ∞

PRINTED IN THE UNITED STATES OF AMERICA

08 09 10 11 12 13 14 15 16 — 10 9 8 7 6 5 4 3 2

Library of Congress Cataloging-in-Publication Data

Barton, John.
    The nature of biblical criticism / John Barton.—1st ed.
        p. cm.
    Includes bibliographical references and index.
    ISBN 978-0-664-22587-2 (alk. paper)
    1. Bible—Criticism, interpretation, etc.   I. Title.
    BS511.3.B37 2007
    220.601—dc22   2007001537

For James Barr, In Memoriam

Contents

Foreword

The core of this book consists of the Croall Lectures, delivered in the University of Edinburgh in September 2005. I am very grateful to my hosts in New College for their great hospitality and for many stimulating discussions.

The idea for the book, however, goes back more than twenty years. In 1984 I wrote a paper called "What Makes Biblical Criticism Critical?" in which many of the essential points of the discussion are already sketched. The paper was intended for a conference in Jerusalem, but a back injury prevented my attending; it was subsequently delivered at the University of Sheffield and at King's College London. Of course I have done a lot of thinking about the subject since then, and this book is the result of material that has accumulated in my files and my head over the intervening period.

A major stimulus for my thinking was James Barr's article "Bibelkritik als theologische Aufklärung,"[1] published in 1982, and his fuller treatment of related issues the following year in *Holy Scripture: Canon, Authority, Criticism*.[2] The present book is in many ways little more than an attempt to develop and spell out in detail points he makes in those two publications. My debt to him over the years has been very great. Contrary to what is sometimes thought, I was never his student in the literal sense, but there is no one from whom I have learned more about the study of the Bible and its place in theology. It is a great pleasure and privilege to dedicate this book to his memory in gratitude and affection.

1. James Barr, "Bibelkritik als theologische Aufklärung," in *Glaube und Toleranz: Das theologische Erbe der Aufklärung*, ed. T. Rendtorff (Gütersloh: Mohn, 1982), 30–42.
2. James Barr, *Holy Scripture: Canon, Authority, Criticism* (Oxford: Oxford University Press, 1983).

Other debts of gratitude must also be mentioned. My teacher in Old Testament studies and doctoral supervisor was John Austin Baker, then chaplain of Corpus Christi College, Oxford, subsequently canon of Westminster and then bishop of Salisbury, and it is from him that I first learned how to read the Bible critically. I must also mention Rudolf Smend, emeritus professor for Old Testament in the University of Göttingen, whose many essential works on the history of biblical studies I have plundered, as will be seen from the numerous citations, and who has also been highly supportive of this and my other projects. Translations from Smend's books, like most other translations from German sources, are usually my own, sometimes even when a published translation already exists.

Some of the reading for the book was done in the University of Bonn while I was Europaeum visiting professor there for a short period in 2005, and I thank my host, Michael Wolter, professor for New Testament, for all his help and hospitality. For the most part, however, I have found the books I needed in Oxford, in the Bodleian Library, the library of the Oriental Institute, and above all in the Theology Faculty Library, where I should like to thank Kate Alderson-Smith, the librarian, and her assistants for their constant helpfulness. I am also grateful to the Theology Faculty Board in Oxford for granting me some sabbatical leave, without which it would have been hard to bring the project to completion.

Finally, thanks to Westminster John Knox Press, and particularly to Philip Law, for accepting the book for publication and working with me on its preparation.

Though New Testament study is not ignored, I am of course an Old Testament specialist, and the book inevitably has an Old Testament slant. I am sure that a New Testament scholar would have written a different book, though I hope the arguments will be felt to apply to the discipline of biblical criticism in general.

John Barton
Oriel College, Oxford
December 2006

1

Introduction

A QUESTION OF DEFINITION

The term "biblical criticism" is now somewhat outmoded. It is common to speak of "biblical studies" and of "biblical interpretation," but for the older term "biblical criticism" it has become more usual to say "the historical-critical method" (occasionally "historico-critical"). As will become clear later, I have reservations about building a historical quest into the very name of the discipline and for that reason prefer the older name.[1] But biblical criticism may in any case be used to mean one of a number of things, and at the outset we should be clear what we are and what we are not talking about.

Biblical criticism could be used, like "literary criticism" in the world of secular literary studies, as the name for any mode of study of the Bible. "Literary criticism" tends to be used to identify all study of and comment on literature: it is not a branch of literary study, but in effect simply another name for it. With whatever philosophy it operates ("New Critical," practical-critical, structuralist, postmodern, etc.), any intellectual study of literature is a form of literary criticism. One may speak freely of ancient literary criticism (Aristotle, Longinus), of medieval literary criticism, or of nineteenth-century literary criticism. On the whole, however, the term biblical criticism has not functioned in a similar way to denote all study of the Bible. It would have sounded slightly odd if Beryl Smalley's famous book *The Study of the Bible in the Middle Ages*[2] had been called instead *The Criticism of the Bible in the Middle*

---

1. Thus also James Barr, "Bibelkritik als theologische Aufklärung," in *Glaube und Toleranz: Das theologische Erbe der Aufklärung,* ed. T. Rendtorff (Gütersloh: Mohn, 1982), 30–42.
2. Beryl Smalley, *The Study of the Bible in the Middle Ages* (Oxford: Basil Blackwell, 1941).

Ages, probably creating an impression that she was writing about medieval attacks on the Bible. (We shall see that some do indeed see hostility implied in the term, even today.) Whereas we freely use the term literary criticism to cover both Aristotle's *Poetics* and the *Times Literary Supplement*, we do not normally talk (for example) of patristic or medieval biblical criticism, but reserve the term for more modern studies (usually those since the Enlightenment). I believe it would be very useful if we could use biblical criticism as the equivalent, in the study of the Bible, of literary criticism, but I do not think this is likely to establish itself. Biblical criticism means a particular *type* of study of the Bible, rather than referring to all biblical studies as such. Accordingly people say that this or that ancient writer "anticipated the conclusions of biblical criticism," rather than saying that he was actually a "biblical critic." And very often the term is used evaluatively, whether for good or ill.

Another use of the term is as the name of one particular *branch* of biblical studies. In this use, it is more or less equivalent to what is commonly known, in a technical sense of the word, as "Introduction" (German *Einleitungswissenschaft*): the study of questions to do with the date, authorship, and stratification of the various biblical books. This is how biblical criticism is defined in the *Oxford English Dictionary*, s.v. "criticism": "The critical science which deals with the text, character, composition, and origin of literary documents, esp. those of the Old and New Testaments." One may thus decide to describe as "critical" those studies of the Bible that are concerned with matters of Introduction, by contrast with works on biblical theology, or the history of Israel or the church, or indeed exegesis of the individual books. Again, however, it may be doubted whether it is only questions of Introduction that come to mind when a scholar is said to practice biblical criticism. It is indeed part of the anticritical case among some that biblical scholars have devoted far too much time to these questions; but most commonly this attack is related to the fact that many such scholars have come to untraditional conclusions, especially about authorship. "Critical scholarship" does not, for most people, *mean* scholarship that concentrates only on matters of Introduction. It denotes a particular style of biblical study. The contrast is not with exegesis or theology or history, but with an anticritical, precritical, or postcritical approach.

It is biblical criticism in this sense—biblical study embodying a critical stance—that this book is concerned with. What is it, we shall ask, that makes biblical criticism "critical"? Most readers will have a clear idea in their minds of books on the Bible that are "critical," and of others that are not: on an ostensive definition there would probably be widespread agreement. But what criteria do we use in making this judgment? To many, the answer to this question is obvious—though different answers seem obvious to different people. It will be necessary to discuss these "obvious" criteria in considerable detail. We shall find that most of them, though they cover some of what is going on in the practice of a critical study of the Bible, will not account for it without remainder, and that exclusive attention to them alone distorts how we see the enterprise. A great deal of ground clearing is thus needed, but along the way many insights will emerge.

To cut a long story short, I shall argue that biblical criticism comes down to attention to the plain meaning of the biblical text. This will seem to some an anodyne conclusion, to others hopelessly naive. Rather like a mathematician covering many pages with calculations in order to show that a theorem is in fact self-evident, I shall have to spend a great deal of detailed discussion to show that such an apparently banal conclusion holds—and that, in reality, it is not banal at all, but pregnant with many exciting possibilities for biblical scholarship. We shall have to establish what is *not* meant by the "plain" sense, as well as what is, to avoid misunderstanding. That will lead us into current debates about literary theory and hermeneutics.

POSSIBLE MODELS

Most biblical scholars probably have their own (perhaps unstated) definitions of what constitutes biblical criticism, and these will have to be discussed at some length.

A first approach, surveyed in chapter 2, sees the critical spirit as consisting in the observation that the text contains difficulties. These may be at the textual level, or may consist of inconsistencies between different books or within particular books. Thus one may say that anyone who notices such difficulties is at least inchoately a biblical critic. On that basis it could not be said that criticism began with the Enlightenment, since difficulties in the text have been noted since very ancient times. Origen, Augustine, and some medieval Jewish writers would qualify as critics. Criticism here is understood to be any attempt to deal rationally with such difficulties.

Secondly, one may follow the now common substitution of the term "historical-critical method" for the older expression "biblical criticism" and argue accordingly that the essence of criticism lies in a concern for historical truth. This is the subject of chapter 3. According to this view, critics are Bible readers whose primary concern is for history, understood as discoverable through a historical method shared with "secular" historians. The rise of biblical criticism is thus the increasing domination of biblical study by historical concerns and by secular methods of satisfying them. Alternatively, it may be said that critics work to establish the historical meaning of the text, "what it meant" rather than "what it means," in Krister Stendahl's famous expression.[3] The contention that biblical criticism is essentially a matter of method is also discussed, and an attempt made to show that this is an unsatisfactory idea, which does less than justice to the concern for empathetic understanding that has been basic to critical study.

Thirdly, it may be argued that criticism focuses on a particular kind of textual meaning. In chapter 4 I examine some possible candidates for this, looking in turn at the original sense, the intended sense, the historical sense, and the literal sense. All capture something that has been true of some biblical criticism. But my contention will be that none of them succeeds in defining the essential nature of the biblical-critical enterprise, since counterexamples to them all can also be found. Where they are true as accounts of biblical criticism, they are true *per accidens*, not because they capture what truly makes criticism critical. My own preference is to say that biblical criticism is concerned with the *plain* sense, but this is a contested term, and needs considerable justification. I argue for an intimate connection between criticism and semantics, and try to show that it is essentially a linguistic and literary operation.

Fourthly, it is impossible to discuss criticism without having some idea of its historical origins. Though this book is not a history of criticism but is analytical in its intentions, it is necessary to examine the development of the art of biblical criticism in a historical perspective. The fact that my discussion somewhat redefines what is meant by biblical criticism means that it may look for its origins in different places from those of other scholars who have worked on the history of criticism. This turns out to be the case, and in chapter 5 I stress the importance of Renaissance, classical, and patristic sources, playing down the traditional association of criticism with the Enlightenment and, to a lesser extent, with the Reformation.

Finally, there are those who regard biblical criticism as essentially an attack on the authority or integrity of the Bible. Criticism is here regarded as being used in its everyday sense of "hostile evaluation." Once it may have been possible for critical scholars to treat anyone who accused them of hostility to the Bible as simply a "fundamentalist." This is certainly not possible today. Now some very sophisticated accounts of how we should read the Bible regard the operations usually known as critical as at best of very limited value. Critics, it is suggested, may not intend to damage the Bible or its standing, but their work has had that effect. What we should be doing is to discover a postcritical mode

---

3. Krister Stendahl, "Biblical Theology, Contemporary," in *The Interpreter's Dictionary of the Bible*, 4 vols. (Nashville: Abingdon Press, 1962), 1:418–32; reprinted with some modifications in *Reading the Bible in the Global Village: Helsinki*, ed. Heikki Räisänen et al. (Atlanta: Society of Biblical Literature, 2000), 67–106.

of Bible reading—one that will not lose such good as there has been in the critical enterprise, but will move well beyond it. A particular concern among those who think like this is that biblical criticism has "taken the Bible away from the church," and should now allow the church to claim it back. Often this is linked to the belief that biblical critics are positivists. They are concerned for nuggets of fact, rather than for the whole sweep of textual meaning. On this view, historical-critical method produces *thin* readings of texts and is concerned to fragment and atomize the text rather than to read it as a rich and complex work. Criticism is a procedure for detaching the text from any possible contemporary relevance and locating it firmly in the past, in which it sheds no light on anything else but is reduced to being a collection of "inert sherds," as Brevard Childs puts it.[4] These issues are discussed in chapter 6. I propose that a critical approach is, on the contrary, the approach that most honors the text in all its givenness, and that it is therefore not inimical to a contemporary appropriation of the Bible, but rather its essential precondition.

TEN THESES

The identification of the quest for the plain sense as the goal of biblical criticism sounds very simple, but it will prove to have many wider implications for biblical study. These may be summed up in the following theses, which will emerge as the discussion proceeds, rather than occupying set places in the book:

1. Biblical criticism is essentially a literary operation, concerned with the recognition of genre in texts and with what follows from this about their possible meaning. It is thus also focused on semantics, but the semantics of whole texts as well as of individual words or sentences.
2. Biblical criticism is only accidentally concerned with questions of "Introduction" or history. Both have in practice been important in the past, but neither is a defining characteristic of a critical approach to the biblical text. The critic must consider the possibility that texts are composite, inauthentic, or unhistorical, but the practice of biblical criticism does not imply a prior commitment to finding this to be so in any given case. Historical reconstruction has often rested on the application of biblical criticism to the texts, but such reconstruction is not of the essence of the critical approach, whose aim, rather, is understanding.

---

4. Brevard S. Childs, *Introduction to the Old Testament as Scripture* (Philadelphia: Fortress Press; London: SCM, 1979), 73. (The text actually has "shreds," but it seems likely that "sherds" was intended.)

3. Biblical criticism is, as is often said, partly the product of the Enlightenment emphasis on reason in the study of texts. But it also inherits the Renaissance turn *ad fontes* and the Reformation emphasis on freedom in reading Scripture, untrammeled by ecclesiastical tradition. And its roots can be traced back even further than this, with clear anticipations in patristic and medieval exegesis. The contrast between critical and precritical interpretation is flawed in suggesting that the difference can be plotted on a timeline; it would be better to speak of critical and noncritical approaches, recognizing that the latter are still very common and that the former did occur before "modernity," even if to a limited extent.

4. Biblical criticism is not reductive or skeptical in essence, though both tendencies may be observed in some practitioners. It does not of itself produce "thin" or positivistic readings of texts, but requires sensitivity to deep meaning and to the possibility of many meanings in certain texts. Reading texts well is similar to understanding other people, not a matter of applying bloodless methods or techniques.

5. Biblical criticism is not the application of "scientific" methods to the Bible, except in the sense that science shares with the humanities a common concern for evidence and reason. It is an example of the kind of criticism that is normal in the humanities.

6. Biblical criticism requires the reader not to foreclose the question of the truth of a text before reading it, but to attend to its semantic possibilities before (logically before, not necessarily temporally before) asking whether what it asserts is or is not true. Attempts to collapse the reading of texts into a single process, as in some proposals to undertake a (postcritical) "theological reading" of the text and in certain "committed" or "advocacy" approaches, are misconceived.

7. Biblical criticism is not, and has not claimed to be, the only worthwhile way of reading biblical texts. It does not preclude moving on to what is traditionally called "application," nor is it inimical to the liturgical or devotional use of the Bible.

8. Biblical criticism is "liberal" in the sense that it recognizes secular reasoning procedures as valid, but it is not necessarily linked to theological "liberalism." The quest for a "critical faith" (Gerd Theissen[5]) favored by some biblical critics is not the same as the pursuit of religious liberalism. Not all "liberal" theologians have been interested in or convinced by biblical criticism.

9. Biblical criticism strives to be "objective" in the sense that it tries to attend to what the text actually says and not to read alien meanings into it. But it does not claim a degree of objectivity higher than is possible in humanistic study generally. Biblical critics have often been less objective than they have claimed to be, but this does not mean that all biblical criticism is hopelessly compromised. Equally, it does not mean that objectivity should not be an ideal at all.

---

5. Gerd Theissen, *Argumente für einen kritischen Glauben*, Theologische Existenz heute 202 (Munich: Kaiser, 1978); ET, *On Having a Critical Faith* (London: SCM, 1979).

10. Biblical criticism is concerned with the "plain" sense of texts, but this is not the same as the "original" sense if that is taken to signify what the text "meant" in the past as opposed to what it "means" now (Stendahl[6]). This distinction misunderstands meaning as something that changes over time, and feeds the idea that biblical criticism is an antiquarian discipline by contrast with something else (e.g., hermeneutics). Rather, biblical critics are concerned with what texts mean, now equally as much as then. The notion that the meaning discovered through criticism then has to be "translated" into a modern idiom misunderstands the nature of textual meaning.

DESCRIPTION AND PRESCRIPTION

There are many voices at present urging that biblical criticism has had its day. As I recorded in the chapter on "historical-critical approaches" in the *Cambridge Companion to Biblical Interpretation*,[7] a number of those I consulted when editing that book advised that there should not be such a chapter, since there was no longer any substantial interest in these approaches, and anyway they were bankrupt. I do not believe this, and in that sense the present book has as one of its aims to argue that biblical criticism is not dead yet. It is important that it should survive and prosper. Attempts to outlaw a critical approach in biblical studies, or to cause it to die of attrition, are in my judgment badly misconceived.

At the same time my intention is not to prescribe what biblical criticism ought to be, but to describe it as it has been and is. There are a number of guides to the history of the discipline, and I have drawn extensively on them.[8] But there does not seem to be any full-blown discussion that is analytical in intention—asking just what *constitutes* a critical approach to the biblical text. This is what I hope to provide. I am not proposing a new program for biblical studies, but rather arguing that the old one is widely misunderstood and is seen as thin, rationalistic, positivistic, and "unliterary," when in fact it has been none of these things except where it has been poorly carried out.

Biblical criticism, seen positively, is a productive and mature discipline,

6. Stendahl, "Biblical Theology, Contemporary."

7. John Barton, "Historical-critical Approaches," in *The Cambridge Companion to Biblical Interpretation*, ed. John Barton (Cambridge: Cambridge University Press, 1998), 9–20.

8. The best known are Hans-Joachim Kraus, *Geschichte der historisch-kritischen Erforschung des Alten Testaments von der Reformation bis zur Gegenwart* (Neukirchen Kreis Moers: Verlag der Buchhandlung des Erziehungsvereins, 1956; 3rd ed. Neukirchen-Vluyn: Neukirchener, 1982), and Werner G. Kümmel, *Das Neue Testament: Geschichte der Erforschung seiner Probleme* (Freiburg: Alber, 1958, 1970); ET, *The New Testament: The History of the Investigation of Its Problems* (London: SCM, 1973).

which sets itself the task of understanding the biblical text. Some at least of the programs that are currently proposed as alternatives to it may better be seen simply as new ways of carrying out that task. I have sought to emphasize common ground wherever possible, and to this extent the book has an irenic intention. It argues that some of the polarities in current discussion of method in biblical studies are exaggerated. This does not mean, however, that "everyone has won, and all must have prizes": some approaches, as their proponents claim, genuinely are incompatible with the idea of biblical criticism. But my aim is to show that the way many people currently conceive of the critical approach is a caricature of how it has really been in the hands of most of those who have practiced it, and that it already includes far more of the current agenda in biblical studies than is widely believed. This is most obviously so in the case of the first thesis above, which states that biblical criticism is essentially a literary operation. Most of those who now press the claims of a literary approach to biblical texts see this as a challenge to how biblical criticism has been. In reality, I shall argue, biblical criticism was a literary movement from the beginning. If this can be made good, there is some prospect of healing some of the rifts within the world of biblical study at the moment—not by corralling scholars into a place where they do not want to be, but by showing them how much they have in common, despite appearances, with those with whom they think they are at odds. Other rifts, of course, remain: some apparently anticritical movements really are so. My hope is that from these pages will emerge a rather new map of biblical studies, one that will offer an encouraging rather than a depressing prospect for the future of the discipline.

2

Difficulties in the Text

A common perception of biblical criticism is that it is concerned with noticing difficulties in the biblical text, and particularly inconsistencies and irregularities. There is a conservative caricature of the biblical critic as someone who sees difficulties everywhere in the text, where a less "hostile" reader will see only order and harmony. But this is not only a conservative perception. Some recent movements, such as rhetorical criticism and discourse analysis/text linguistics, tend also to think that traditional criticism has been far too ready to see discrepancies, through a rather "flat" reading of the Bible. Most critics will respond to this by saying that there are indeed many more inconsistencies and awkwardnesses in the text than such approaches allow, and that it is the task of the critic to register them and devise solutions to the problem they present. Thus the identification of biblical criticism with the detection of irregularity in the biblical text is widely agreed by both its proponents and its opponents.

One possible way of responding to the accusation that biblical criticism is the imposition of a "modern" mind-set on the Bible is to argue that, seen from this perspective, approaches we can call "critical" have existed from very ancient times. On the purely textual level, for example, one can point to Origen's work in compiling the Hexapla as an example of textual criticism that long antedates the Renaissance concern for establishing the best text of Scripture, and one that proceeded by noting inconsistencies among the various biblical texts available at the time. Where questions of a more "higher-critical" kind are concerned, the argument will take the form of pointing out that readers have always been aware of difficulties within the biblical text, the kind of difficulties (mainly internal inconsistencies) that in modern times have led to hypotheses such as the four-source theory about the compilation of the Pentateuch—the so-called Graf-Wellhausen hypothesis—or source analysis of the Gospels.

9

But does the observation of such difficulties in fact constitute biblical criticism? The aim of this chapter will be to show that, although criticism certainly does involve the ability to spot difficulties in the text, the crucial issue is how these difficulties are perceived, and what kinds of hypotheses are developed to account for them. The recognition of "problems" in the Bible is not in itself a sufficient condition for us to speak of "biblical criticism." There must also be present a certain approach to solving such problems, and it is the aim of this chapter to analyze what that approach is.

AWARENESS OF PROBLEMS IN THE TEXT

One use of the word "critical" is by way of contrast with "naive" or "superficial." Modern biblical critics have noticed difficulties within the biblical text that do not strike people who read the texts quickly or superficially. Critical observations in this sense would include, for example, the inconsistencies between Kings and Chronicles, the impossibility of Moses' having written an account of his own death, the problem of reconciling the chronology of Paul's ministry according to Acts with what emerges from the epistles, the question of how Cain managed to have children when he was the only person alive in his generation. Now it is not hard to show that such questions were asked in the ancient world and are not the product of modern skepticism. In this sense it is perfectly proper to say that *critical* study of the Bible has existed from the time when the Bible was first received as canonical Scripture.

This point is well made by John Rogerson in *Beginning Old Testament Study*, a student's guide to Old Testament study to which I also contributed. Seeking to counter the fears of more biblically conservative students that modern Old Testament study is an invention of unorthodox biblical scholars, Rogerson shows very carefully that in the sense currently being discussed such Old Testament study is already present in the work of Augustine, a theologian whom conservative Christians are likely to hold in honor and not to suspect of unorthodoxy. In *City of God*, book 15, Rogerson points out, Augustine shows that problems of the kind that have concerned careful modern readers of the Bible were already a live issue for him. Augustine there tackles the historical difficulty of the extreme longevity of the patriarchs, the enormous stature of the giants who lived before the flood, and the advanced age at which people in the early chapters of Genesis produced their first children. He adopts various procedures to resolve these difficulties. He compares parts of the biblical texts with other parts, to show that the years of those who lived before the flood really were of the same length as in later times. He suggests that the text omits some information that would be relevant to answering our questions: for example, it is certainly said that the patriarchs produced children in old age, but it is not positively asserted that they had not had any children before. And he appeals to "secular" evidence, such as the still extant tombs of ancient heroes, which confirm (so he argues) that the stature of people in times gone by really was greater than it is now. "These explanations may seem crude to us," says Rogerson. "But the methods used by him [comparing text with text, noting possible omissions, and appealing to external evidence] did not differ fundamentally from those used by critical scholars today."[1]

Now with the positive point being made here I am fully in accord. It is not a particularly modern achievement to have spotted discrepancies, puzzles, and apparently tall stories in the Bible. This needs to be said repeatedly in the present climate of discussion, to guard against a misunderstanding of biblical criticism prevalent in two quite different and opposing groups among serious students of the Bible.

On the one hand, biblical conservatives need to be reminded that it is not the rationalism of the Enlightenment, or the materialism of the nineteenth century, or the supposed skepticism of modern German theology, that have discovered the inconsistencies and historical difficulties in the biblical text and have led to "critical" theories about it. Careful readers have always noticed such things. Far from being an invention of modern scholars who are trying to detract from the authority of the Bible, they are features of the text that have always cried out for explanation and have always been felt to do so. One may wonder whether scholars who argue that criticism proceeds from lack of commitment to the Bible as a book of faith, have really taken this point to heart.[2] Ordinary people in the churches certainly ask such questions, and ask them not out of disenchantment with the Bible, but precisely because they take it so seriously that it worries them to find discrepancies and implausibilities in the text.

On the other hand, there can be a kind of rhetoric of biblical criticism, perhaps less heard now than it once was, which goes to the other extreme and exaggerates the contribution of modern biblical study in order to commend rather than to condemn it. One sees this, for example, in Kraus's work, which represents the growth of biblical criticism as the triumph of light over darkness. A student taught in this way can easily get the impression that all "precritical" scholarship was naive, dogmatic, and blind: that no one before (say) Colenso ever gave a moment's thought to the logistical difficulties Noah

1. See *Beginning Old Testament Study*, ed. John W. Rogerson (London: SPCK, 1983), 9–11.
2. See the discussion in chapter 6.

must have faced at feeding time, or that it is only since Copernicus, or Newton, that anyone saw the slightest difficulty in believing that the sun stood
still for Joshua or moved backwards for Isaiah. The traditional organization
of handbooks on biblical study, in which the patristic and medieval periods
are credited with only occasional glimpses into the historical problems of the
text, does need to be countered, and Rogerson does this very effectively. As
we shall see in chapter 5, critical study of the Bible in the modern senses did
indeed already occur in ancient times. The impression that results if the
rhetoric I have described is left unchallenged is, paradoxically, rather similar to the conservative perception of biblical criticism as a modern, secular
procedure; the difference lies only in the value judgment expressed about
this. It can become a kind of critical "orthodoxy." Brevard Childs in particular is right to have challenged such attitudes, though I am not sure that in
practice they are as widespread as he thinks.

Against the rhetoric of both right and left on this issue, Rogerson's argument that "biblical study has always been critical" is clearly important. The
difficulties in the biblical text that modern scholars deal with were noticed in
ancient times, not just sporadically, but with deep and serious interest.

But to call what was going on in this interest biblical criticism may suggest to a careless reader that there has in principle been nothing new in modern critical study at all, nothing that was not already clear to Augustine or
Origen or the great medieval Jewish commentators; that we have improved
the tools and have access to more information, but nothing has changed deci-
sively. This, I believe, is not the case. To try to show this, I shall not return
to the examples Rogerson cites from the *City of God*, but I shall look at some
Jewish examples of handling inconsistencies in the Old Testament and examine a more extended example from Augustine, his discussion of the discrepancies between the Gospels in *De consensu evangelistarum*, at the same time
looking at later harmonies of the Gospels. We shall see that there are truly
two different mind-sets at work as between the attitude that led to harmonization and the critical impulse. This observation may help to get us closer
to seeing just what is the defining feature of biblical criticism. I should stress,
however, that the point is not to contrast "ancient" with "modern" perceptions as such. Rogerson is correct in thinking that a critical attitude did exist
in the ancient world, as I shall go on to show in chapter 5, just as noncritical approaches exist in great profusion today. The true contrast is between
critical and noncritical, not between critical and precritical. It is true,
though, that evidence for what we are calling criticism in antiquity is not
widespread; as we shall see, if Augustine shows some critical awareness in the
City of God, in *De consensu evangelistarum* much of what we may define as a
critical sensibility is lacking.

HARMONIZATION OF TEXTS

From ancient times Bible readers have been aware of apparent inconsistencies in the biblical text. Jewish scholars discussed contradictions between the various bodies of legislation in the Pentateuch, and between the Pentateuch and Ezekiel;[3] everyone knew that Kings and Chronicles tell differing stories; and Christians were confronted by their opponents with the accusation that the Gospels were mutually inconsistent. The discovery of such inconsistencies is not the work of modern biblical critics, but of many ordinary readers of the Bible from time immemorial. We know from Origen that pagans mocked Christians for having inconsistent stories about their founding figure, and already at the beginning of the third century Hippolytus had to deal with a proposal by a certain Gaius that John and Revelation should not stand in the New Testament canon because they contradicted Paul and the Synoptics.[4] Earlier still, one of the motives behind Marcion's reduction of the Gospels to one seems to have been the desire to avoid inconsistencies in the account of the life of Jesus. In fact the most sophisticated work in antiquity was done in the harmonization of the Gospels, and this has continued into modern times: a new harmony of the Gospels was published as recently as 1996.[5]

The attitude lying behind Gospel harmonies is summed up by Dieter Wünsch in his article "Evangelienharmonie" in the *Theologische Realenzyklopedie*, published in 1982, as follows: "The presupposition of every literary Gospel harmony is an assumed *objective* harmony, in other words the assumption that the canonical Gospels do not contradict each other in any significant respect."[6] Or, as S. J. Patterson puts it in the *Anchor Bible Dictionary*, "a gospel harmony

---

3. On apparent self-contradictions in Ecclesiastes, see Babylonian Talmud *Shabbat* 30b. In *Numbers Rabbah* 2:14–15 a similar alleged self-contradiction in the prophets is explained away. (Of course, a great deal of rabbinic discussion focuses on apparently conflicting principles in the Torah and seeks to render them harmless.) Cf. David Weiss Halivni, *Revelation Restored: Divine Writ and Critical Responses*, Radical Traditions: Theology in a Postcritical Key (London: SCM, 2001), 101: "Inconsistencies and unevenness in the Pentateuchal scriptures are not the discovery of modern textual science alone . . . the earliest stewards of Torah, including some of those represented in the Bible itself, were aware of discrepancies in the tradition."

4. See Bruce M. Metzger, *The Canon of the New Testament: Its Origin, Development, and Significance* (Oxford: Clarendon Press, 1987), 104–5.

5. O. E. Daniel, *A Harmony of the Four Gospels* (Grand Rapids: Baker Book House Co., 1996).

6. "Voraussetzung jeder literarischen Evangelienharmonie ist die angenommene *objektive* Harmonie, also die Annahme, daß die kanonischen Evangelien sich in nichts Wesentlichem widersprechen" (Dieter Wünsch, "Evangelienharmonie," in *Theologische Realenzyklopedie* [Berlin: W. de Gruyter, 1982], 1: 626–36). Detailed studies of some medieval Gospel harmonies can be found in Christoph Burger, August den Hollander, and Ulrich

rests on the supposition that the four canonical gospels are in fundamental or substantive agreement . . . in their presentation of the life of Jesus."[7] That is to say, the harmonizer is aware that there *appear* to be contradictions among the different versions of the story, but believes it can be shown that they are only apparent. If there were no awareness of the contradictions, the question would not arise in the first place; the awareness itself is not at all a modern phenomenon. Harmonization is an attempt to deal with this awareness by showing that, contrary to appearances, it is actually a false perception of the textual data. Gospel harmonization proceeds along lines similar to those of Jewish harmonization of the legal sections in the Hebrew Bible, which are similarly known to contain apparent discrepancies. The hero of the Jewish enterprise is one Hananiah ben Hezekiah. According to the Babylonian Talmud, Hananiah consumed three hundred barrels of oil to keep his lamp alight while he worked to show that there were no inconsistencies between Ezekiel and the Torah, as there appear to be (*b. Shabbat* 13b).

The major exponent of Gospel harmonization in the ancient church was Augustine, whose work *De consensu evangelistarum* was to become normative in Western Christianity. Its great predecessor, Tatian's *Diatessaron*, was widely influential in both East and West, and in the Syrian churches was apparently used instead of the four separate Gospels down to the fourth century, but it has survived only in fragments and in quotations in other writers.[8] It is also not clear that it rested on the great assumption of an objective harmony: it may rather have been intended as a replacement for the Gospels, which would imply that Tatian believed they really did conflict as they stand.[9] Augustine's work, on the other hand, is fully extant, and undoubtedly assumes that the Gospels conflict only in appearance. His work is a lengthy and tightly reasoned

---

Schmid, *Evangelienharmonien des Mittelalters* (Assen: Royal Van Gorcum, 2004). The beginning of modern study of harmonization in the Gospels is the article by C. Pesch, "Über Evangelienharmonien," *Zeitschrift für Theologie und Kirche* 10 (1886): 225–44 and 454–80.

7. S. J. Patterson, "Harmony of the Gospels," in *Anchor Bible Dictionary*, ed. David Noel Freedman (New York: Doubleday 1992), 3:61.

8. On the *Diatessaron*, see Tjitze Baarda, "Factors in the Harmonization of the Gospels, Especially in the Diatessaron of Tatian," in *Gospel Traditions in the Second Century: Origins, Recensions, Text, and Transmission*, ed. W. L. Petersen, Christianity and Judaism in Antiquity 3 (London: University of Notre Dame Press, 1989), 133–56; idem, *Essays on the Diatessaron* (Kampen: Kok Pharos, 1994); W. L. Petersen, *Tatian's Diatessaron: Its Creation, Dissemination, Significance, and History in Scholarship*, Vigiliae Christianae Supplement 25 (Leiden: Brill, 1994).

9. This is really a different sense of "harmonization": on the distinction, see my "Unity and Diversity in the Biblical Canon," in *Die Einheit der Schrift und die Vielfalt des Kanons/The Unity of Scripture and the Diversity of the Canon*, Beihefte zur Zeitschrift für die neutestamentliche Wissenschaft 118, ed. John Barton and Michael Wolter (Berlin: W. de Gruyter, 2003), 11–26.

attempt to convince the worried Christian that the inconsistencies are not real but merely apparent.

For the most part, this work is not a Gospel harmony in the sense of a continuous retelling of the Gospel story in the words of Scripture, but rather a detailed discussion of apparent points of inconsistency in the Gospels—though Augustine does, as a sample of how the task could be accomplished, write out a harmonized birth narrative containing all the elements in both Matthew and Luke arranged in a coherent order. This represents more or less what the average Christian probably still thinks of as the details of the events surrounding the birth of Jesus, with Matthew and Luke blended into a smooth story.

Augustine deploys two main strategies in dealing with discrepancies between the Gospels. Where similar incidents or sayings occur that nevertheless have significant differences, he tends to argue that they reflect two separate but similar occasions. Thus Jesus twice told Simon that he would be called Peter, once early in his ministry, as recorded in John, and again at Caesarea Philippi, as reported in the Synoptics (*De consensu* 2:17). He preached two similar sermons, one on the mount, one on the plain (ibid.). At the tomb on the day of resurrection Mark tells us there was an angel inside the tomb, Matthew that there was one outside, and both are correct; the two accounts are not incompatible (3:24). From silence we may not infer absence, so that when Matthew tells us that two blind men were healed and Mark mentions only Bartimaeus, we may be sure that there were indeed two: Mark simply mentions the one who was known to his readers (2:65). Thus, much that we would regard as a variant tradition can be explained on the assumption that many similar things occurred or were said and that the evangelists were selective in which they reported, different evangelists making different selections. This first strategy of Augustine results in a very much elongated Gospel narrative, and probably requires that the events of Jesus' life were spread over a longer period than any one Gospel suggests.

The second strategy Augustine adopts has a rather more modern appearance. He suggests that neither the *order* of events nor the exact *wording* of sayings was particularly significant to the evangelists. So far as order is concerned, we find him dealing with the variation between Matthew and Luke in the temptation stories by arguing that the order simply did not matter to the evangelists: "nihil tamen ad rem, dum omnia facta fuisse manifestum sit" (2:12)— the basic matter of the story is not affected by the variation in order, since it is clear that all three temptations did happen. Probably each evangelist remembered things in a different order, but this does not detract from the historical facticity of each event: "it is quite likely that each of the evangelists believed that he ought to tell the story in the order in which God had resolved to put into his mind the very things he was narrating, in those matters for which, after all, the order, whether this or that, in no way detracts from the authority and truth of the Gospel."[10]

In a similar spirit, what matters in sayings of Jesus or others is not the exact words but the *res*, the content being communicated, and it does not matter if that is not recorded exactly. The *veritatis integritas*, "the integrity of the truth," or, as Augustine sometimes puts it, the *sententia*, the meaning communicated, matters more than the precise words. "We should understand," he says, "that what is to be sought and embraced is not so much the truth of the words but of the things communicated."[11] In the same chapter Augustine discusses the words of John the Baptist: did he say he was unworthy to untie Jesus' sandals or to carry them? Perhaps he said both on different occasions, or perhaps he said both at the same time, but in any case the same point (*sententia*) is made by the two sayings, namely, that John recognized his own inferiority to Jesus, and "salubriter discimus nihil aliud esse quaerendum quam quid velit qui loquitur": we learn that we should seek only what John intended when he spoke, and not worry too much about the exact words.

> Origen appealed to similar principles in treating differences between the Gospels: In the *Commentary on John*, Origen tackles the discrepancy between John and the Synoptics over the Cleansing of the Temple. . . . He 'conceives it to be impossible for those who admit nothing more than the history in their interpretation to show that these discrepant statements are in harmony with one another.' He demonstrates the implausibility of the Johannine narrative, and then, having explained the deeper meaning of the Johannine story by allegorising its details, Origen proceeds to apply narrative criticism to the Matthaean story, showing that that too is unpersuasive taken as it stands. In the end the deeper intent of each evangelist must be attended to, rather than the history they purport to report.[12]

This is a slightly dangerous principle, which could lead to a certain indifference to the exact text of the Gospels; nevertheless it serves well enough to deal with a good many of the inconsistencies between them. It reappears at the Reformation in the harmonistic work of Chemnitz, who argued against any *ordinis et temporis anxia ratio* ("anxious calculation of the temporal order of

---

10. "Satis probabile est quod unusquisque evangelistarum eo ordine credidit debuisse narrare, quo voluisset Deus ea ipsa quae narrabat eius recordationi suggerere in eis dumtaxat rebus, quarum ordo, sive ille sive ille sit, nihil minuit auctoritati veritatique evangelicae" (2:14).

11. "Intelligeremus non tam verborum quam rerum quaerendam vel amplectandam esse veritatem" (2:12).

12. Frances M. Young, *Biblical Exegesis and the Formation of Christian Culture* (Cambridge: Cambridge University Press, 1997), 88, referring to Origen, *Commentary on John*, 10:130.

events").[13] It can also be found in patristic times in Theodore of Mopsuestia, commenting on the discrepancies among the Gospels over the events surrounding the resurrection of Jesus:

> If indeed [the Gospels] exhibit . . . a perfect harmony—since they all preach the resurrection and indicate the same day and say that the women came to the tomb—why they wish to waste time discussing the *minutiae* I do not know. Indeed, in my opinion, nothing else is required for the confirmation of the truth of what is said than that the various accounts exhibit a great harmony in the essentials; in the unimportant things and in those things which small men value, their words are by no means in perfect accord.[14]

Augustine's first approach to harmonization occurs again in the great *Harmonia evangelica* of Andreas Osiander, published in 1537, which Wünsch thinks is probably the first work to use the word "harmony." This completely eschews Augustine's second method (indifference to exact ordering and wording) and insists that every word in the Gospels is to be taken as a literal record, pressing the matter much further than Augustine had done. Every variant account of an action or saying, however small, must refer to a separate event or utterance. As Wünsch writes, "As opposed to the Augustinian tradition, Osiander is unable to concede any distinction between essential and inessential elements in Holy Scripture. Exact attention is paid not only to the contents of each pericope, but also to the external circumstances conveyed by it, since they too are inspired";[15] and again, "Osiander is unable to honor the Gospels theologically as differing writings. For him, on the contrary, the Gospel writers are simply delivery men providing the building blocks for a harmony."[16]

The result is, to our way of thinking, comic. Jesus heals the servants of two different centurions, cleanses the temple three times, and cures four blind men in Jericho. His ministry includes four Passovers, for only so can all the events of the Gospels be accommodated, once it is assumed that every variant of a

---

13. See Wünsch, "Evangelienharmonie," 634.

14. Theodore, *Commentary on the Gospel according to John*, quoted in Rowan A. Greer, *Theodore of Mopsuestia: Exegete and Theologian* (London: Faith Press, 1961), 116, from J.-M. Vosté, "Le commentaire de Théodore de Mopsueste sur Saint Jean, d'après la version syriaque," *Revue biblique* 32 (1923): 244–45.

15. "Anders als in der augustinischen Tradition kann Osiander keine Unterscheidung zwischen Wesentlichem und Unwesentlichem in der Heiligen Schrift zugestehen. Nicht nur der Gehalt einer Perikope, sondern auch die in ihr mitgeteilten äußeren Umstände verdienen genaue Beachtung; denn auch sie sind inspiriert" (Wünsch, "Evangelienharmonie," 631).

16. "Osiander kann die Evangelien als unterschiedliche Schriften nicht theologisch würdigen, sondern die Evangelisten sind für ihn die Lieferanten, die die Bausteine für die Harmonie beibringen" (Wünsch, "Evangelienharmonie," 631–32).

story represents a separate incident. Osiander set the tone for the many harmonies produced in the years of Lutheran orthodoxy, though Augustine's second, more "liberal" approach did sometimes reassert itself.

But Osiander and Augustine are at one in their commitment to the "objective harmony" of the Gospels. They do not feel free to change anything in order to bring harmony about; on the contrary, they argue that complete harmony already reigns, even if sometimes, according to Augustine, it is a *concors diversitas*. The casual reader may *think* there are inconsistencies between the Gospels; but the casual reader is mistaken, as detailed work on the texts can demonstrate.

Our discussion has a clear bearing on how the four-Gospel canon was regarded in the early centuries. Niels Astrup Dahl in 1971 wrote an article entitled "Contradictions between the Gospels, an Old Hermeneutical Problem."[17] Following Oscar Cullmann, he suggested that the hermeneutical problem of inconsistencies was solved, in the case of the Gospels, by adopting a kerygmatic interpretation of them as four alternative tellings of the single story of salvation. We may see this in the titles, which do not say "the Gospel of Mark," but "the Gospel according to Mark." But the evidence I have discussed tends to suggest rather that in early times the Gospels were not read as independent self-contained witnesses. Instead, they were treated as compendia of stories and sayings, from which material could be excerpted and recombined. What is even more surprising is that such a perception of the Gospels continued even after the fourfold canon was a fixed and accepted entity. Augustine did not feel free, as Tatian had done, to rewrite the Gospels into a harmonized form, but only to demonstrate their mutual consistency as they stand. Yet there is little sense that each is a unique record of the kerygma. He does, it is true, explain the selection of some incidents in Matthew and Luke respectively by suggesting that Matthew is more interested in Jesus Christ as king, Luke in Jesus Christ as priest; that accounts, for example, for the different emphases of the genealogies (*De consensu* 1). But in general he treats the Gospel accounts as all cut from much the same cloth, and as (to change the metaphor) simply four files from each of which information about Jesus can be extracted. Wünsch puts it very well when he says, "The authors of Gospel harmonies presuppose that there is no distance between the life of Jesus and its presentation."[18] The same assumption can be seen very clearly in Osiander.

17. Niels A. Dahl, "Widersprüche in der Bibel, ein altes hermeneutisches Problem," *Studia theologica* 25 (1971): 1–19.
18. "Bei den Verfassern von Evangelienharmonien wird keine Distanz zwischen dem Leben Jesu und der Darstellung desselben vorausgesetzt" (Wünsch, "Evangelienharmonie," 626).

The problem for a modern reader is this: there is no sense in any of the harmonists that each Gospel tells a separate story that is incompatible at many points with the story told in the others. To say that Jesus healed one blind man really is to say that he did not, on the same occasion, heal two; to say that there was an angel inside the tomb really is to say that there was not one outside. This is because we think that a writer who went to the trouble of recording the presence of the one angel would not have simply overlooked the presence of the other; and that one who wrote that one blind man was healed meant not one at least, but precisely one—that being part of the convention of telling stories. To our perception, the harmonistic attempt to combine the stories produces simply a fifth story that is incompatible with all the other four. This is because we have a clear sense of how the telling of a story works; we have a sense for genre. Even though we do not know exactly how to classify the Gospels generically,[19] we know that they are not simply files containing facts, but constructed accounts of the life of Jesus with a plot and a shape.

Now it is this, it seems to me, that constitutes our approach as *critical* in a way that Augustine's or Osiander's is not. It is not in noticing inconsistencies that biblical criticism consists, for the ability to do this is presupposed by all harmonizing attempts. Without such an ability, the problem to which harmonies are a solution would not present itself in the first place. Biblical criticism consists in understanding the nature of a written text such as a Gospel as a finished whole, with its own internal dynamic and logic. Augustine and Osiander are like lawyers adding up evidence from many sources to make a case; biblical critics are like (indeed, are) readers of literature, who ask how a complete account hangs together. There is no common ground between these two procedures.

There are anticipations of such a critical approach in the Fathers, most notably in Origen. Thus, for example, he explains the omission of the temptations and of the agony in the garden of Gethsemane in the Fourth Gospel by arguing that John had a "divine" picture of Jesus with which these accounts of human weakness would not blend—in this he was developing Clement of Alexandria's famous description of John as a "spiritual" Gospel. There is here an anticipation of redaction criticism. But such explanations are rare in the Fathers. There is very little sense of what we might call the integrity of each Gospel as a complete story in its own right. The Gospels are seen as providing raw materials for the harmonizer to work with, not as literary works.

19. Though a case for them as modeled on the Hellenistic *bios* (biography) is made in Richard A. Burridge, *What Are the Gospels? A Comparison with Graeco-Roman Biography* (Cambridge: Cambridge University Press, 1992).

If I am correct in the contrast I am drawing between the Fathers and the modern biblical critic, then the essence of the critical spirit consists in a particular kind of literary perception.[20] The critical biblical scholar cannot accept harmonization because it ignores the character of the Gospels. From a purely historical perspective, it is conceivable (if improbable) that Jesus cleansed the temple three times; it is not conceivable that any of the evangelists thought he did, because each tells the incident in such a way as to make it clear that it is a unique event. It is *the* cleansing of the temple, not *a* cleansing of the temple. The fact that John places it at the beginning of Jesus' ministry and the Synoptics toward the end is a real problem, because the two placings contribute to two radically different stories of Jesus. And the discrepancy cannot be reconciled either by suppressing one of the accounts, as Tatian may have done, or by constructing an account in which both appear, as in Osiander. A critical approach to the Bible has to recognize honestly that the Gospel accounts are incompatible. This is not a historical so much as a literary point, and it is related to an ability to distinguish between the actual life of Jesus and all the accounts of it, that is, to recognize the evangelists as authors, not merely collectors of tradition. One might say that it depends on an ability to recognize the genre of texts. There is of course much discussion of just what genre the Gospels belong to, but in rejecting harmonizations of them we are showing that we do regard them as (at any rate in some sense) coherent narratives, not merely as databases of sayings and stories; for if we regarded them as that, harmonization would not be so objectionable. And this perception of them is essentially a literary matter, not a historical one.

I may be able to illustrate the point here with another example, this time from harmonization not of the biblical texts but within the Bible itself.[21] In Exodus 12:9 the Passover sacrifice is to be roasted—neither raw nor boiled in water. But in Deuteronomy 16:7 boiling is actually commanded. In 2 Chronicles 35:11–13 the Chronicler shows that he cannot tolerate this discrepancy. Accordingly, in recording how the Passover was celebrated under Josiah, he declares that the sacrifice was "boiled in fire." The practical effect of this is nonsensical, and it results in reporting an event that actually conforms to *nei-*

20. This perception runs exactly contrary to what is often supposed to be typical of the "historical-critical method"! Contrast Fernando F. Segovia, *Decolonizing Biblical Studies: A View from the Margins* (Maryknoll, NY: Orbis Books, 2000), 13, who writes that in historical criticism "there was little conception of the text as a literary, strategic, and ideological whole." On the contrary, it seems to me, it is only because the critics approached the text with an expectation it would be such a whole that they were struck by the features that often mean it cannot be so. They did not set out to find "aporias"; they noticed them just because they were trying to read the text as coherent.

21. See the discussion in Benjamin Sommer, "Inner-biblical Interpretation," in *The Jewish Study Bible*, ed. Adele Berlin and Mark Z. Brettler (New York: Oxford University Press, 2004), 1832–33; and in Halivni, *Revelation Restored*, 25.

ther of the laws—just as Gospel harmonizations produce in effect a fifth Gospel that conforms to none of the four. But the important thing for the Chronicler was evidently that the laws had been harmonized, however ineptly. (Later rabbinic discussions produce other, more satisfactory, solutions to the problem.) As Sommer puts it, the authors of Chronicles, unlike most modern scholars, "view the Torah not as an anthology of differing opinions (comparable to the Talmud), or as a compendium of different sources, but as a single work, written by Moses. . . . Consequently they deny that a legal disagreement . . . can occur in the Torah."

This example, even more clearly than the harmonization of the Gospels, shows how much the harmonizing motive is a literary one. The process has nothing at all to do with history, and nor have the modern reader's objections to it. We do not consider the Chronicler's solution to the difficulty unsatisfactory because he did not realize that the texts in question come from different periods, for example, but because he disregards the integrity of each text and treats them as mere raw material that can be recombined, even if the result is nonsensical. This again is essentially a literary perception.

Rabbinic literature provides many examples of textual harmonization. In the Babylonian Talmud *Shabbat* 30b there is a discussion of the text in Proverbs 26:4–5: "Do not answer fools according to their folly, or you will be a fool yourself. Answer fools according to their folly, or they will be wise in their own eyes." On the surface there seems to be an inconsistency here, but it is resolved by saying that verse 4 refers to the discussion of words of Torah, while verse 5 refers to discussion of secular matters. To the modern interpreter, Proverbs is made up of the kind of material in which wisdom is communicated by sometimes opposing aphorisms, rather as in the English pair of proverbs "Many hands make light work" and "Too many cooks spoil the broth." Both are true, and wise conduct consists in knowing how to apply each in appropriate circumstances. A modern interpreter would take something like this to be the meaning of the verses in Proverbs. Once again, it may be noted, this is a question of *genre*. A book such as Proverbs is to us the kind of book where riddling contradictions are to be expected. To the rabbis, it was a work like the Torah as they conceived that: divine instructions for good living, which could not contain any *real* contradictions. The attitude is very similar to that of Augustine to the Gospels. All the material must teach a consistent message, and there is no awareness of the different genres of different texts. Here the critical impulse has certainly nothing to do with history, but altogether with the literary character of the work.[22] (It

22. A classic Jewish attempt to harmonize biblical inconsistencies may be found in the work of Rabbi Manasseh ben Israel, the Lisbon-born rabbi who came to England in 1655 and successfully petitioned Oliver Cromwell for Jews to be allowed to return to

should especially be noted that it is a critical perception of the text that allows the "inconsistencies" to stand and is *not* concerned by them in this case, and it is the *non*critical reader for whom they are a problem.)

Is not the same true of critical attitudes to the pentateuchal sources? Great use has been made of the four-source hypothesis in reconstructing the history of Israel. The most obvious example of this is the work of Julius Wellhausen. By correlating each of the four sources with a particular period in the history of Israel, he was able to produce an account of the history of Israel's life and thought that is strikingly at variance with the surface account that can be gained from a straightforward reading of the text. Of course Wellhausen's work was focused on history, and one can understand the use of the term "historical-critical method" in reference to the way he used the results of source analysis. But this only makes it the more striking that source analysis itself was not produced by a historical impulse at all, but by a desire to understand how the text came to contain inconsistencies, and to explain them without recourse to harmonization. One of the basic source-critical insights is that Genesis 1 and Genesis 2 do not simply provide raw material from which details of the creation can be worked out, but tell two different—and incompatible—stories about the creation. A story in which humankind is created after the animals and a story in which humankind is created before the animals are simply incompatible stories. It was the accumulation of perceptions such as this that led to the now traditional source analysis, and it was only because that task had been accomplished—partly, indeed, by Wellhausen himself—that he was able to use its results in constructing his account of Israel's history.

The original impulse, however, was not a historical but a *literary* one. One of the very earliest attempts at source criticism of Genesis, by Jean Astruc, did not even question the Mosaic authorship of the text, but spoke of "the original memoirs Moses appears to have used" in writing Genesis.[23] In the nineteenth century, history did indeed take center stage, but the roots of biblical criticism go back well before the nineteenth century, into a period when historical concerns were far less marked. The question that marked the beginnings of biblical criticism was not a question about history, but a question

---

England. His work discusses hundreds of examples—189 in Deuteronomy alone, for example. See E. H. Lindo, *The Conciliator of R. Manasseh ben Israel; A Reconcilement of the Apparent Contradictions in Holy Scripture*, 2 vols. (London, 1842). Manasseh's first example is the discrepancy between Gen. 1:1 and 2:4—was heaven or earth created first? His guiding principle is that "the Bible being in the highest degree true, it cannot contain any text really contradictory of another" (p. 1).

23. Jean Astruc, *Conjectures sur les mémoires originaux dont il paroit que Moyse s'est servi pour composer le livre de la Genèse* (Brussels, 1753).

about how to read and understand texts: it was a hermeneutical or, I would say, a literary question.

The point that harmonizers in particular and precritical interpreters in general fail to grasp may be put like this: certain types of text provide certain types of information. One cannot go to a text looking for a simple transcript of events; every text tells a story and does so in its own unique way. This is essentially a perception of the genre of texts. One finds this realization already in so early a critic as Matthias Flacius Illyricus (1520–75), who remarks that in reading a text one must decide "whether it deals with a narrative or history, a piece of teaching or instruction, a text offering consolation or an accusation, the description of something, or a speech or something similar."[24] It may be a historical observation or problem that points the reader toward such a question. Thus, in the criticism of the Pentateuch, the sentence "at that time the Canaanites were in the land" (Gen. 12:6) pointed many early scholars, both Christian and Jewish, to a realization that the chapter in question could not very well be by Moses, since it could have been written only in a time after the expulsion of the Canaanites. But this led to the question how such texts came to be written, if Moses was not their author. And this question could be solved only by a literary analysis of the texts. As Wellhausen himself remarked in a review written in 1897, "the supporters of the Graf hypothesis simply wish to place the three legal and tradition strata in the Pentateuch in the right order [historically right, he means]. *But the problem is a literary one, and must be solved by literary means,* through an inner comparison among the sources themselves as well as by a historical correlation with the securely transmitted facts of Israelite history."[25] Certainly history comes into the matter, but the primary emphasis is literary; the question may be a historical one, but the answer is a literary answer.

If I am right about this, then the primary thing differentiating critical from noncritical reading is sensitivity to literary genre. Critical scholars recognize what *kind* of text they are dealing with. In the case of the Gospels, they recognize that they are confronted by narrative texts that do not consist merely of

24. "Ob es sich um eine Erzählung oder Geschichte, um eine Unterweisung oder irgendeine Lehre, um eine Trostschrift oder eine Schelte, um die Beschreibung irgend einer Sache, um eine Rede oder etwas ähnliches handelt" (M. Flacius Illyricus, *De ratione cognoscendi sacras litteras*, ed. L. Geldsetzer [Düsseldorf: Stern Verlag, 1968], 97).

25. My italics. "Die Anhänger der Grafschen Hypothese . . . wollen nur die drei Gesetzes- und Traditionsschichten des Pentateuchs in die richtige Folge bringen. Das Problem ist ein literarisches und muß auf literarischem Wege gelöst werden" (Review of R. Hommel, *Die israelitische Überlieferung in inschriftlicher Beleuchtung,* cited in Lothar Perlitt, *Vatke und Wellhausen. Geschichtsphilosophische Voraussetzungen und historiographische Motive für die Darstellung der Religion und Geschichte Israels durch Wilhelm Vatke und Julius Wellhausen,* Beihefte zur Zeitschrift für die alttestamentliche Wissenschaft 94 [Berlin: W. de Gruyter, 1965], 166).

potentially recombinable nuggets of information, but stories that have a certain kind of plot or shape. The antiharmonizing atmosphere of biblical criticism thus in a sense leads quite naturally toward what we might call redaction criticism. Put another way, traditional criticism anticipates much that we now call a newer literary approach, seeing the Gospel texts as coherent stories in which it does not make sense to impute gaps into which material from other Gospels can be slotted. Even if for some critics the aim is to discover the truth about the historical Jesus, they do not treat the Gospels as transcripts of the historical facts—as noncritical, harmonizing readers did—but regard them as constructed literary works at one remove from the facts they claim to report. A critical approach asks first, What kind of text is this?

Another way of looking at this might be as follows. It is sometimes suggested that one of the effects of biblical criticism is to "atomize" the text—to divide it up into smaller sources, sometimes very minutely—whereas precritical reading was more "holistic" and thus had more respect for the text in its finished form. That some pentateuchal criticism in particular did divide the text into very small pieces cannot be doubted, and the prevailing redaction-critical style of criticism in the German-speaking world still tends to go in for minute differentiations between small pieces of text. But in essence the critical approach begins with the very opposite of an atomizing tendency. Where precritical interpreters reconcile difficulties in the text by looking at the story the text tells in a piecemeal way, and arguing that this verse can be made compatible with that, biblical criticism has regard to the whole gestalt of the text in question, and asks how the story in its entirety hangs together. Once this is done, it becomes apparent that many noncritical solutions will not work, that the discrepancies are real ones. Critical readers have in their minds an idea of what makes for coherence in a literary work and quickly observe that such coherence is not present in many biblical texts.

It can of course be objected that the ideas about coherence being invoked are essentially modern ideas, and that the biblical authors worked with different notions of what it was for a text to cohere.[26] But this itself is a critical argument, which tries to identify how texts held together in the ancient mind, and

---

26. Cf. my article "What Is a Book? Modern Exegesis and the Literary Conventions of Ancient Israel," in *Intertextuality in Ugarit and Israel: Papers Read at the Tenth Joint Meeting of the Society for Old Testament Study and Het Oudtestamentische Werkgezelschap in Nederland en België, Held at Oxford, 1997*, ed. J. C. de Moor, Oudtestamentische Studiën 40 (Leiden: Brill, 1998), 1–14. One modern scholar who particularly pressed this line of objection to the work of biblical critics was Umberto Cassuto; see his *The Documentary Hypothesis and the Composition of the Pentateuch* (Jerusalem: Magnes Press, 1961; from Hebrew original of 1941; Jerusalem: Hebrew University).

in effect is an accusation of anachronism against the critical scholar: it is not in any way a defense of precritical reading but a plea for biblical criticism to be more sensitive to ancient literary genres than it is. I believe that this plea is in some measure well founded; scholars are too ready to assume that ancient writers had our own rather tightly defined ideas of what constitutes a "well-formed" literary genre. But this is not an argument against biblical criticism in itself, simply an accusation that it has sometimes in practice been too tin-eared in its reading of ancient texts. The basic critical perception, that one can understand a text only by recognizing its genre, is not undercut by such an objection.

One can see from all this, by the way, why certain manifestations of "biblical archaeology" strike many scholars as essentially noncritical, because they do not ask the crucial question about genre, but instead treat the texts simply as repositories of potential facts. I do not wish to imply that all biblical archaeology has had this character, but simply to say that when people accuse some of it of being uncritical, if we probe the accusation, this is what it amounts to. For example, it is quite common nowadays to say that a number of the writings of the Albright school, such as John Bright's *History of Israel*,[27] are insufficiently critical. I am not sure whether this is so; it is far from being merely a retelling of the biblical story. But if it is so, then this is because Bright does not ask what kind of literature the Old Testament is and therefore how far it is legitimate to use it in reconstructing the history of Israel. His dispute with Martin Noth—which nowadays seems rather tame, since compared with modern so-called minimalists Noth was scarcely less conservative than Bright!—was essentially about the literary character of the Old Testament. For Noth, the stories of the patriarchs were simply not the kind of material from which history could be written, but legends, as Hermann Gunkel had called them (*Sagen*). The argument was not about the facts on the ground as established by archaeology, but about the nature of the texts with which archaeology was being brought into association. This is a literary question.

Similarly with the Pentateuch. Here harmonization has already occurred within the biblical text itself. The critical move is to notice that the finished product is not a coherent work, and this is a literary perception. It is from this perception that the hypothesis of originally distinct sources derives. What source analysis does is to separate out strands within the narrative that do cohere, with a unity of theme and purpose and plot, and to suggest that these have been combined in very much the way Tatian combined the four Gospels to produce the *Diatessaron*. There is nothing especially *historical*-critical about this procedure; it is, rather, a *literary*-critical approach.

27. John Bright, *A History of Israel* (London: SCM, 1960; 3rd ed. 1981).

The study of biblical harmonization thus has implications well beyond its own apparently limited interest. It reminds us what we mean by calling an approach to the Bible precritical. We do not mean that it was unconcerned for historical inquiry: indeed, one of the chief preoccupations of Augustine or Osiander was precisely to produce a coherent historical picture of the life of Jesus. It is biblical criticism that stressed on the contrary the difficulties for historical reconstruction presented by the discrepancies among the Gospels. Nor do we mean that it was uninterested in the questions our opening definition from the *Oxford English Dictionary* identified as critical concerns, such as the origins and development of the biblical text. These too are matters in which precritical interpreters took an interest, as do their heirs today in conservative Christian communities. Very few critical scholars are as interested in, say, the date of Daniel or the authorship of the Pastoral Epistles as are noncritical or fundamentalist Bible readers. No, what makes approaches precritical is their inability to engage with the literary character and genre of the biblical texts. By contrast, critical reading attends closely to just this question. Ordinary readers of the Bible can be just as critical, in this sense, as professional biblical scholars, by showing that they know what sort of questions biblical books can and cannot answer. Biblical criticism has its technicalities, but the underlying attitude that makes it possible is available to all.

My arguments in this chapter have one consequence that could be significant for the discipline of biblical studies. They suggest that the currently perceived rift between what is called historical criticism and the newer literary approaches may be more apparent than real. Historical critics, so-called, have got into the way of emphasizing the historical aspects of their work, and literary critics into emphasizing the nonhistorical character of theirs. The difference may be summed up in the now customary contrast between diachronic and synchronic modes of biblical study. There are indeed examples where such a distinction is clear, but I suspect they are not nearly so common is as often thought. Biblical criticism has at its heart an essentially literary focus, which can be traced back to its beginnings in a period that had not yet embraced nineteenth-century scholarship's interest in the historical. The correlation of biblical criticism with historical study is an important part of the development of the discipline, but essentially an accidental one, by no means given in the origins of a critical approach. Modern literary critics of the Bible have more in common with how biblical criticism has been than they sometimes recognize.

Two further features of biblical criticism emerge from the discussion of harmonization. One is the importance of semantics: not just the semantics of individual words, important as that undoubtedly is, but what may be called the macrosemantics of whole texts. The perception of genre in texts is intimately related to the ability to perform a close reading, that is, to establish the overall meaning of a complete text. To understand a text is to see how it hangs together, to grasp its drift, how one section leads to another, how the argument moves forward, and what kind of overall sense it makes—to follow what German scholars call its *Duktus*. (Rhetorical criticism has moved this question into the spotlight but has not seen, I believe, how much it was already the concern of earlier biblical critics.) Even if the text is to be used in the task of historical reconstruction, it needs first to be understood; otherwise one will not be able to make an appropriate use of it. Here again the parallels between biblical and wider literary criticism are much closer than people often think.

Secondly, the question of a passage's truth needs to be bracketed out while it is studied, not out of skepticism but as a procedural matter. In the harmonizers, a premature concern for the truth of the Gospel stories is in many ways the factor that gets in the way of a due literary understanding of them. Augustine wants to know what Jesus actually did and said, before he has stopped to ask what kind of stories he is dealing with. He already "knows" that the different and discordant accounts in the four Gospels must be reducible to a single concordant one before he has examined them, and so he forces them into a framework that derives from none of them. He approaches the biblical texts from what is now sometimes called a confessional or confessing point of view, already convinced that they convey absolute truth; his task is then simply to demonstrate that truth by reading them in a way adapted to produce it. Biblical criticism is the opposite of this. It studies the text in a value-neutral manner, trying to understand it before passing judgment on matters of truth and falsehood, relevance or irrelevance. As we shall see in chapter 6, this characteristic of criticism is now under fierce attack in some quarters. But the attack itself suggests that the characteristic is indeed present. I shall argue later that the neutral, bracketing-out approach proper to biblical criticism not only is essential, but actually expresses more respect for the text than does a so-called theological hermeneutic. My concern at present, however, is not so much to commend a critical approach as to identify its defining characteristics, and thereby to shift attention from a concentration on history toward what I see as a more accurate definition, of which the older term biblical criticism is a better expression. The term historical-critical method will be the subject of the next chapter.

CRITICISM AND INCONSISTENCIES

I hope to have shown that the essence of biblical criticism does not reside in the recognition of difficulties in the text, for there were many precritical commentators who were intensely aware of such difficulties and strove hard to explain them. What characterizes the critical approach is a particular way of handling the difficulties, a way driven by a literary perception of the genre of the texts in which they appear. To this point—that noticing difficulties is not in itself a critical procedure—may be added an equal and opposite one: that there are many undoubtedly critical commentators who have not been interested in difficulties in the text in any case. The idea that critical scholars spend all their time on the lookout for incongruities in the text is a caricature.

The caricature draws its strength from a concentration on the Pentateuch. Here traditional biblical criticism has concentrated on source division, and there is no doubt that much of the evidence for that comes from minute observation of doublets that clash with each other and inconsistencies such as the use of different divine names with no apparent rationale. From the work of Richard Simon onward, pentateuchal study has indeed been interested in "difficulties" in the text. Even so, it would be odd to deny the description critical to form-critical work, which is not focused on such matters at all, or to redaction criticism, which asks rather how a semblance of unity and coherence has been imparted to disparate materials.

But if we move away from the Pentateuch and consider other biblical books, most critical work has not been concerned with difficulties and inconsistencies anyway. Take a book such as Job. There do exist source-critical studies of Job, arguing that this or that chapter is inauthentic: chapter 28, and the speeches of Elihu (chaps. 32–37) are widely said to come from different hands from the bulk of the book, and many commentators argue that the prose and verse sections did not originate at the same time. As with pentateuchal criticism, some of these arguments at least do rest on noticing inconsistency—as when it is said, for example, that the prose prologue and epilogue deal with a somewhat different theological issue from the verse speeches. (The prose tale is concerned with the question whether a person can be disinterestedly pious, the verse dialogue with possible reasons for the suffering of the righteous.) But the majority of critical commentaries on Job are concerned primarily to provide a coherent reading of the book without spending much time on the inconsistencies. Most such commentaries are critical in that they ask about the meaning of the book as it is in itself, rather than about its typological function as foreshadowing Christ (by contrast with a classic such as Gregory the Great's *Moralia in Iob*) or about its historical truth as a report of real events. They do this because they have perceived that the book is *not that kind of thing*: neither a historical report nor a piece of prophecy, but a wisdom book, albeit a rather unusual one, which deals with questions about the meaning and purpose of human existence. Once again, what makes such readings critical is their attention to the book's genre.

Even in the case of the Pentateuch, by no means all critical commentators have been interested in questions of source criticism. Von Rad's great commentary on Genesis, for example, does indeed present the sources in different fonts.[28] But his exposition is not concerned with the source analysis in itself. He concentrates on the theological contents and implications of each passage as he expounds it and does not draw much attention to differences between the sources. Yet it would be distinctly odd to say that von Rad was not a critical scholar. The major series of commentaries on the Old Testament—Das Alte Testament Deutsch, the Old Testament Library, Hermeneia, the Word Biblical Commentaries—are all critical and would be called so by any biblical scholar. Yet for the most part their essential concern is with the theological meaning of the text, not with the observation of difficulties such as we have discussed in this chapter.

If we turn to the New Testament, the point is even clearer. Commentaries on the Pauline letters are not critical only if they suggest (as often in the case of 2 Corinthians, for example) that the letters are full of inconsistencies, while being noncritical if they read the letters "straight." With the exception of chapter 16, there are few parts of Romans that are often regarded as needing a source-critical explanation in terms of separate underlying documents. Yet it would be odd indeed to suggest that most critical commentaries on Romans are therefore not critical at all. To take the limiting case in the Pauline corpus, probably no one has ever suggested that Philemon is composite or anything but a unified and coherent composition. Yet a reading of Philemon could still be critical or noncritical. It will be critical if it attends to the fact that this is a letter, not a theological treatise; if it shows awareness of its historical context as determining what it can mean (on this see chap. 4); if it is interested in the overall drift and does not interpret each verse atomistically as though the text were a collection of aphorisms or proof texts. A noncritical reading of Philemon would on the contrary be one that ignored its specific literary character as a letter, or read it simply as a section of the New Testament, treated as a single text in which the individual books are like the chapters of a large book, lacking specificity. A noncritical reading would pay no attention to the text's plain sense (see again chap. 4), divorcing it from its context in the life of Paul and forcing it to answer questions that were not his questions.

CONCLUSION

We may sum up like this. First, the observation of difficulties is not in itself evidence of a critical approach; it depends how the difficulties are dealt with. And second, there is much critical work that is not concerned with difficulties

28. Gerhard von Rad, *Genesis: A Commentary* (London: SCM, 1961, 2nd ed. 1972; translated from *Das Erste Buch Mose, Genesis* [Göttingen: Vandenhoeck & Ruprecht, 1956]).

in any case. In short, the observation of difficulties is neither a necessary nor a sufficient condition of a critical approach to the Bible.

What, then, is biblical criticism? It is an inquiry into the biblical text that takes its starting point from the attempt to understand, a desire to read the text in its coherence and to grasp its drift. This is essentially a literary operation. Unlike precritical and some postcritical interpreters, however, biblical critics do not assume that all texts can in fact successfully be read in this holistic way, but are prepared to encounter frustrations in reading. Such frustrations meet noncritical interpreters, too, in the form of inconsistencies and irregularities in the text which on the face of it thwart the attempt at holistic reading. When this happens, noncritical and critical interpreters diverge in their approach. Noncritical readers take the givenness (whether religious or literary) of the text to authorize or even demand harmonization, even if the result is to produce an "unreadable" (because unclassifiable) text. The critical response is to ask about the genre of the text, and on the basis of the answer to decide how the inconsistencies are to be regarded. The solution may be that there is no solution, that is, that the text must simply be composite. But it is not this conclusion that constitutes the study as critical, but rather its concern for the kind of text that is being read, and an awareness of what questions it is appropriate to ask of it. For this reason it is quite possible for there to be critical readings of texts that do not identify difficulties at all.

So the attempt to define biblical criticism as attention to difficulties in the text fails. Biblical critics have often been interested in difficulties, but so have others whom we would not call critics; while not all biblical-critical work has been concerned with difficulties anyway. There is some correlation between criticism and a concern with difficulties, but the latter cannot be part of the definition of the former. We must therefore examine other possibilities, and a number of strands have already suggested themselves. Above all, I have argued that biblical criticism is by definition a *literary* operation. But this conflicts sharply with a prevailing definition of it in terms of a concern with history; and that will concern us in the next chapter.

3

The "Historical-Critical Method"

Biblical critics quite often present themselves as historians rather than as theologians,[1] while opponents of criticism, or those who think the time has come to "move on" from it, regularly regard its historical character as the root of what is objectionable about it: biblical criticism, both agree, is history, not theology.

For many people working in biblical studies, this seems fairly obvious. It can be seen in the preferred description of biblical criticism as the "historical-critical method." The use of this term, which has all but replaced "biblical criticism" in much academic writing about biblical study, points to the belief that a critical approach to the Bible consists in applying to it a method essentially at home in the study of history. For many, perhaps most, scholars it is axiomatic that traditional biblical criticism has been dominated by historical concerns.[2] Those who are now urging that a literary approach to the Bible should be encouraged often speak of the need to replace the historical-critical paradigm with a literary one. Proponents of the so-called canonical approach suggest that biblical study has become exclusively historical in its concerns and should

1. See E. P. Sanders, *The Historical Figure of Jesus* (London: Allen Lane, Penguin Press, 1993), 2–3; Geza Vermes, *Jesus the Jew: A Historian's Reading of the Gospels* (London: Collins, 1973), passim.

2. In Robert Morgan with John Barton, *Biblical Interpretation*, The Oxford Bible (Oxford: Oxford University Press, 1988), the development of criticism is focused very much on the increasing concern with historical questions, with chapters entitled "Criticism and the Death of Scripture," "History and the Growth of Knowledge," and "History of Traditions," all concentrating on the interest in history as that which has diverted biblical interpretation from embracing a more theological task. As this chapter will show, I have since come to think this emphasis misplaced, though that is not to say that the evidence assembled in the book is in any way wrong in itself.

31

become more theological. People who favor a holistic or synchronic reading of the biblical text often contrast this with the historical or diachronic approach that has prevailed until now in biblical studies. Feminist and liberation theologians, who believe passionately that the Bible should be read to promote human freedom and emancipation from oppression, often contrast this with the "purely historical" methods of traditional academic study. On all sides it is agreed that history has provided the normative models for studying the Bible since the rise of critical study in the European Enlightenment. Both those who attack biblical criticism and those who defend it generally do so by emphasizing its essentially historical character.

Such was certainly Karl Barth's understanding of the matter; he belongs to the attackers. Here are his comments on his colleague Hugo Gressmann:

> Gressmann is *not* a theologian, not in *any* sense; as a self-confessedly "heathen" historian he gets exercised about my exegesis, and with just the same "righteous anger" I have to confess that I do *not* believe in his *bona fides* as a claimant to the title of "theologian." It is a *lie* to call oneself a theologian and to sit in a theological faculty if one has *no* understanding of theological questions and *no* interest in theological tasks, but on the contrary has one's *entire* love as a scholar *only* for historical study. *Sunt certi denique fines*, and in Gressmann's case these have certainly been transgressed. . . . One might as well hold discussions with a wooden peg as with this man, who has never thought it necessary to devote even five minutes' thought to the question "What is Theology?" Where this man is concerned my dearest wish would be that he would leave us in peace and just talk to the philologists about *their* problems.[3]

In this chapter I shall examine how far the term "historical-critical method" really does justice to the task that biblical critics undertake. This has two

---

3. "Greßmann ist *kein* Theologe, in *keinem* Sinn, und mit demselben 'sittlichen Zorn,' mit dem er sich als bewußt *heidnischer* Geschichtwissenschaftler über meine Exegese aufregt, bekenne ich, daß ich an seine bona fides, sich Theologe nennen zu dürfen, . . . *nicht* glaube. Es ist eine *Lüge*, sich Theologe zu nennen und in einer theologischen Fakultät zu sitzen, wenn man wie er für theologische Fragen *kein* Verständnis und für theologische Aufgaben *kein* Interesse, sondern seine *ganze* Liebe als Wissenschaftler *nur* bei der Geschichtswissenschaft hat. Sunt certi denique fines, und die sind bei Greßmann überschritten. . . . Man könnte ebensogut mit einem Holzpflock diskutieren wie mit diesem Mann, der über die Frage: Was ist Theologie? noch keine fünf Minuten nachzudenken für nötig gehalten hat. Und an diesen Mann selbst hätte ich auch keinen anderen Wunsch als den, daß er uns in Ruhe ließe und sich mit den Philologen über *ihre* Probleme unterhielte" (*Karl Barth–Martin Rade, Ein Briefwechsel*, ed. C. Schwöbel [Gütersloh: Mohn, 1981], 218; quoted in Rudolf Smend, "Karl Barth als Ausleger der Heiligen Schrift," in *Theologie als Christologie: Zum Werk und Leben Karl Barths. Ein Symposium*, ed. H. Köckert and W. Krötke [Berlin: Evangelische Verlagsanstalt, 1988], 9–37; quotation, 18–19).

aspects. First, how far is a concern for *history* a defining characteristic? Granted that much critical work on the Bible has certainly been historical in its interests, is that what makes such work critical? Secondly, is critical biblical study the application of a *method*? Both proponents and opponents often seem to think it is, but we shall see reason to question this.

CRITICISM AND HISTORY

"History" as the focus of biblical criticism may, I think, bear one of two senses, and it is important to be clear which we are talking about. Any given critic may have been concerned with both, but they are conceptually distinct.

According to the first sense, biblical criticism is historical in that critics have been concerned to reconstruct the historical events underlying the biblical text. They may be concerned with the history of Israel, the historical Jesus, or the historical development of the early church.

A second possibility is that they have been interested in the historical development of the biblical text itself, in its underlying strata and sources: which parts of (say) Isaiah really go back to the prophet, and which are later additions; how the Pentateuch came to be compiled, and from what underlying source materials.

We need to hold these two senses apart in our minds if we are to obtain any clarity about the use of the expression "the historical-critical method."[4]

1. Historical Events

The most obvious reason for calling biblical criticism the *historical*-critical method is a belief that its most characteristic task has been the reconstruction of historical events and their evaluation.

On this understanding the typical critical work will be a history of Israel, a work on the historical Jesus, or a history of the church in the New Testament period. There are many such works, produced by people whom anyone would call biblical critics. In looking to the founding fathers of modern biblical study, one thinks, in the case of the Old Testament, of Julius Wellhausen. The work we now refer to as *Prolegomena to the History of Israel* was originally

---

4. There is a possible and very important third sense: it may be said that biblical critics have been interested in the "historical meaning" of texts, that is, the meaning that texts had in their original context. This rests on the belief that a text is not free-floating but belongs in a historical context. We shall explore this in chapter 4.

called *Geschichte Israels I* (*History of Israel*, volume 1).[5] Where the New Testament is concerned, the work of David Friedrich Strauss, some half a century before Wellhausen, is the most obvious example.[6] In both cases the scholars named were in a line that stretched back into earlier times: Wellhausen is unimaginable without the work of W. M. L. de Wette,[7] and Strauss's hypotheses owe much to the explosive "Wolfenbüttel Fragments" of Reimarus.[8] In modern times one may think of the various quests for the historical Jesus, where the recognition that the true story cannot be simply read off from the text of the New Testament, but requires examination with the tools of historical method, might be seen as the classic instance of biblical criticism as history.

It has been normal, in writing histories of biblical criticism, to concentrate very strongly on these examples.[9] But two points may be raised here. First, though many critical scholars have indeed been concerned with history, this has by no means been the only concern of the critical movement in biblical studies. Many critical scholars have written on biblical theology; others have been interested in the literary forms of the text; others again have studied particular types of material in the Old and New Testaments—wisdom, prophecy, apocalyptic, Gospels, epistles—without any great stress on their "diachronic"

---

5. Julius Wellhausen, *Geschichte Israels I* (Berlin: G. Reimer, 1878); 2nd ed. 1883 as *Prolegomena zur Geschichte Israels*; ET, *Prolegomena to the History of Israel* (Edinburgh: A. & C. Black, 1885).

6. David Friedrich Strauss, *Das Leben Jesu* (Tübingen, 1835); ET, *The Life of Jesus Critically Examined* (London: SCM, 1973).

7. W. M. L. de Wette, *Beiträge zur Einleitung in das Alte Testament*, 2 vols. (Halle: Schimmelpfennig, 1806–7). See J. W. Rogerson, *W. M. L. de Wette, Founder of Modern Biblical Criticism: An Intellectual Biography* (Sheffield: JSOT Press, 1992).

8. H. S. Reimarus, *Fragments* (Philadelphia: Fortress Press, 1970).

9. For the Old Testament, see especially Hans-Joachim Kraus, *Geschichte der historisch-kritischen Erforschung des Alten Testaments von der Reformation bis zur Gegenwart* (Neukirchen Kreis Moers: Verlag der Buchhandlung des Erziehungsvereins, 1956; 3rd ed. Neukirchen-Vluyn: Neukirchener Verlag, 1982). K. Lehmann points out that the term "source," which from the Renaissance onward had had the sense of "authoritative original starting-point" (*fons*), has in modern biblical studies come to mean one of the underlying documents in composite texts (hence we speak of the "sources" of the Pentateuch, and of "source criticism"). This bespeaks a shift from biblical study as the exploration of the Bible, seen as the source of faith, to biblical study as a type of critical history. See K. Lehmann, "Der hermeneutische Horizont der historisch-kritischen Exegese," in *Einführung in die Methoden der biblischen Exegese*, ed. J. Schreiner (Würzburg: Echter Verlag, 1971), 40–80. Francis Watson, in *Text, Church and World: Biblical Interpretation in Theological Perspective* (Edinburgh: T. & T. Clark, 1994), 257, thinks that New Testament scholarship has typically had historical reconstruction as its main aim—and that it has reconstructed history in a reductive manner.

dimension. This point has already been made by James Barr, and I simply call attention to it again here.[10] Much that has been written on Paul or the Gospels does not belong to any historical genre, but is thematic or theological or literary; and the same is true, preeminently, of the Old Testament Wisdom literature, where it is indeed hard to see how much can be said about historical matters at all, given the difficulties of dating involved. Thus though there is plenty of critical history writing based on an examination of the Bible, it is hard to argue that an interest in history is the defining characteristic of critical scholarship. Many questions other than history have been the subject of critical questioning in the study of the Bible.

Indeed, one of the greatest contributions to reconstructing the history of Israel, that of Julius Wellhausen, depended crucially on the fact that other kinds of critical work on the biblical text had already been accomplished, namely the source-division of the Pentateuch. This went back several centuries before Wellhausen himself, at least to the work of Richard Simon and of Jean Astruc, though Wellhausen himself of course contributed greatly to it. It was his discovery (or hypothesis) that P was the latest of the sources that led directly to his particular reconstruction of Israel's history, its central plank being the shift from "ancient Israel" before the exile to "Judaism" after it. Whether or not Wellhausen's hypothesis was correct, it rested on work that was not in itself directly historical, that is, on the painstaking identification of the sources of the Pentateuch.[11] That is much more a literary than a historical procedure. Wellhausen built a history of Israel upon it; but his primary critical move was to adopt such a source-division, not the fact that he used that division as a basis for a reconstruction of history. Source-division itself clearly long antedates any interest in reconstructing a history of Israel by critical investigation of the Old Testament.

Secondly, and conversely, there has been a great deal of study of the history of Israel that few would describe as critical. John Rogerson identifies de Wette's signal contribution as having provided the first history of Israelite religion that diverged significantly from the story of Israel as the Bible tells it.[12] But if that is so, then most scholars would probably regard a lot of the historical writing

10. James Barr, *Holy Scripture: Canon, Authority, Criticism* (Oxford: Oxford University Press, 1983), 105–6.

11. On this point, cf. F. W. Dobbs-Allsop, "Rethinking Historical Criticism," *Biblical Interpretation* 7 (1999): 235–71.

12. John W. Rogerson, *Old Testament Criticism in the Nineteenth Century: England and Germany* (London: SPCK, 1984), 29: "De Wette's *Contributions* is the first work of Old Testament scholarship to present a view of the history of Israelite religion that is radically at variance with the view implied in the Old Testament itself."

before de Wette as uncritical.[13] It is uncritical, not because it is not historical, but because its authors were unable, or at any rate failed, to question the text and simply retold the story. It is worth mentioning here again that John Bright's *History of Israel*[14] has often attracted much the same criticism: that it is comprehensive and well informed but not *critical* in the true sense, because it essentially gives the reader simply an expanded version of the Old Testament story, much enriched with, for example, the findings of biblical archaeology, but does not raise the possibility that the biblical text may be simply misleading or mistaken. Whether this is fair to Bright is not the point here. The point is that the *critical* impulse is being detected not in the mere fact of being concerned with history, but in approaching history from a particular stance. This stance is one in which the text is subject to critical questioning. It may prove to be essentially accurate—questioning is not the same as disbelief or skepticism—but its accuracy is not a given; it can be established or demolished only through inquiry.

These two points taken together suggest that a concern for reconstructing history is not in itself part of the *definition* of biblical criticism. The idea that biblical critics are as a class interested in history (rather than, say, theology) is wide of the mark; but even when they are, what marks them out as critical is not that interest in itself, but the spirit in which they inquire into history. As a matter of fact, rather few biblical scholars have any historical training; they mostly come to theology and biblical studies from a literary or linguistic background, traditionally via the study of classics but in more recent times often from the study of literature or modern languages. Barth could condemn Gressmann as being a historian rather than a theologian, but it is doubtful whether Gressmann himself would have seen himself as a historian; probably he would have called himself a philologist.[15] In recent years E. P. Sanders and Geza Vermes have both famously claimed to be historians, not theologians; but most secular historians would probably read them not as historians in the ordinary sense of the word, but rather as theologians applying historical principles. When the *Times Literary Supplement* publishes reviews of books

13. Frances Young points out that patristic and classical authors were often concerned with *to historikon*, "but to jump to the conclusion that *to historikon* is some kind of historico-critical exegesis is misplaced: I submit that too many discussions of patristic exegesis have jumped to conclusions about historical interest where such terminology is used, for it does not necessarily imply what we mean by historical" (Frances M. Young, *Biblical Exegesis and the Formation of Christian Culture* [Cambridge: Cambridge University Press, 1997], 79).

14. John Bright, *A History of Israel* (London: SCM, 1960; 3rd ed. 1981).

15. Rudolf Smend, *Deutsche Alttestamentler in drei Jahrhunderten* (Göttingen: Vandenhoeck & Ruprecht, 1989), 173–81.

on biblical history, it includes them in a section called Religion, not History. This may be a misperception, but it is a very common one, and probably reflects the fact that reconstructions of biblical history do not strike secular historians as very much like what they do themselves.[16]

Even those biblical scholars who are correctly perceived as historians were often appreciated by their contemporaries because they were felt to be contributing to the *theological* appropriation of the Bible. Thus Rudolf Smend remarks of Albrecht Alt—surely important for his reconstructions of the history of early Israel and its institutions—that his historical investigations into ancient Israel were valued in the theological world precisely because they seemed to show that we had firm ground under our feet after all in dealing with the oldest period of Israelite history, "and wasn't that marvelously usable by theologians writing sermons?"[17] It also fitted well into the "revelation as history" approach current in Alt's time in German theology.

Similar things might be said of the quests for the historical Jesus. However much their practitioners stress that their concern is historical, their efforts are perceived by others as primarily of theological importance. In this connection, one may get a rather misleading impression from a classic such as Van A. Harvey's *The Historian and the Believer*.[18] This is concerned chiefly with research into historical matters, preeminently indeed with the quest for the historical Jesus, and thus rightly concentrates on the historical aspect of biblical scholarship. But in the process Harvey tends to write as though this were the main or even the only type of work that biblical scholars do, and to describe biblical criticism exclusively in terms of the historical.[19] The perceived conflict between criticism and faith is portrayed as one between (as the title indicates) historians and believers, and in the process all biblical scholars are seen primarily as historians. If we broaden out from the question of the historical Jesus to look at the other kinds of work biblical scholars do, the epithet "historian"

16. In this connection it is interesting to note the comments of Philip Davies on the concept "ancient Israel" in *In Search of 'Ancient Israel,'* Journal for the Study of the Old Testament: Supplement Series 148 (Sheffield: JSOT Press, 1992), which he regards as essentially a theologically constructed entity, not corresponding to any ancient reality. One of E. P. Sanders's criticisms of biblical scholars is that they are often not nearly historians enough: they read Paul, for example, as if he were a systematic theologian, with far too shaky a grasp of his historical setting.

17. "Und war das alles nicht für den Theologen bis hin zur Predigt herrlich verwendbar?" See Smend, *Deutsche Alttestamentler in drei Jahrhunderten*, 205.

18. Van A. Harvey, *The Historian and the Believer: The Morality of Historical Knowledge and Christian Belief* (London: SCM, 1967).

19. This tendency is also very marked in Paul S. Minear, *The Bible and the Historian: Breaking the Silence about God in Biblical Studies* (Nashville: Abingdon Press, 2002).

seems much less appropriate. And even research into the historical Jesus seldom uses "normal" historical methods, but has developed a methodology all
its own—for example, the principle of dissimilarity—which secular historians
often find rather puzzling.[20]

Even where biblical scholars genuinely *are* primarily concerned with history, not all can be said to have approached historical questions in a critical
spirit. Already we are beginning to see wherein such a spirit resides. It involves
treating the accuracy of the biblical account as an open question. But if the
question is open, how is it to be decided? Only by examining the historical
sources—a procedure that involves as many literary processes as directly historical ones. Before Wellhausen could ask whether the presentation of the
early history of Israelite institutions in P was "true," he had to establish when
P was written, but also what kind of source P was. Thus we meet again the
question of genre, which lies at the root of historical work, as well as of work
that is in itself more obviously literary.

Nevertheless, Wellhausen was indeed primarily a historian, who saw himself as doing for Israel what the great classical historians of his day—Niebuhr,
Ranke, Mommsen—were doing or had done for the history of Greece and
Rome. As Smend observes, in the nineteenth century it was entirely natural
that biblical criticism had as one of its chief fruits the possibility of historical
reconstruction; in that period any attempt to grasp the Bible (studied by critical methods) as a whole was more or less bound to conceive that whole in
terms of history.[21] Nothing I have been saying is meant to detract from this
obvious fact. Few before or since have, however, been quite so single-minded
in their refusal to broach theological questions[22] or in an insistence that history was their concern. Most biblical historians turn out to be theologians in

---

20. See Gerd Theissen and Dagmar Winter, *The Quest for the Plausible Jesus: The Question
of Criteria* (Louisville, KY, and London: Westminster John Knox, 2002), for details of how
this principle has worked in practice.

21. Rudolf Smend, "Nachkritische Schriftauslegung," in *Parrhesia. Karl Barth zum 80.
Geburtstag*, ed. E. Busch, J. Fangmeier, and M. Geiger (Zurich: EVZ-Verlag, 1966), 215–37;
also in Smend, *Die Mitte des Alten Testaments* (Munich: Kaiser Verlag, 1986), 212–32; and in
Smend, *Bibel und Wissenschaft* (Tübingen: Mohr Siebeck, 2004), 230–50; see 235.

22. Wellhausen was highly unreceptive to the idea of a theology of the Old Testament.
Rudolf Smend found in the cover of an edition of Hitzig's commentary on Isaiah a proposed
youthful book by Wellhausen of which part of the title read "A Criticism of So-called Old
Testament Theology as an Academic Discipline" ("Kritik des s.g. ATl. Theologie als wis-
senschaftlicher Disziplin"); see Rudolf Smend, "Theologie im Alten Testament," in *Verifikationen. Festschrift für Gerhard Ebeling zum 70. Geburtstag*, ed. E. Jüngel, J. Wallmann,
and W. Werbeck (Tübingen: J. C. B. Mohr [Paul Siebeck], 1982), 11–26; reprinted in R.
Smend, *Die Mitte des Alten Testaments* (Munich: Kaiser, 1986), 104–17; the reference is on
105 of the last-mentioned publication.

disguise, contrary to the impression given by many who attack historical criticism in biblical studies. But when we say that Wellhausen was a *critical* historian, we are identifying his contribution as lying in the way he questioned his sources. After all, the authors of those sources themselves—the J, E, and P writers—were also interested in history; but no one would call them "critical." In a later section we shall have to ask where the critical principles applied by Wellhausen and his successors derive from, since a particular theory about this has also been alleged to define critical biblical study.

Thus it is not in a concern for history per se, but in a particular style of studying history, that biblical scholars have been "critical." Historical study, where that is the concern, can be either critical or noncritical; and critical study can be historical or nonhistorical. This suggests that the term "historical-critical method" is an awkward hybrid and might be better avoided.

2. The History of the Biblical Text

A second possible theory about the essentially historical nature of biblical criticism will point to its concern for what Robert Alter calls "excavative" work on the text.[23] The suggested analogy is with archaeology (and we recall Childs's complaint that biblical critics treat the text as if it were "inert sherds" lying in the ground[24]). The critic, it is said, is interested in the earlier stages of the biblical texts rather than in their final form (i.e., the form that now lies before us). This is also a historical interest, in that it concerns itself with how the text used to be, rather than in how it now is. To be a critical scholar is thus again to be *historical*-critical in one's interests—only that history now means not political or social history, but the history of the text.

In some ways this is not unlike the idea that critics are mainly concerned with "Introduction," an idea already mentioned in chapter 1.[25] The suggestion is that work which defines itself as critical is interested in getting back behind the text to the earlier documents from which it was composed. In the case of prophetic texts, it means identifying and "deleting" passages that cannot claim to go back to the prophet himself. In the case of the Pentateuch and other historical books, it means dividing the text up into its underlying sources and seeking to date them. In every case the quest is for some original text that is earlier than the text in its present form, and the critic's task is then to trace how the present form developed from the earlier source material.

---

23. Robert Alter, *The Art of Biblical Narrative* (London: George Allen & Unwin, 1981).
24. See above, p. 5.
25. See p. 2.

This identification of how critical scholars work usually occurs in polemical works that disapprove of the critical operations thus identified and seek to realign scholarship on the basis of interest in the text's final form. Is biblical criticism in fact so focused on the quest for the original components of texts, and does that justify its being called historical-critical?

There is no doubt that some critical scholars have focused very strongly on the earliest stage of a text that can be reconstructed. The tendency is perhaps more obvious today in the German-speaking world than among Anglophones, with verses still being split up among several sources or "hands," deletion still recommended, and verse numbers marked with an asterisk to indicate a hypothetical earlier phase in the text's formation at which it lacked some elements that are now there. As long ago as 1951, C. R. North was complaining about this tendency, in his survey of pentateuchal criticism in *The Old Testament and Modern Study*.[26]

But it is doubtful whether this digging beneath the surface is the distinguishing mark of historical-critical scholarship. It is not true of many books or articles that anyone beginning biblical study today would be expected to read. And it is far from clear that the founders of nineteenth-century criticism saw the matter in this way.[27] To some extent the insistence that biblical criticism has been interested only or chiefly in the earliest strata of texts is an aspect of

26. C. R. North, "The Pentateuch," in *The Old Testament and Modern Study: A Generation of Discovery and Research*, ed. H. H. Rowley (Oxford: Clarendon Press, 1951), 48–83. In the literary realm a similar complaint can be found in J. R. R. Tolkien's classic study *Beowulf: The Monster and the Critics (The Sir Israel Gollancz Lecture for 1936)* (Oxford: Oxford University Press, 1958). Tolkien urges that Beowulf has been too long in the hands of historians, interested only in the background of a text that they did not appreciate as poetry; it is time to consider it again as a work of art. Interestingly, however, he is not averse to questions of "Introduction," as the biblical critics would call them: "I accept without argument throughout the attribution of *Beowulf* to the 'age of Bede'—one of the firmer conclusions of a department of research most clearly serviceable to criticism: inquiry into the possible date of the effective composition of the poem as we have it" (p. 20). Note the similarity to our argument about the "principal" author of texts in the phrase "the effective composition of the poem as we have it."

27. Cf. James Barr, "Jowett and the Reading of the Bible 'Like Any Other Book,'" *Horizons in Biblical Theology: An International Dialogue* 4 (1982): 1–44, esp. 3: "It is remarkable how little the essay [sc. Jowett's essay "On the Interpretation of Scripture," in *Essays and Reviews*, 1860] has to say about the task of historical reconstruction of the original situation, and how little it seeks to prove that the task of the biblical interpreter is an essentially *historical* one at all." See also Barr's shorter piece "Jowett and the 'Original Meaning' of Scripture," *Religious Studies* 18:433–37, esp. 433: "It is difficult to believe . . . that Jowett, when he spoke of 'recovering the original' meaning, intended any such process of historical research. His essay says very little about historical criticism, and it presents no guidance to the reader about a historical process by which the 'original' might be recovered."

the conservative theory that it has been preoccupied with matters of Introduction. Introduction has indeed been excavative, but it is only a small part of the whole critical enterprise.

In fact the interest of biblical scholars of the critical school has not been uniformly in either the earliest or the latest stages in the composition of biblical texts, but has varied as among different books. It is perhaps only in the case of the classical prophets that there has been a serious concentration on the words of the original prophet, and it is mainly here that the dreaded word "deletion" will be found. In the case of the Pentateuch there has certainly been (until recently) a general unwillingness to talk much about the meaning of the *final* form; but nor on the other hand has interest centered on the very earliest elements. There are many studies of the four sources J, E, D, and P, and it is on these *intermediate* stages between the earliest strata and the finished product that scholarly concern has been focused. In the Wisdom literature, interest has been about equally divided between individual sayings and larger collections, though in the case of Job and Ecclesiastes it has long been usual to concentrate on what might be called the "principal author." Form criticism of course deals with small units, but has never restricted its concern to the earliest versions of these, being much interested (on the contrary) to show how they developed and expanded over time. And redaction criticism makes sense only if one can not only isolate the original components of a text but also discover the intentions of those who edited them into a finished whole. Indeed, if we call redaction criticism a critical method, we thereby make it crystal clear that we are not using critical to mean reconstructive or concerned with the earliest form of the text, for redaction criticism is precisely an attempt to discover meanings later than the original one.

Can we be more specific about which stage in the growth of biblical texts has been of most interest to critical scholars? If we look at the differences just noted among prophets, Pentateuch, and Wisdom literature, we might well be drawn to James Barr's way of formulating the matter: that the author in whom biblical critics have usually been most interested is the author who gave the text its "dominant literary character," rather than the earliest or latest author. As an example of this, take Gerhard von Rad's book on the Priestly document.[28] Here the raw materials and earlier, smaller collections on which the Priestly compiler drew are designated Pg (g=*Grundschrift*), and contributions to the continuing P tradition that postdate the main document are called Ps (s=*Supplementum*), but P, standing alone, is used as the siglum for what comes

---

28. Gerhard von Rad, *Die Priesterschrift im Hexateuch literarisch untersucht und theologisch gewertet* (Stuttgart and Berlin: Kohlhammer, 1934).

between these two stages, the coherent work from which we derive our over-all impression of priestly theology. Similar things might be said about the Deuteronomistic History. Those who write on this are interested in its under-lying sources, and also in the ways it was later expanded and adapted; but the focus of concern is with the document between these stages, the "basic" D his-tory to which Martin Noth devoted his seminal book.[29]

The main reason why scholars in the past did not attempt a "holistic" read-ing of the Pentateuch, until modern literary theory and the canonical approach together made it inevitable, had nothing to do (I would suggest) with a preju-dice in favor of the "earliest" or "original" meaning, nor with a sort of archae-ological desire to burrow beneath the surface of the text. It was quite simply that a holistic reading of the Pentateuch makes little sense, unless one is pre-pared to set up literary conventions very different from those within which modern readers normally approach texts, and thus guarantee in advance that a satisfactory meaning for the whole will be forthcoming. If you are used to reading postmodernist writing, then the collected works of Moses may well seem rather unified. But if your previous experience is in reading Thucydides or Livy, you can hardly fail to notice certain awkwardnesses in the Pentateuch; and if you tackle these awkwardnesses in a systematic way, you may well end up with something like the Graf-Wellhausen hypothesis. Then you will feel that you have before you not one incoherent work, but four reasonably coher-ent ones, coherent enough to be attributed to writers who gave them shape and structure. As an intelligent, "critical" reader of the Bible, your interest is likely to focus on those strata in the texts which, like the works of classical or modern authors, are relatively complete works that convey some continuous and consistent meaning. This is not a question of antiquarianism, historicism, or opposition to the final form, but of the application of normal literary per-ceptions to the Bible.

If we look at the last century or so of biblical study from this perspective, a lot of untidy features will begin to make sense. Take, for example, the book of Isaiah. It is true that, until very recently, no one had attempted to read this book "holistically."[30] No critical scholar thought it worth trying, because even a superficial look at the book makes it clear that it is composite and anthological

29. Martin Noth, *Überlieferungsgeschichtliche Studien I*, Schriften der Königsberger Gelehrten Gesellschaft 18 (1943), 43–266; 2nd ed., Tübingen, 1957, 1–110; ET, *The Deuteronomistic History*, Journal for the Study of the Old Testament: Supplement Series 15 (Sheffield: JSOT Press, 1981).

30. See Benjamin Sommer, "The Scroll of Isaiah as Jewish Scripture, or, Why Jews Don't Read Books," in *SBL Seminar Papers: 132nd Annual Meeting* (Atlanta: Scholars Press, 1996), 225–42.

in character. However, it is not true, on the other hand, that people took an interest only in the words of the original prophet, Isaiah son of Amoz, so far as these could be reconstructed. On the whole that is what has mainly interested students of Isaiah 1–39, who have spoken of deleting passages deemed not to come from the prophet himself—though even then they have recognized various smaller collections as having their own literary integrity, for example, the so-called Isaiah apocalypse of chapters 24–27. But in looking at Isaiah 40–66 there has been no thought of deleting these chapters from the book of Isaiah because they are not original. On the contrary, scholars have recognized here one or perhaps two major independent works of Old Testament prophecy, to which they have given names, though admittedly not very inventive ones: Deutero- and Trito-Isaiah (some German scholars will even speak of *das Deuterojesajabuch*, as though the Bible actually contained a book called Deutero-Isaiah). This is because they have quite correctly realized that these chapters do not amount to mere appendices or additions to the words of Isaiah of Jerusalem, but are self-contained works bearing the stamp of a single creative mind.[31] They may well, in turn, be made up of older, small units—or it can be plausibly argued that they are—but no one thinks we should therefore ignore the finished product and concentrate all our energies on the original components.

On the other hand, until the rise of the canonical approach and other "holistic" approaches, it did not occur to scholars that it was in any sense improper to isolate Deutero- and Trito-Isaiah from chapters 1–39 and to examine them as the separate works they so manifestly appeared to be. For most critics the Old Testament contains not a book of Isaiah but three books of Isaiah, each deserving study in its own right. Within each collection one may sensibly speak of older fragmentary material or redactional additions, but there is no commitment to the original prophet Isaiah such that the whole of chapters 40–66 has to be called a redactional addition. Just the same way of thinking has led to such less used but equally acceptable terms as Deutero-Zechariah (Zech. 9–14), the appendix to Ezekiel (Ezek. 40–48), and the book of consolation (Jer. 30–31). Other critical titles such as the Succession Narrative and the Deuteronomistic History proceed from exactly the same way of approaching the material. So far from its being a desire to fragment the text or get back to an original stratum that results in these names for extended portions of it, these

---

31. Even if Hugh Williamson is correct in thinking that Deutero-Isaiah was planned as an addition to Isaiah 1–39, it is still true that this work has an integrity of its own and is quite unlike a series of fragmentary add-ons: see H. G. M. Williamson, *The Book Called Isaiah: Deutero-Isaiah's Role in Composition and Redaction* (Oxford: Clarendon Press, 1994).

titles are evidence of a successful attempt to find unity and coherence in collections of material that are superficially disordered and lacking in structure. The willingness of many biblical conservatives to accept at least the Deutero-Isaiah hypothesis is eloquent testimony that they have seen this themselves and that, at least in this kind of critical judgment, they can recognize the desire to read the Bible as a set of works with a real internal unity rather than as an inspired jumble.

To sum up: a concern for the history of the biblical text, and within that for original sections, is not of the essence of biblical criticism. Critics have certainly sometimes divided up the text in the quest for the earliest fragments and have taken an interest in how these fragments came together to form the books we find today. But what makes this kind of work *critical* is more the search for coherence and unity than a desire to carry out textual archaeology. The hypothesis that a text is made up of fragments represents a frustrated attempt to see it as coherent and is not an end in itself. Rather, critics try to read each text as cohering; but when that fails, they resort to theories of fragmentation. (Whether or not a given text is actually fragmentary is an open, empirical question; critics do not automatically expect to find it so.) Even so, critical approaches have typically been most interested in stages of the text at which some coherent unity can be discerned. The whole Pentateuch fails to be read as a unity, but each of the supposed sources can be so read, and once that is so, critics are more interested in them than in the underlying fragments from which they may have been put together. Job contains some elements of disorder, but a typical biblical critic is more interested in the meaning imparted by the principal author than in the meaning of the disorderly sections. Isaiah is something of an anthology, but critics have looked for coherent sections and in the process have produced the hypothesis of Deutero- and Trito-Isaiah.

HISTORICAL METHODS

So far I have tended to argue that the basis of biblical criticism is to be found more in literary than in historical perceptions of the text. It is clear, however, that many biblical scholars have been interested in history—the history of the text or the history of Israel, Jesus, or the church—even if it is true to see this as true *per accidens* rather than as the essence of a critical approach. In this section we must discuss the common assertion that in studying history, scholars have used historical methods shared with secular historians. One could of course be interested in history without following a modern scientific method in reconstructing it; but it is widely suggested that in practice inquiry into the various histories just mentioned has been conducted according to the principles of modern historical inquiry. Very often the name of Troeltsch is mentioned in this connection.

In one sense I believe this contention is obviously true. When they have been concerned with history (and this, as we have seen, is less often than many people think), biblical critics have certainly tried to adopt approaches similar to those they would use in any other field of historical inquiry. For example, they have argued that historical sources cannot be taken as true simply because they claim to be, but must be sifted and weighed, and not combined with each other in a harmonizing way.[32] When, as we have seen, John Bright's *History of Israel* is accused of being uncritical, what people have in mind is his tendency to assume that the biblical account will always turn out to be true in some sense, though it may need tweaking at some points, and that all the accounts of an event will somehow prove to be compatible. Or again, critics have believed that any writer has a *Tendenz*, something that he or she is attempting to persuade the reader of, and that this should be allowed for and discounted. It is also presupposed that historians themselves have a desire to prove or disprove certain things, and that they must allow for this desire and so far as possible set it aside. A further point is an awareness of anachronism as calling into doubt the accuracy of accounts that contain it.[33] All these are general principles not simply of historical study but of any kind of intellectual inquiry in the humanities or (mutatis mutandis) the natural sciences. This is sometimes captured by describing history written on these principles as scientific history, though the usage is rather misleading in English (and possibly rests on a mistranslation from German, where *wissenschaftlich*, here rendered "scientific," means rather "intellectually rigorous"[34]).

Any account of how criticism operates would be bound to include such points as these, and they justify the use of the term "historical-critical method" where critics have been concerned with the reconstruction of history, which (as we have argued) some, but not all, have been. Often, however, more is meant than this. It is often alleged as a criticism of criticism that it depends on a particular formulation of historical principles, those to be found in the work of Ernst Troeltsch. This is argued in detail, for example, in Peter Stuhlmacher's *Schriftauslegung auf dem Wege zur biblischen Theologie*:[35]

32. In this connection it is amusing that Wellhausen describes harmonizers such as Hitzig as examples of "the historical-critical school" (*Prolegomena*, 221).

33. The earliest use of the term "anachronism" attested in English, according to the *Oxford English Dictionary*, is in 1816 (Coleridge), but the concept is undoubtedly older.

34. See the discussion of Gadamer, pp. 55–58.

35. Peter Stuhlmacher, *Schriftauslegung auf dem Wege zur biblischen Theologie* (Göttingen: Vandenhoeck & Ruprecht, 1975); ET, *Historical Criticism and Theological Interpretation of Scripture: Toward a Hermeneutic of Consent* (Philadelphia: Fortress, 1977).

We have recalled that an aspect of the treatment of texts in historical enquiry is the application of the system of methods belonging to historical criticism: i.e., a guiding understanding of history, including at least what Troeltsch called the ground-rules—criticism, analogy, and reciprocity.[36]

Troeltsch's three principles, usually rendered in English as "criticism," "analogy," and "correlation," are summed up as follows by Van Harvey:

(1) the principle of criticism, by which he meant that our judgments about the past cannot simply be classified as true or false but must be seen as claiming only a greater or lesser degree of probability and as always open to revision; (2) the principle of analogy, by which he meant that we are able to make such judgments of probability only if we presuppose that our own present experience is not radically dissimilar to the experience of past persons; and (3) the principle of correlation, by which he meant that the phenomena of man's historical life are so related and interdependent that no radical change can take place at any one point in the historical nexus without effecting a change in all that immediately surrounds it. Historical explanation, therefore, necessarily takes the form of understanding an event in terms of its antecedents and consequences, and no event can be isolated from its historically conditioned time and space.[37]

These principles involve approaching historical narratives with a fixed belief that they should be treated skeptically, that we can believe nothing in them that is not encountered in ordinary life (which rules out miracles, for example), and that no historical events can operate outside the "normal" context of cause and effect. Those who are opposed to biblical criticism see these principles as inherently reductionist and rationalistic. On this basis the Bible is reduced, it is said, to a collection of fables in which no one can be asked to believe. Stuhlmacher's own response to this reduction of biblical narrative is to argue that we should follow Rudolf Bultmann in seeing the text as primarily concerned with existential questions, so that it can still speak, even when its historical value has been removed: that is, he accepts that biblical criticism has the reductive effect just outlined, but argues that this does not matter for faith, because faith does not depend on the verifiability of this or that historical fact:

36. "Wir haben uns darauf besonnen, daß zur geschichtswissenschaftlicher Behandlung von Texten das Methodensystem der historischen Kritik, d.h. ein leitender Geschichtsbegriff und mindestens die von Troeltsch so benannten Grundregeln der Kritik, Analogie und geschichtlichen Wechselwirkung gehören" (Stuhlmacher, 24).

37. Harvey, *The Historian and the Believer*, 14–15, citing Ernst Troeltsch, *Gesammelte Schriften* (Tübingen: J. C. B. Mohr, 1913), 2:729–53; and his article "Historiography," in *Encyclopedia of Religion and Ethics*, ed. James Hastings (New York: Charles Scribner's Sons, 1914), 6:716–23.

The great thing about Bultmann's system of existential interpretation is that in this system he retains these tried and tested rules of historical criticism, yet at the same time is able in this way to take up the question of the unconditional claim of the word of God on humanity.[38]

The reductive effect of Troeltschian criticism results, according to Stuhlmacher, from the fact that it depends on an essentially rationalistic view of history:

As a consequence of its roots in the history of ideas, the historical-critical method implies . . . its own system of assigning value. Its results also depend in the strongest way on the conception of history in the framework of which it is practiced.[39]

But if we do not accept Bultmann's existentialist solution to the problem this raises, then we are left with a severely reductionist view of historical study and no way back to any kind of religious faith in the texts of the Bible. This is the difficulty that scholars in a more Anglo-Saxon tradition tend to feel, since they generally think that actual historical fact matters, even for faith.

My own question is whether biblical criticism, when it does deal with matters of history, is in fact in thrall to Troeltsch. Troeltsch was himself a professor of (systematic) theology, not a secular historian in any normal sense of the word, but paradoxically he seems to have somewhat exaggerated the more positivistic and skeptical aspects of historical study. It is well known that when secular historians have studied biblical narratives, they have often come to rather less skeptical conclusions than their theological colleagues![40] They certainly apply what Christian Hartlich described as "the universally accessible conditions for knowledge of truth to statements about events from the past."[41] But

38. "Das großartige an Bultmanns System der existentialen Interpretation von Texten ist es nun, daß er in diesem System diese bewährten Regeln der historischen Kritik einhalten, zugleich aber die Frage nach dem den Menschen unbedingt angehenden Wort Gottes auf diese Weise aufgreifen kann" (Stuhlmacher, 24).

39. "Die historisch-kritische Methode impliziert . . . von ihren geistesgeschichtlichen Wurzeln her ein eigenes System von Wertsetzungen. Ihre Ergebnisse hängen außerdem aufs stärkste ab von der Geschichtskonzeption, in deren Rahmen sie praktiziert wird" (Stuhlmacher, 97). Cf. Francis Watson, Text, Church and World, 257, who argues that New Testament scholarship has typically been historically reconstructive and theologically reductionist.

40. See, for example, Amélie Kuhrt, "Israelite and Near Eastern Historiography," in Congress Volume Oslo 1998, ed. A. Lemaire and M. Sæbø, Supplements to Vetus Testamentum 80 (Leiden: Brill, 2000), 257–79; on the New Testament, compare the now classic comments of A. N. Sherwin-White, Roman Society and Roman Law in the New Testament (Oxford: Clarendon Press, 1963).

41. Cited in William Yarchin, History of Biblical Interpretation: A Reader (Peabody, MA: Hendrickson, 2004), 304. See Christian Hartlich, "Historisch-kritische Methode in ihrer

these conditions do not in themselves depend on the interpreter's being "a Cartesian, Kantian, Positivist, Atheist, or any other such label"[42]—nor, one may add, a Troeltschian. Where miracles are concerned, for example, the average biblical scholar does not venture an opinion but simply says, "The historian cannot adjudicate in this matter"—this is specially notable where the resurrection of Jesus is concerned, and is particularly striking in the case of E. P. Sanders, who writes: "That Jesus' followers (and later Paul) had resurrection experiences is, in my judgement, a fact. What the reality was that gave rise to the experiences I do not know."[43] This is not very much in the spirit of Troeltsch, whose more rigid principles lead rather to a denial of the possibility of resurrection and to explanations in terms of corporate delusion. Sanders is indeed much more in the mold of any other secular historian, as he himself claims to be, operating with critical methods but without any particular ideology about them: "I shall discuss Jesus the human being, who lived in a particular time and place, and I shall search the evidence and propose explanations just as does any historian when writing about a figure of history."[44]

One accusation often leveled against the application of historical methods to the Bible is that it represents a claim to extreme objectivity that in fact conceals much prejudice and self-interest. This has been the main basis of the attack on critical scholarship by Walter Wink. Wink argues that the historical-critical method is "ensnared in an objectivist ideology" that can never do more than "simply refer the data of the text away from an encounter with experience and back to its own uncontrolled premises."[45] "By detaching the text from the stream of my existence, biblical criticism has hurled it back into the abyss of an objectified past. Such a past is an infinite regress. No amount of devoted study can bring it back."[46]

This complaint is not unlike that made by some who support "advocacy" readings, whether liberationist or feminist: they argue that traditional biblical criticism has claimed to be objective[47] but in fact has been skewed in the direction of powerful men, who hide their hegemony under a cloak of objectivity. R. S. Sugirtharajah writes, "Though historical criticism was liberative partic-

---

Anwendung auf Geschehnisaussagen der Hl. Schrift," *Zeitschrift für Theologie und Kirche* 75 (1978): 467–84.

42. Cited in Yarchin, 304.

43. E. P. Sanders, *The Historical Figure of Jesus*, 280.

44. Ibid., 2.

45. Cited in Yarchin, 355. See Walter Wink, *The Bible in Human Transformation* (Philadelphia: Fortress, 1973).

46. Cited in Yarchin, 354.

47. There is another sense of "objective" in literary criticism that has nothing to do with detachment and will concern us in chapter 4.

ularly to the Western, white and middle class, it had a shackling and enslaving impact on women, blacks and people of other cultures."[48] The need rather is to read the biblical texts in an engaged manner. Objectivity is not only a sham; it is actually undesirable.

The difficulty is that a Western male responding to this accusation cannot be taken seriously in his doing so, since the terms in which the disagreement is set up preclude any possibility of dialogue and allow only capitulation (and serve you right, such writers might argue). But one might perhaps venture the suggestion that objectivity is here being used as something of a straw man. Few biblical critics have ever claimed the degree of objectivity they are being accused of. What they have argued for is reasonable objectivity, that is, a refusal simply to read one's own ideas into the text or to have no sense of detachment from it even for the purposes of study. In a way, advocacy readings have an interest in promoting such a degree of objectivity, since they presumably want to say that the text really does confront the interpreter with a challenge, and it is hard to see how that can be so if there is no way of encountering the text other than one already totally colored by one's own presuppositions. To put it another way, an advocacy reader saws off the branch on which he or she is sitting by denouncing objectivity. If the claim is that male or dominant readers have not been as objective as they should have been—that their claim to be objective is false and that they should actually be more objective, not less—then the attack hits home. But in that case, objectivity—a certain measure of detachment—is the price we pay for being able, later in the process, to criticize readers for failing to see that the texts undermine their own comfortable lives.

As we have seen, Bultmann argued in a directly opposite direction: the aporia induced by objective historical method was precisely the means needed to point the interpreter to the need to read the texts existentially, and that made historical criticism not merely acceptable but actually desirable. For Wink, on the other hand, the claimed objectivism of the historian represents a kind of "false consciousness," in which skepticism reigns but disguises the fact from itself by pretending to be simply objective. I feel sure that this does sometimes happen, but believe the cure is more objectivity, not less.

One feature widely thought to characterize historical criticism may be called *positivism*. What this amounts to is the accumulation by the critic of discrete, uninterpreted facts—"hard facts," as some might call them—rather than

---

48. R. S. Sugirtharajah, "Critics, Tools, and the Global Arena," in *Reading the Bible in the Global Village: Helsinki*, ed. H. Räisänen et al. (Atlanta: Society of Biblical Literature, 2000), 49–60; quotation, 52.

any attempt at deeper levels of interpretation. In the nineteenth century, it may be said, the alternative to positivism was idealism, and modern scholars, especially in the English-speaking world, are certainly not idealist: so it makes sense to claim that they are positivists.

That there is positivism in biblical studies seems to me undeniable. The most obvious example might be the work of the Jesus Seminar, where each individual recorded saying of Jesus is assessed for authenticity by a process that in the end involves majority voting. It is probably fair to say that, by contrast with German biblical studies, Anglo-American scholarship is in a somewhat positivistic phase at the moment. In the study of the Old Testament, the dominance of the Albright school in North America was (is) to some extent the dominance of positivist attitudes. Albright and his school answered the question of how true the Old Testament is largely in terms of how far individual recorded events could be verified by external evidence, and Bright's *History of Israel* could be called positivist by comparison with, say, that of Martin Noth. Indeed, it is hard to see how archaeology, and history based upon it, can avoid being in some sense positivistic. Either a given stratum is there or it is not; either it contains artifacts or it does not; and reporting on these data is simply misleading if it detaches itself from the straightforwardly factual question. Textual study, I would urge, also has its own proper kind of positivism—either a given word occurs in a text or it does not; and even the Jesus Seminar is right in thinking that Jesus either did or did not utter any given recorded saying—however far it may be from having established adequate criteria for deciding the matter, and however much its work needs complementing with an attempt to interpret the significance of what is discovered on this level.

But an interest in the historical dimension of the Bible—and hence a historical-critical approach—does not seem to me to correlate very strongly with positivism. When Elisabeth Schüssler Fiorenza speaks of "the positivist value-neutral stance of historical-critical studies,"[49] she seems to me to be exaggerating, as also when she speaks of a "scientistic, value-detached, epistemological 'rhetoric of fact'" that "covertly advocates a scholarly political practice that does not assume responsibility for its own engagements and interests."[50] (This is the point we have already discussed about objectivity.) Every biblical scholar knows colleagues who are in practice positivists, but I do not believe that they constitute the majority or that positivism is in any way of the essence of biblical criticism. H. Barth and O. Steck are surely nearer the

---

49. Elisabeth Schüssler Fiorenza, "Biblical Interpretation and Critical Commitment," *Studia Theologica* 43 (1989): 5–18; see Yarchin, *History of Biblical Interpretation*, 386.
   50. Schüssler Fiorenza, ibid.

mark when they write, in a standard textbook, "Exegesis does not maintain its rigorously academic character by orientating itself toward the experimental and empiricist sciences and tying itself to their ideal of exact and objective knowledge; if it did, it would have to restrict itself to the analysis and description of the linguistic surface of texts."[51] Biblical criticism is intellectually rigorous, but it is not therefore positivistic.

This may be seen if we concentrate again on Julius Wellhausen, surely a *historical* critic if anyone was. His comparative lack of interest in theological interpretation might make us expect that in him above all we would find the positivism of which Schüssler Fiorenza complains. The more so, as Wellhausen was rather free from the Hegelianism that had characterized some earlier scholars, notoriously Vatke. (The old canard that his approval of Vatke's historical work indicates that Wellhausen was himself a Hegelian has been laid to rest by Perlitt, though one still hears it said.[52]) Wellhausen followed the classical historians Niebuhr, Ranke, and Mommsen, precisely in their attempt to *free* historiography from its domination by any kind of philosophy, as expressed in formulations such as Vatke's "The historical serves to illustrate the conceptual."[53] In Wellhausen, as Perlitt puts it, we have "a change of climate from philosophy to history, from systematization to plain exegesis."[54] Here if anywhere we should surely find positivism. Yet, as Perlitt shows, the German historians, Wellhausen included, took nothing from positivism:

> The first requirement of positivism—to convey the facts as precisely as possible—was something that the German historians did not need

---

51. "Exegese wahrt ihren wissenschaftlichen Charakter allerdings nicht dadurch, daß sie sich an den experimentellen und empirischen Wissenschaften orientiert und sich an derer Ideal exakt-objektiver Erkenntnis bindet; sie müßte sich dann auf Analyse und Deskription der sprachlichen Oberfläche der Texte beschränken" (H. Barth and O. H. Steck, *Exegese des Alten Testaments: Leitfaden der Methodik (Ein Arbeitsbuch für Proseminare, Seminare und Vorlesungen)* [Neukirchen-Vluyn: Neukirchener Verlag, 1971; 9th ed. 1980], 1).

52. Perhaps the best demonstration of this comes from Wellhausen's own work, where he says that the Deuteronomistic presentation of history is unrealistic in a way reminiscent of Hegel: "One is reminded of 'thesis, antithesis, synthesis' when one listens to the monotonous beat with which history marches on or turns round in circles: rebellion oppression repentance rest, rebellion oppression repentance rest" ("Man wird an Satz Gegensatz und Vermittlung erinnert, wenn man sich den einförmigen Takt in's Ohr klingen läßt, nach dem hier die Geschichte fortschreitet oder sich im Kreise dreht. Abfall Drangsal Bekehrung Ruhe, Abfall Drangsal Bekehrung Ruhe") (*Geschichte Israels I*, 240). No one who was a Hegelian himself could have written that scornful sentence! See Perlitt, *Vatke und Wellhausen*, 187–88.

53. "Das Historische dient der Illustrierung des Begrifflichen" (Perlitt, 129).

54. "Der Klimawandel von der Philosophie zur Historie, von der Systematik zur bloßen Exegese" (Perlitt, 152).

to learn here; the other requirement—to draw from the facts conclusions about general laws—seemed to them to be so similar in their
results to the deductions of the philosophy of history that they were
happy to jettison the inductive methods that positivism strove for. The
basic stance of positivism was hardly enticing in any respect as a contribution to historical presentation.[55]

In a quite unpositivistic way, Wellhausen traced development at a deep level
in ancient Israelite conceptions and approaches to the world. He provided a
complete model for understanding the changes that occurred after the exile. He
did so in a way that is so unpositivistic that it is only too often condemned as the
imposition of a philosophical concept on the text—evolution and anti-Semitism
have both been alleged as lying behind it, though there is nothing much in either
accusation. Wellhausen's application of biblical criticism is interpretative, rich,
anything but thinly positivistic. He certainly believed in objectivity, but he was
as far as possible from any preoccupation with "bare facts."

Thus I find myself wanting to adopt a somewhat complex position. On the
one hand, it seems to me that biblical criticism, in its historical mode (by no
means the only mode it has), does indeed work by principles shared with secular historiography. But, on the other hand, these principles do not seem to
me nearly so skeptical as their formulation by Troeltsch implies; nor do they
mean seeing history as devoid of any meaning beyond facts that can be established on the basis of maximal skepticism, analogy, and correlation. Perhaps
the last word can be left to Lothar Perlitt in his comments on Wellhausen:

55. "Die erste Forderung des Positivismus, die Fakten so präzise wie möglich zu ermit-
teln, brauchten die deutschen Historiker nicht erst hier zu lernen; die andere Forderung,
aus den Tatsachen auf allgemeine Gesetze zu schließen, schien ihnen im Ergebnis mit den
Deduktionen der Geschichtsphilosophien so verwandt zu sein, daß sie die vom Positivismus
eigentlich angestrebte inductive Methode gerne auch noch dreingaben. Die positivistischen
Grundtendenzen verlockten kaum in irgendeiner Hinsicht zur historischen Darstellung"
(Perlitt, 84–85). Edgar Conrad, *Reading the Latter Prophets: Toward a New Canonical Criticism*, Journal for the Study of the Old Testament: Supplement Series 376 (London: T. & T.
Clark International, 2003), 44, speaks of "the historical positivism represented by the father
of historical criticism, Julius Wellhausen"—a positivism, he argues, criticized by Gunkel. On
35–36, however, Wellhausen is called an idealist, as are other Old Testament scholars such
as Martin Noth. It is difficult to be a positivist and an idealist at the same time. But as Perlitt comments, sometimes any stick will do to beat Wellhausen with: "Wellhausen is criticized on the grounds that he reconstructs the history of Israel perversely or from motives
that have nothing to do with objective attention to the matter in hand; that he is an evolutionist; that he is a victim of Hegelian philosophy (through Vatke's influence); or even (*horribile dictu*) that he is all these things at once" ("Wellhausen habe die Geschichte Israels
willkürlich oder aus sachfremden Motiven konstruiert, er sei Evolutionist, er sei—
durch Vatkes Einfluß—ein Opfer der Hegelschen Philosophie oder, horribile dictu, er sei
alles das zugleich") (Perlitt, *Vatke und Wellhausen*, 2–3).

For Wellhausen, the witness that history bears to God lies—hidden, yet at the same time clearly revealed—in its givenness and in its natural course, in such a way that the 'earthly nexus' of events resists any attempt to spiritualize or theologize it. Because God's activity in history cannot be grasped with one's hands, but only with faith, Wellhausen writes the history of Israel as a 'profane' history, analogous to any other history, and renounces any attempt to demonstrate special 'revelations' in it with the tools of the historian. But for him this 'profane' history does not exclude 'religious' history, but on the contrary includes it. The historian cannot write salvation history [*Heilsgeschichte*]; but this is because 'salvation history' is simply secular history, seen with the eyes of faith.[56]

When biblical scholars reconstruct history, they do so using the same methods as secular historians. But a great deal of their time is not spent in reconstructing history anyway, and to call biblical criticism the historical-critical method skews our awareness of this. The methods that historians do use are seldom used in the cause of positivism by most historians working today, and nor are they so used by biblical scholars who use them. The term "the historical-critical method" is not the best one to use in analyzing the work of biblical scholars, raising as it does the expectation that such work will be essentially skeptical and reductionist. A great good would be served by reverting to the older term "biblical criticism."

TRUTH AND METHOD

So much for the contention that biblical criticism consists in applying to the Bible the particular methods of study analyzed by Troeltsch. I should now like to broaden the discussion, since those who attack biblical criticism allege that at its heart lies a whole theory about the necessity of method in textual study that goes beyond the specifics of what was advocated by Troeltsch and involves a worldview deeply inimical to what is proper in the humanities—and especially in theology, seen as in many ways the ultimate humanities discipline.

---

56. Cf. Perlitt, *Vatke und Wellhausen*, 232: "Das Gotteszeugnis der Geschichte liegt für Wellhausen in ihrer Faktizität, in ihrem Ablauf derart verborgen und zugleich zutage, daß der 'irdische Nexus' einer Vergeistlichung oder Theologisierung widerstrebt. Weil man Gottes Geschichtshandeln nicht mit Händen, sondern nur im Glauben ergreifen kann, schreibt Wellhausen die Geschichte Israels, in Analogie zu aller Geschichte, als Profangeschichte und verzichtet darauf, besondere 'Offenbarungen' mit dem Handwerkzeug des Historikers nachzeichnen zu wollen. Diese 'Profanität' der Geschichte schließt für ihn die Religionsgeschichte nicht aus, sondern ein: Der Historiker kann keine Heilsgeschichte schreiben. Heilsgeschichte: das ist Profangeschichte mit den Augen des Glaubens" (my translation, in Robert Morgan with John Barton, *Biblical Interpretation*, 87–88).

The idea that criticism is the application of method to the theological task—and hence also to the study of the Bible—has been discussed at length by Andrew Louth in his book *Discerning the Mystery*.[57] This is a profound and important book, and in much of what it positively asserts it is highly illuminating. If I take issue with what it says about biblical criticism, this is done despite gratitude for having learned much from Louth's discussion.

Louth argues that theology, and within theology the reading of Scripture, is concerned with insight and wisdom of a kind that can come only from personal commitment, and that an attempt to subject it to the requirements of method is to assimilate it to the natural sciences, in which progress in understanding comes from methodical inquiry. Theology, on the other hand, belongs very centrally to the humanities, and in the humanities an Enlightenment model of intellectual progress brought about through the application of correct method is a chimera. Knowledge in the humanities is subjective knowledge, the knowledge of truth or texts by someone who seeks to enter into them with imaginative commitment, not objective knowledge, the knowledge of a supposedly detached and impartial observer:

> Science is concerned with objective truth, that is, with truth inhering in the object of knowledge. Such truth is independent of whoever observes it, and it is precisely this that the use of the experimental method seeks to achieve. As we have seen, the experimental method seeks to elide the experimenter by the principle that experiments must be repeatable by other experimenters. Objective truth, in this sense, seeks to be detached from the subjectivity of the observer. In contrast to such objective truth, subjective truth is a truth which cannot be detached from the observer and his situation: it is a truth which is true for me, and which cannot be expressed in such a way that it is true for everyone. Put like that, it seems at first sight obvious that objective truth is real truth, and subjective truth falls short of such ultimacy. But further reflection suggests that so to suppose is to over-simplify. When Kierkegaard claimed that all truth lay in subjectivity, he meant that truth which could be expressed objectively (so that it was the same for everyone) was mere information that concerned everyone and no one. Real truth, truth that a man would lay down his life for, was essentially subjective: a truth passionately apprehended by the subject. . . . If, then, we concede that the humanities are concerned with subjective truth, as opposed to the objective truth sought by the sciences, this need not imply that they are concerned with what need not be true, what is not absolute, but it does imply (and this is the most important sense of subjective truth) that the humanities are not primarily con-

57. Andrew Louth, *Discerning the Mystery: An Essay on the Nature of Theology* (Oxford: Clarendon Press, 1983).

cerned with establishing objective information (though this is important), but with bringing men into engagement with what is true.[58]

A false aim of objectivity, Louth believes, is precisely what is implied in
adherence to the historical-critical method. The aim in the humanities
should be the kind of knowledge of which interpersonal understanding, not
scientific detachment, is the paradigm case, and this cannot be attained
through the practice of *method*, for method is the attempt to abstract from
interpersonal knowledge and apply a series of techniques to material that is
conceived of as inert and open to detached observation. Theology is in many
ways the paradigm of the humanities, since it is concerned with knowledge
of God, who can never be an object amenable to our detached study, but is
only ever a Subject with whom we have to interact. Insofar as the study of
the Bible is part of theology, and not merely a quest for antiquarian factual
information, it cannot possibly be adequate to conceive it after the scientific
model of historical-critical method.

As Louth makes explicit, he has been greatly influenced by Hans-Georg
Gadamer's great work *Truth and Method*,[59] which "puts forward an analysis of
the legitimacy of (in his own words) 'an experience of truth that transcends the
sphere of the control of the scientific method.'"[60] For Gadamer, the picture
of scientific progress through the refinement of methodical procedures and
detached objectivity is wholly inappropriate in relation to knowledge in the
humanities, which requires a prior commitment to an immersion in the material being studied, and in which tradition—the slow accumulation of deeply
felt responses over time by other committed interpreters—replaces objective
detachment.

We may leave aside here the question whether science does in fact proceed
by the kind of detached study here being hypothesized. Some scientists would
now deny the possibility of a detached observer and in that sense would bring
scientific inquiry closer to what Gadamer understood to be the essence of
humanistic study. If such scientists are right, that would in a sense be even
more grist to Gadamer's (and Louth's) mill. The model of the detached scientist is important in their discussion mainly for heuristic reasons: it paints a picture of what, in their view, knowledge in the humanities is not, whether or not
this picture is actually to be found in the world of the natural scientist. And for

58. Ibid., 27–28.
59. Hans-Georg Gadamer, *Wahrheit und Methode: Grundzüge einer philosophischen
Hermeneutik*, 4th ed. (Tübingen: Mohr, 1975); ET, *Truth and Method* (New York: Crossroad,
1975).
60. Louth, xii, quoting Gadamer, *Truth and Method*, xii.

the study of the Bible, the effect, according to Louth, is to oppose historical-critical method as wholly inappropriate to the subject matter of Scripture, which is not the accumulation of facts but the knowledge of God, the ne plus ultra of committed, humanistic knowledge.

My own reaction to Louth's work, which made a great impression on me when I first read it in 1983, is a complicated one. On the one hand, he seems to me to have grasped correctly the nature of knowledge in theology as self-involving, the very opposite of cool detachment. Yet, on the other hand, I do not really recognize in his account of historical-critical method the practice of biblical criticism as I have experienced it. I find myself wanting to say that his strictures on what he calls historical-critical method have a great deal in them, yet that such historical-critical method is something of a straw man. In fact, I feel much as any scientist skeptical of the alleged complete objectivity of science would feel about Louth's account of scientific method: that he has correctly identified an ideal type of intellectual activity that is not applicable in the humanities, but has not shown that it actually exists. In short, I doubt not only whether biblical criticism should be called historical-critical, but also whether it is correct to call it a method in the sense that term has in science as described by Louth. Louth's criticisms, I want to say, would hit the mark if biblical criticism were actually the pseudoscientific methodical kind of inquiry he supposes it to be, but in reality that is not how most biblical critics understand their own work.

It is not hard to understand why Louth has the impression he has of biblical criticism. There are—of course—critics whose approach is more or less positivistic and who would fully accept Louth's account of what they are aiming to do, maintaining that their work is indeed scientific in Louth's sense. One should be on one's guard about the mere use of the term "scientific," since sometimes in biblical studies this is used to render the German *wissenschaftlich*, which (as we saw above) more accurately means something like "intellectually rigorous." There are, after all, *Geisteswissenschaften* (humanities) as well as *Naturwissenschaften* (sciences), and Gadamer himself will have used *wissenschaftlich* to refer to work in the former, even though he was quite clear that such work was emphatically not scientific in the sense that term normally bears in English. But even allowing for such possible linguistic confusion, there are biblical critics who think of their work as scientific.

Most biblical critics would also want to affirm that there can be progress in biblical studies, and this is one of the aspects Louth regards as belonging to a scientific paradigm of knowledge. As he rightly points out, in the humanities one constantly returns to past writers, in a way that scientists do not. In science, there is a clear distinction between actual scientific work, which draws on past work only insofar as it lays the foundations for present work, and the history of science, which is a branch of history rather than of science. But in the humanities, past writers are continually rediscovered and reinterpreted: "Philosophers continue to discuss Plato, for instance; the problems that he raised are not problems that admit of the kind of solution which would enable us to leave them behind and pass on to other problems."[61] Yet Louth himself concedes that there are areas in which there can be progress in humanistic study: "Of course, there *is* a certain sort of advance: there is a place for the kind of problem-solving faculty we have found lying at the root of the sciences. It represents the 'detective' element in the researches of the humanities: trying to piece together bits of evidence, or follow up clues; but to refer to it as the 'detective' element indicates that it is not central—it is a peripheral, if important and time-consuming, activity."[62] But on the issue of fact, there is probably not much difference in practice between Louth's proposal and the position of most biblical critics. They might stress the possibility of progress, even in understanding the text and not merely in the detective-like activities of questions of Introduction, for example, but they would mostly agree that we do detective work on precisely these texts because they have continued importance and resonance; just as he would agree that even important and resonant texts require detective work. This is a matter of degree and of emphasis, not of head-on confrontation.

But however positivistic and scientific biblical criticism may look to some outsiders, I doubt in fact whether Louth has correctly captured its *self*-understanding in his assimilation of it to scientific method. Biblical critics who are self-reflective do not in general, I think, see themselves as scientists of some kind. They are aware that work on the Bible belongs to the humanities, and this means that its methods differ, in at least some of the ways Louth outlines, from scientific method. But my case here is not based on counting heads. Even if biblical critics did generally believe their own work to be the application of historical-critical *method* understood in a scientific way, they would be wrong. Biblical criticism is not, in fact, the application of method to the biblical text. It contains within itself an approach which is already a good deal closer to what Louth proposes than he himself recognizes.

Biblical criticism is not a matter of *processing* the text, but of *understanding* it. Any procedures that are applied to the Bible are in the interests of understanding.[63] Later in this chapter I shall look at a number of so-called biblical

61. Louth, 67.
62. Ibid.
63. There is an implication in the way Louth writes that biblical critics are trying to become the *masters* of the text, rather than standing before it and listening to it openly. It is perhaps here that my own perception of what biblical criticism is about differs most sharply

"methods" and shall argue that "method" is the wrong word to apply to them. In this I shall return to a theme argued at some length in my book *Reading the Old Testament*[64] some twenty years ago. But first I want to deal with the question of method in more general terms. How far is there in reality a historical-critical method in biblical studies?

As I shall argue further below, biblical criticism contains in essence three central features: (a) attention to semantics, to the meaning of words, phrases, sentences, chapters, whole books; (b) awareness of genre; and (c) bracketing out of questions of truth. Of these, only the third seems to me to be amenable to discussion in terms of method. When we attend to the meaning of a text before asking whether what it asserts is true, we are in a sense applying a procedure—a postponement of an evaluation of the text's truth. But I am not clear that this procedure counts as a method in the vicious sense condemned by Louth, who would surely also recognize that apprehension of meaning precedes judgments about truth. Certainly elsewhere in the humanities such a procedure normally operates; we do not approach Plato, for example, with a settled conviction that whatever he says will turn out to be true. It is, indeed, perhaps only in the case of the Bible (and for some Christians certain other texts, such as creeds and conciliar definitions, or confessions) that the opposite principle operates and there is a prior expectation of truth. In most spheres where criticism is applied to texts, one would take it for granted that the issue of truth arrives only after the meaning has been established, so that if we have had to insist on this in the case of biblical criticism, that is a peculiarity of its being *biblical*.

So far as the other two matters are concerned, it seems to me that criticism is the application, not of method, but rather of a sort of intuition. One cannot establish through any method what a text means: one has to grasp it by an intuitive appropriation of the combination of words that make it up. The larger the unit whose meaning is being sought, the more this is apparent. It might be said (though the point would be rather trivial) that one can come to understand a particular word by looking it up in a dictionary, which is a kind of method. But there is no technique that will deliver the meaning of a whole passage and reveal its overall drift, still less one that will demonstrate what a whole

---

from his, for I perceive biblical criticism as quite precisely an attempt to avoid trying to master the text, but instead to allow it its own space, to make its own points in its own way, and to receive it without the distortion that is produced if we try to control it and twist it to our own ends. It is interesting and perhaps puzzling that two people, both of whom have read a lot of biblical criticism, can receive it in such different ways.

64. John Barton, *Reading the Old Testament: Method in Biblical Study* (London: Darton, Longman & Todd, 1984; 2nd ed., 1996).

book means. Genre, similarly, is hopelessly elusive if one tries to get at it in any methodical way. Granted that we recognize certain phrases as revealing genre—"once upon a time," for example, as the marker of a fairy story—there is no method that will guarantee recognition of less obvious genres, and of course none that will reveal that a given fairy story is actually a parody or an ironic use of the genre. How would we convince a doubter that *Gulliver's Travels* is not a children's tale? It requires an overall appropriation of the whole work by a critical intelligence to make it clear that it is in fact a subversion of its apparent form in the interests of a satirical intent. No term other than intuition seems to me to be adequate, and certainly there is no method that will help; we might recall the much-quoted remark of T. S. Eliot, "The only method is to be very intelligent."[65]

My argument would be that what biblical or literary critics do in establishing the meaning and genre of a work is already not far from what Louth thinks they *ought* to be doing: entering into the text at a deep level, recognizing the shared humanity of the author, so that *cor ad cor loquitur* (heart speaks to heart). The best model for understanding a text is interpersonal understanding. Such understanding, contrary to an emphasis on the subjective dimension, requires also a high measure of objectivity—not in the sense of objectifying the other person or the text, but in the sense of recognizing their otherness from ourselves. Hugo Gressmann, so derided by Barth as a "mere" biblical historian without an ounce of theology in his soul, summed it up in these words: "True objectivity always presupposes love."[66] This is not the expression of a positivistic attitude

---

65. Compare Wellhausen's maxim, quoted in Rudolf Smend, *Julius Wellhausen: Ein Bahnbrecher in drei Disziplinen* (Munich: Carl Friedrich von Siemens Stiftung, 2006), 48: "It is not just a question of the spectacles, but of the eyes" ("Es kommt nicht bloß auf die Brille an, sondern auch auf die Augen").

66. "Wahre Objektivität setzt immer Liebe voraus" (quoted in Rudolf Smend, *Deutsche Alttestamentler in drei Jahrhunderten*, 179). The reference is to an article of Gressmann's in *Zeitschrift für die alttestamentliche Wissenschaft* 42. Compare Manfred Oeming, "'Man kann nur verstehen, was man liebt': Erwägungen zum Verhältnis von Glauben und Verstehen als einem Problem alttestamentlicher Hermeneutik," in *Altes Testament und christliche Verkündigung: Festschrift für Antonius H. J. Gunneweg zum 65. Gerburtstag*, ed. Manfred Oeming and Axel Graupner (Stuttgart: Kohlhammer, 1987), 165–83 [the title means "one can only understand what one loves"], citing Goethe: "One cannot come to know anything unless one loves it; and the deeper and more complete the knowledge is to become, the stronger, more powerful, and livelier must that love, indeed passion, be" ("Man lernt nichts kennen, als was man liebt, und je tiefer und vollständiger die Kenntnis werden soll, desto starker, kräftiger und lebendiger muß Liebe, ja Leidenschaft sein"). Oeming's own conclusion in this article is that love is necessary, insofar as it means a commitment to studying this or that text, but that rational detachment is *also* essential—a conclusion with which I would agree. The two attitudes can coexist; not all love is blind!

to the biblical text. Of course there are positivistic elements in biblical criticism, all the work that Louth describes as "detective-like," but that is not the sum total of what criticism amounts to. Criticism focuses in essence on a deep understanding of the text.

Schleiermacher is the source, via Dilthey, of many ideas in Gadamer and hence in Louth, but he is also the ancestor of modern biblical critics. In Schleiermacher we find an opposition to the idea that hermeneutics is a theory about understanding that starts with the assumption that we can easily grasp the meaning of texts, and instead presupposes that all textual understanding is difficult. Misunderstanding, he believed, is the normal condition of humankind when faced with the utterances of others, whether contemporary or enshrined in historical texts. As Heinz Kimmerle puts it, "The work of Schleiermacher constitutes a turning point in the history of hermeneutics. Till then hermeneutics was supposed to support, secure, and clarify an *already accepted* understanding. . . . In the thinking of Schleiermacher, hermeneutics achieves the qualitatively different function of first *making understanding possible*, and deliberately *initiating understanding* in each individual case."[67] Schleiermacher recognizes the *alien* character of whatever is written by another person to our own understanding; for him, successful interpretation is always achieved, not simply given. This is because it requires a penetrative grasp of the text, not mere openness to something whose meaning is obvious.[68]

67. For this formulation, see Anthony C. Thiselton, "The New Hermeneutic," in *New Testament Interpretation*, ed. I. H. Marshall (Carlisle: Paternoster, 1977), 308–33, at 310–11, referring to H. Kimmerle, "Hermeneutical Theory or Ontological Hermeneutics," *Journal for Theology and the Church* 4 (1968): 107. Contrast with this the words of Gerhard Ebeling, "Interpretation—and therefore hermeneutics—is required only in cases where the word-event is disturbed for some reason" ("Interpretation, und deshalb Hermeneutik, ist nur in dem Fall erforderlich, wenn das Wortgeschehen aus irgendeinem Grunde gestört ist") ("Wort Gottes und Hermeneutik," *Zeitschrift für Theologie und Kirche* 56 [1959]: 224–51). This presents hermeneutics as the solution to a problem, as though normally texts yielded up their secrets without difficulty, whereas Schleiermacher—correctly, in my judgment—saw that *all* texts are difficult texts, precisely because they are produced by someone other than ourselves, and hence are inherently hard to understand.

68. F. D. E. Schleiermacher, *Hermeneutik und Kritik*; see Manfred Frank, *Schleiermachers Hermeneutik und Kritik* (Frankfurt am Main: Suhrkamp, 1977), 18: "Ist jedoch die Vernunft selbst ein Institut des Sinns, so vermag sie das Verstehen nicht zu überspringen. Eben darum ist das Nicht-Verstehen für Schleiermacher nicht mehr als Ausnahme des Umgangs mit fremder Rede zu behandeln, sondern muß grundsätzlich als Regelfall der Begegnung mit fremdkonstituiertem Sinn unterstellt werden. Zu solcher Askese zwingt die Vernunft nicht irgendeine methodisch zu übende und bloß provisorisch aufrechtzuerhaltende Skepsis. Sie entspringt vielmehr der alltäglichen Erfahrung unversöhnter Strittigkeit der Äußerungen und Ansichten miteinander kommunizierender Partner und der Relativität des allgemeingültigen 'Wissen' in bezug auf die Zustimmung durch alle Subjekte, die hinsichtlich seiner

To my mind the essential nature of biblical criticism is thus a deep and imaginative understanding of the text, not very unlike what Louth himself is calling for. To sink oneself in a text until its meaning becomes lucid involves all the exercise of imagination and intuition that for Louth are the mark of the humanities (as opposed to the sciences, on his interpretation of science). It also involves, and I do not at all wish to deny this, technical skills such as knowledge of languages and the ability to piece together the solutions to puzzles about authorship, date, composition; but Louth does not disregard these features either. In a given critic the latter kinds of skill may be much more apparent than the former. But even such seemingly positivistic critics must necessarily have the ability to reconstruct in themselves the meaning of the text, to grasp its semantics, its overall drift or *Duktus*, its genre; or else their work will be simply a series of unconnected *aperçus*. There are very few critics of whom that has really been the case.

Louth's intention is to tell critics that they should cease to be critics and become instead deep readers of texts; my own proposal is that critics should be encouraged to become more what they already are, which is not far from what Louth would like them to turn into. I believe he misreads the situation in biblical studies, in a way by accepting at face value some of the scientific rhetoric in which critics do sometimes engage, especially when they are faced with challenges from a quite different direction from Louth's—from fundamentalists and other conservative forces. But rhetoric is what it is; biblical criticism is no more scientific than any other pursuit in the humanities, but is predicated on empathy and understanding.

This is perhaps made most clear by Schleiermacher in the very place where he does seem to equate criticism with such external aspects of texts as

---

diskursiv übereinkommen" ("Yet if reason is itself an institute of sense, then it cannot bypass understanding. For just that reason, nonunderstanding is for Schleiermacher no longer to be treated as an exception to dealing with communications from others, but must fundamentally be acknowledged as the normal case in contact with meaning constituted by others. It is reason that compels us to such an asceticism, not some kind of skepticism that is to be practiced methodically and maintained merely provisionally. It arises, rather, from the everyday experience of the irreconcilable questionability of the assertions and points of view of partners in communication with each other, and from the relativity of universally valid 'knowledge' where consent by all subjects who come to an agreement by discussion is concerned"). This, as Frank argues, tends against the case sometimes made for a special hermeneutic for this or that type of text (for example, the New Testament) on the grounds that it presents unusual difficulties for interpretation: *all* texts present unusual difficulties for interpretation! Cf. also Frank, 92: "Die strenge Praxis geht davon aus, daß sich das Mißverstehen von selbst ergibt und das Verstehen auf jedem Punkt muß gewollt und gesucht werden" ("Rigorous praxis presupposes that misunderstanding happens of its own accord, whereas understanding must at every point be actively desired and sought after").

authorship and context. He says that hermeneutics is "the art of correctly understanding another person's discourse, above all in writing" ("die Kunst, die Rede eines andern, vornehmlich die schriftliche, richtig zu verstehen"), whereas criticism is "the art of correctly judging the authenticity of writings and writers" ("die Kunst, die Echtheit der Schriften und Schriftstellern richtig zu beurteilen"). Yet he then immediately states that one cannot have criticism without hermeneutics: "Since criticism can recognize the importance of the witnesses in their relation to the contested work only through an appropriate and correct understanding of the latter, its practice presupposes hermeneutics."[69] We do not *first* decide on the authenticity of a document and *then* go on to understand it; understanding is a precondition of decisions about authenticity. And this point can be generalized to all critical operations. Again, there are certainly biblical critics who would deny this, and against them Louth is right to issue his challenge. But I believe such critics are mistaken. Understanding is at the beginning of all criticism, not something that comes in later, and understanding is a self-involving exercise.

To make these rather abstract discussions more concrete, I should like to look in more detail at specific modes of criticism in biblical studies, trying in each case to show that what is involved is not a method in the pseudoscientific sense but something altogether more humanistic.

Source Criticism

Source criticism is perhaps everyone's paradigm case of thin, bloodless historical-critical method. One takes texts that have a rich finished shape and character and dissects them into originally independent sources. This is felt to be a procedure involving no "understanding" of the texts, but only the application of a quasi-scientific technique based on observations about word frequencies and distributions, and perceptions of inconsistencies between passages on a superficial, literal-minded level. So runs (and has always run) the anticritical opposition to source analysis.

As I tried to show in *Reading the Old Testament*, this is a caricature of the approaches of source critics.[70] What comes first in source analysis is always an act of understanding, or rather of *attempted* understanding. Source criticism did not arise from a theoretical idea about how the biblical text should be studied. It arose from an attempt to understand the biblical narratives, espe-

---

69. "Da die Kritik die Wichtigkeit der Zeugnisse in ihrem Verhältnis zum bezweifelten Schriftwerke nur erkennen kann nach gehörigem richtigen Verständnis der letzteren, so setzt ihre Ausübung die Hermeneutik voraus" (Frank, 71).

70. *Reading the Old Testament*, 25–26.

cially those in the Pentateuch, as finished wholes, an attempt that the texts themselves seemed systematically to frustrate. The problem in understanding was of long duration; as we saw earlier in this book, Augustine, not to mention a number of Jewish commentators, had already wrestled with some of the difficulties in the text to which source criticism eventually emerged as the solution. The breakthrough occurred when critics began to ask how one would solve the problem if one attended to the types of text involved, and bracketed out the question of their truth long enough for the possible implications of their contradictions to surface properly in the mind. It then emerged that one explanation for the oddity of the texts might be that they were an amalgam of several earlier, in themselves coherent, texts.

As now taught, source criticism is often presented as though it were a rational procedure like a scientific method, which can be (and ought to be) applied in principle to any text. But in origin, source criticism is not a method but a hypothesis. And the way in which the hypothesis is tested is not scientific, but humanistic: its truth or falsity depends on whether the individual sources isolated by the hypothesis can be read with understanding. If they cannot, then the "solution" is no solution at all but leaves us back where we began, with incoherent texts. The characteristic way of trying to refute source criticism then consists precisely in seeking to show, on the one hand, that the Pentateuch is perfectly coherent as it stands or, on the other, that the hypothesized sources are not themselves internally coherent—or, of course, both. Nowhere in this process, so far as I can see, is any particular method involved. There is no set of procedures one can apply to the text that will yield the classic four-source hypothesis about the Pentateuch. It results from *noticing* certain things about the text that others had overlooked or explained away too quickly. We may fully grant that now, when source criticism has been established for a couple of centuries, students can be preconditioned to see the inconsistencies that form the basis of the theory, even coerced into seeing them; and in this way source criticism can be turned into a kind of method that anyone can practice. However, it did not originate as a method, but as a series of observations made by people who, *ex hypothesi*, did not till then believe in a source-critical method. Source analysis began, as we might put it, from the bottom up, not from the top down. It was not a method arrived at prior to being applied, but a theory generated from the frustrating experience of trying to understand a text and failing to do so.

Form Criticism

With form criticism even more than with source analysis, the importance of genre is obvious. The small *Gattungen* that form critics detect in longer texts are examples of texts that have in each case a particular genre that sets them off from the literary context in which they are now placed and enables us to argue that they will have had an earlier discrete existence. In the Old Testament such *Gattungen* are etiological stories, legal formulae, liturgical hymns, and prophetic oracles; in the New, the various types of story encountered in the Gospels (paradigms, miracle stories, parables) and, again, prophetic words (embedded in the epistles) and liturgical texts (such as the hypothetical Christ hymn in Phil. 2). Again, form criticism is a set of hypotheses rather than a method. Recognizing that a particular verse marks the beginning of a text different in genre from the preceding verse, and one that can then be classified and compared with similar texts found elsewhere, is painstaking work, but it is not best characterized as the application of a method. One cannot set out rules that will generate the identification of literary forms; one comes upon them serendipitously in reading the Bible with a certain kind of openness to its literary character.

Again, once form criticism has been discovered, it can be learned. Students can acquire the ability to reel off the different forms Bultmann identified in the Gospels. But to be a form critic is not to have acquired this body of information, but, rather, to read the text with an awareness of genre, which (as I have argued) is one of the defining features of criticism. I cannot see that there is any method or procedure that will enable one to identify *Gattungen*; it is a matter of literary perception, the result of asking certain sorts of question that did not occur to most people before the late nineteenth century. It is not even a *quasi*-scientific undertaking. And what has been built upon it is also not scientific. The aspect of form criticism of the Gospels that most people are familiar with, especially in the English-speaking world, is its tendency to historical skepticism. Once one has said that Jesus' miracles are related in a manner analogous to that of all other miraculous events, one seems to have reduced their probable historicity. It is not, as a matter of fact, clear that this need be so; if there is only one way of telling a miracle story, then it would follow that a true miracle story would have to have the same form as a false one. A form critic is bound to classify the Synoptic accounts of the Last Supper as etiological stories explaining the origins of the Eucharist, but few (though not none) are prepared to go on to draw the conclusion that therefore the Last Supper did not happen. As pioneered by Gunkel, form criticism of narratives helped the reader to understand how such narratives came to be told within religious communities, and deflected interest from their historicity. But form criticism is not a method for investigating early communities; it is, again, a set of hypotheses about them, rooted in a particular way of seeking to understand and enter into texts, or what lies behind them.

In the cases of both source and form criticism, there is clearly, *in addition to* the drive to understand the text generically and holistically, some of what

Louth calls detective work, a problem-solving mentality. This means that biblical critics would be right (supposing that source- and form-critical hypotheses are correct) to claim that there is progress in assimilating and applying them, and this may fall under Louth's condemnation, since according to him the humanities are not susceptible to progress. I believe this is an exaggeration, justifiably pointing to the fact that human understanding such as the humanities enshrine does not "date," but making this into a hard and fast rule according to which humanistic understanding does not advance at all. Most people who, like Louth, might defend Gadamer's emphasis on tradition would not go so far as to deny all possibility that understanding might advance in at least some respects. We do not "improve" on Shakespeare, admittedly, in the sense that Einstein improves on Newton. But our grasp of Shakespeare himself may certainly improve through the asking of new questions or the production of better editions. Surely Louth would not deny this. My main point here, however, is that whether or not we can truly speak of progress, where the understanding of biblical texts is concerned, through the labors of source and form critics, the improved understanding that may be called progress is secured through a form of cognition that is itself entirely humanistic. The greater understanding is achieved—through understanding; that is, through entering more closely into the nature of the text, an entering in that requires imagination and intuition, not scientific method.

Textual Criticism

It is probably textual criticism that comes nearest to most people's idea of a scientific method in biblical studies and in the study of the humanities in general. What could be more objective than establishing the original text of a literary work or document? It is interesting, however, that practicing textual critics tend to talk of their own work as an art rather than as a science, because the idea that establishing the "correct" text precedes judgments about meaning, though it has a certain heuristic value, appears to those actually engaged in the text-critical task to be a misunderstanding. Textual critics are constantly making decisions about the meaning of texts. Such a basic text-critical principle as preference for the harder reading—far from being a piece of method that can be applied without any entering into the meaning of the text—makes sense only if it can be assumed that the critic already understands what the text means, for only so can one judge a particular reading to be "harder," that is, less intuitively probable in its context and therefore less likely to have been introduced by a copyist.

Furthermore, there is an overlap with "higher," that is, source, criticism, which we have already seen not to be driven by a quasi-scientific method. In the case of the Gospels, for example, there are places where the variation among manuscripts of one of the Synoptics is as great as, or greater than, the variation between the parallel passages in two Synoptics.

> It is very important to take note of the fact that there are as many dif-
> ferences between D and B in Luke 6.1ff. as there are between the two
> texts in D of Mark 2.23ff. and Luke 6.1ff. . . . . Are there two separate
> texts of Luke and one of Mark, or one called Luke and two of Mark,
> or three separate texts? Or are they all one text?[71]

In such a case, the kind of judgment needed to establish the more probable reading in, say, Mark, is exactly the same kind of judgment needed to form a hypothesis about the earlier version of the Synoptic parallel, which would traditionally be called a source-critical judgment. In both cases the critic cannot make any progress without a perception of what the texts mean; nothing can be accomplished by any sort of mechanical operation. Parker, it may be noted, is occasionally willing to use the word "scientific" to describe textual criticism. But it is plain that he does not mean by that the application of mere techniques, but rather rigorous and informed judgment. And if textual criticism, which stands at the "harder" end of the spectrum of critical approaches, depends on humanistic judgment, how much more the other varieties of biblical criticism.

The upshot of this discussion is, I believe, that biblical criticism is not correctly seen as any kind of method, and as such does not rightly attract the kind of critique leveled at it by Louth. It is not hard to see why people think of it as a scientific method, and some of its own proponents have used language that suggests this, though (I would argue) more rarely than one might suppose from Louth's discussion. Closer analysis reveals, however, that it is scientific only in the sense of being *wissenschaftlich*. Like science, biblical criticism appeals to evidence; it weighs probabilities; it judges between what is more and what is less probable. But there is no divide between the sciences and the humanities in this respect; both are intellectually rigorous. When it is suggested that biblical criticism sees itself as essentially simply a problem-solving set of techniques, however, the analogy with science breaks down (if indeed science itself is correctly seen in those terms). Study of the Bible in a critical mode requires just the kind of deep understanding of the meaning of texts that Louth contrasts with biblical criticism. Criticism is a semantic operation, and grasping

71. David C. Parker, *The Living Text of the Gospels* (Cambridge: Cambridge University Press, 1997), 46–47.

the macrosemantics of entire texts is not a task for which there is any method; it requires empathy and imagination. Of course, this does not mean on the other hand that it is simply a matter of unfocused emotion. Detailed attention to questions of language, historical context, and authorship is required. But these questions in turn cannot be settled by method; they too require informed judgement. There is a kind of rhetoric of biblical criticism, perhaps less common now than it was, that tries to pretend that such matters can be settled scientifically; but the rhetoric should not take us in. It has often been deployed to ward off accusations from those in the sciences to the effect that biblical studies are a "soft" subject, but it does not do justice to the actual workings of biblical criticism on the ground. I conclude this discussion of Louth with some words of Patrick Lambe:

> Louth has fallen into the same trap as the fundamentalist in holding to an undifferentiated view of critical method as it is represented, or rather caricatured, by rationalist debunkers, Troeltschian positivists, or the spiritual aridity of specialist journals. In fact . . . there is nothing inherently wrong with the method *per se* (rather the contrary), and the faults of its practitioners or of the ideology it is used to serve should not be transposed upon the method itself. [It will be seen that Lambe also calls criticism a "method," which we have seen cause to doubt.] For the subservience to ideology, whether it be scientific (in the sense that Louth attacks) or positivist, is itself inherently *anti*-critical, in that it is a petrification of the critical faculty into set forms and pre-aligned results. . . . Insofar as criticism becomes subservient to the scientific ideology Louth describes, then to that extent it is bad criticism, *inauthentic* criticism.[72]

CONCLUSION

The historical-critical method thus proves to be a less than ideal term for communicating what biblical criticism is about. In essence, criticism is neither historical nor a method. There has been a strong correlation with history, at least since the nineteenth century, and there has frequently been a tendency to speak as though criticism has methodological implications. But in itself the critical approach to the Bible is not a method but a series of explanatory hypotheses,

72. Patrick Lambe, "In Defence of Criticism," unpublished paper, 1983. For a discussion of the nature of literary criticism that similarly argues that it is not merely the application of ruthless logic-chopping to texts, see Colin Radford and Sally Minogue, *The Nature of Criticism* (Brighton: Harvester Press, 1981).

driven by a particular attitude toward texts and textual meaning. Though crit-icism certainly entails situating texts in the context of their origin, it does not necessarily involve the reconstruction either of historical events or of the his-tory of the text's development. There are many examples of genuinely critical work that has little interest in either kind of history. And on the other hand, as pointed out early in this chapter, there has been and is plenty of interest in his-tory that is not at all driven by a critical mind-set. We therefore need to look elsewhere for a definition of the essential nature of biblical criticism.

4

The Plain Sense

A major thesis of this book is that biblical criticism is primarily concerned with the "plain sense" of the text. This is, however, a highly contested idea, both in biblical studies and in wider literary studies—so contested indeed, that some readers may hardly believe that anyone can propose it as a viable notion at the beginning of the twenty-first century. We shall have to take a circuitous route to discover just what it can reasonably mean. This will require us first to distinguish it from several other possible "senses" that can be attributed to texts.

THE ORIGINAL SENSE

It is common to hear it said that biblical critics are concerned with the original sense of texts,[1] by contrast with senses that the texts may have acquired later. For example, critics may be interested in the meaning of a pentateuchal passage as it stood in the J source, rather than as it now stands in the finished Pentateuch; or in what Isaiah meant by a particular oracle, as opposed to what the editors of Isaiah took it to mean, or forced it to mean by placing it in a new context. Similarly, they may want to know what Jesus meant by one of his sayings, by contrast with what the early church took it to mean. Biblical criticism is here seen on a rather archaeological model, as a discipline that strips away later layers of meaning and gets back to the original level—hence Robert

---

1. See the discussion of Benjamin Jowett in James Barr, "Jowett and the 'Original Meaning' of Scripture," *Religious Studies* 18:433–37, and "Jowett and the Reading of the Bible 'Like Any Other Book,'" *Horizons in Biblical Theology: An International Dialogue* 4 (1982): 1–44.

Alter's use of the term "excavative" to describe it. In part this goes with the characterization of biblical criticism as primarily historical in orientation, an idea we have discussed at some length already. I suggested that critics have only intermittently been concerned with the earliest strata in texts. Certainly part of the critical operation has been what is known as Introduction, and this does have as one of its tasks to establish whether texts are composite and, if so, what the component parts of these texts are. However, there are many biblical texts in which no earlier underlying sources have been discovered, but where questions of Introduction—place and time of composition, authorship, and literary context—still need to be studied.

But in any case, biblical criticism goes beyond matters of Introduction to a consideration of meaning and implication. And here it is by no means always the earliest levels of a text that concern the critic. As we have seen, often critics have been most interested in levels of the text that lie between the earliest strata and the finished product; for example, in the meaning of J rather than *either* of its underlying components *or* of the final Pentateuch. In this they have been concerned not with the *original* meaning of individual verses or passages, but with the meanings these have taken on as parts of a larger composition.

Thus, insofar as the expression "the original sense" is used to point to the fact that critics have not practiced "final form" exegesis, it is saying something both true and important. But, taken strictly, it fails to register that some texts have passed through a number of stages before reaching this final form, and that the critic may be concerned with its meaning at a number of these different stages, not only at the earliest we can reconstruct. In practice, the level at which the meaning is sought tends to vary among different kinds of text. It is mainly in the prophets that students of the Bible have been concerned with the original message, and studies of the prophetic books have often concentrated on stripping away later accretions to get back to what the prophet originally said, making that the prime aim. But in the study of Wisdom books, for example, there has been no such universal concern. Critics have seldom been particularly interested in the meaning of the individual proverbs lying behind Proverbs in any supposed original context, but have usually been content to expound them as they stand within the collection. With Job, as we have seen, the widespread acknowledgment of a complex compositional history has not prevented most commentators from discussing primarily the meaning of the "main" author, whose work is less than the absolutely complete book but much more than the individual sayings and speeches that make it up. And in some books, such as the Psalms, the concern until very recently was normally with each psalm taken individually (now scholars are starting to be interested in the compilation of the Psalter), but not very much with the fragments out of which some psalms may have been composed. Thus the term "original sense," taken to refer to the meaning of the earliest textual strata, does not capture very much of what biblical criticism has been concerned with.

"Original sense" may be intended in another way, however: the sense that the text has when considered in its own historical setting, rather than as taken by later generations. Here there may be no privileging of "early" strata, but simply a concern that the text should not be read anachronistically. I shall argue that this is indeed an important aspect of critical study, part of its concern for semantics.[2] In this meaning of the term, "original sense" does capture something that has been important in biblical criticism. I shall suggest, however, that the term "plain sense" does more justice to this than "original sense"—partly because of a possible confusion with the idea that criticism is concerned with the earliest layers in the text, which has just been considered, and partly because the word "original" tends to set up a contrast between what the text means and what it meant, a distinction which I shall go on to argue can be misleading (see the discussion below of Krister Stendahl[3]).

THE INTENDED SENSE

One of the ways in which biblical critics are often accused of being out of touch with wider literary studies is in their supposed attachment to authorial intention. The "intentional fallacy" was identified so long ago in literary criticism that it is hardly interesting any longer to most people in the literary world. It is simply taken for granted by most students of literature that authors have no special proprietary rights over the meaning of what they write; rather, in writing a work, they set it free for interpretation by readers. This was one of the pillars of the so-called New Criticism in the middle of the twentieth century and was already expressed quite clearly by T. S. Eliot and his contemporaries. I have written extensively, in my *Reading the Old Testament*, on possible implications of realizing that "intention" is a fallacy and will not repeat all that material here.[4] Intentionalism is also a target for attack

2. Cf. Barr, "Jowett and the Reading of the Bible 'Like Any Other Book,'" 16: "[In traditional readings of the Bible] the effect that disturbed Jowett was a semantic one. It was not so much that ideas had changed—for that could be justified as necessary and salutary—but that the meanings of words, as they were used within the later theological structures, were now being read back into the Bible as if they were their meanings there."

3. See below, pp. 80–84.

4. Barton, *Reading the Old Testament*, 147–51.

in much French structuralism and poststructuralism, epitomized in the title of Roland Barthes's work "The Death of the Author."[5]

Biblical critics, on the other hand, have certainly tended to be interested in what biblical authors meant by their writings. To say they have been intentionalists is oversimple. There is a tradition that runs back via Dilthey to Schleiermacher that speaks of the interpreter understanding the author's meaning better than he does himself, which strictly speaking goes beyond the claims of intentionalism.[6] Yet it is still the *author's* meaning that is being sought, and to that extent this hermeneutical doctrine is still an intentionalist one. It is not hard to find formulations of the business of biblical criticism that stress a quest for what the author meant. A good example would be this definition by W. H. Schmidt:

> A text is the assertion of a human person, transmitted in writing—a person who can no longer defend himself against misunderstanding. Who can step forward as his advocate if not historical criticism? Criticism tries, as well as it is able, to preserve the rights of the text, and in its name to counter misinterpretations. Indeed, there is no other possible way of allowing the text, as the word of another person, the freedom to speak for itself.[7]

5. Roland Barthes, "The Death of the Author," can be found in *Modern Criticism and Theory: A Reader*, ed. David Lodge with Nigel Wood, 2nd ed. (Harlow: Longman, 2000), 146–50.

6. "Die Rede zuerst ebensogut und dann besser zu verstehen als ihr Urheber" (*Schleiermacher: Hermeneutik und Kritik*, ed. F. Lücke [Berlin 1838], 32).

7. "Ein Text ist die schriftlich überlieferte Äußerung eines Menschen, der sich gegen Mißverständnis nicht mehr selbst wehren kann. Wer anders könnte als sein Anwalt auftreten als historisch-kritische Forschung? Sie versucht, soweit sie es vermag, das Recht des Textes zu wahren und in seinem Namen gegenüber Fehldeutungen Widerspruch einzulegen. In der Tat gibt es keine andere Möglichkeit, dem Text als Wort eines anderen Menschen die Freiheit zukommen zu lassen, selbst zu reden" (W. H. Schmidt, "Grenzen und Vorzüge historisch-kritischer Exegese," "Zugänge zur Bibel," *Evangelische Theologie* 45 [1985]: 469–82; quotation, 476–77). The guidelines for authors in the series the International Critical Commentary, issued in 1985 by J. A. Emerton and C. E. B. Cranfield, say in a similar vein that "the primary concern of these volumes is the elucidation of the meaning of the text as intended by its writers," while allowing that the commentator should remain aware of his own location in the modern world, so as to write intelligibly for his readership. Schleiermacher regarded the author's intention as important: "Hermeneutics and rhetoric belong together because every act of understanding is the reverse of an act of speaking, in which there has to come into one's consciousness what thought lay at the bottom of the speech" ("Die Zusammengehörigkeit der Hermeneutik und Rhetorik besteht darin, daß jeder Akt des Verstehens die Umkehrung eines Aktes des Redens ist, in dem in das Bewußtsein kommen muß, welches Denken der Rede zum Grunde gelegen"); see Frank, *Schleiermachers Hermeneutik und Kritik*, 76.

That biblical critics have often been intentionalists does not seem to me in doubt. One could respond to the arguments of the previous chapter by saying: Granted that criticism has not always been concerned with history, yet it has been concerned with intention (which *is* historical in a way, since the intention is that of people who lived in the past).

But is a concern for the author's intention a *defining* characteristic of biblical criticism? Or is the association, like that between criticism and history or historical method, frequent but contingent? My argument will be that it is contingent. There are two prongs to this argument: first, a great deal of biblical interpretation that we should have no hesitation in describing as critical has not in fact been intentionalist; and second, there have been biblical interpreters who were concerned with intention, yet whom we would not normally call critical.

First, nonintentionalist critics. I return here to the question of form criticism. Gunkel held that we should be concerned with the intentions of the original writers of the biblical psalms. But that was because he thought these psalms, although they derived from standard types of composition, were themselves lyrics by specific authors—very much the idea of the psalms that was normal in his day. It was Mowinckel who for the first time suggested that the biblical psalms were actually examples of just the multipurpose, "community"-produced texts of which Gunkel thought they were imitations. On Mowinckel's understanding, the psalms have no authors in the ordinary sense of that term, but represent the endpoint of a process of development shaped by many generations of anonymous "tradents." With the exception of the "learned" psalms such as Psalm 119, the psalms arose within a worshiping community that endlessly reshaped them to express its corporate religious sentiments.[8]

Very much the same can be said of a particular development from form criticism, the "traditio-historical criticism" practiced by, for example, Martin Noth and Gerhard von Rad. If we were to deny the title "critical" to these scholars, it is hard to see to whom we would apply it. Yet their interest in the traditions of the Pentateuch and the Deuteronomistic History is again an interest in tradents rather than in authors. It is true that both of them speak as though the writers we call J and E, or the compiler of the finished Deuteronomistic work, have something of the author about them, so much so that we might think they should really have called them authors.[9] But they present their own work as a study of the

8. See Sigmund Mowinckel, *The Psalms in Israel's Worship* (Oxford: Blackwell, 1962), i, esp. 23–41. (The work is a translation of *Offersang og Sangoffer* [Oslo: Aschehoug, 1951].)
9. See the detailed discussion in John Van Seters, *The Edited Bible* (Winona Lake, IN: Eisenbrauns, 2006), esp. 256–76.

transmission of tradition; Noth's books are called *Überlieferungsgeschichte des Pentateuch*[10] and *Überlieferungsgeschichtliche Studien*,[11] stressing the emphasis on tradition rather than on individual authorship. Noth and von Rad are both, indeed, interested in the meanings intended by the final compiler or redactor, but that by no means exhausts their interests. Both wanted to know about the earlier stages in the transmission of the traditions about Israel's history, and in these stages there can be no question of *authors*. The stories of early Israel or of the monarchic period are supposed to have come together slowly over an extended period of time, and no one person was ever responsible for them: they are an expression of a folk memory. This means that there can be no investigation into intention, in anything like the sense the term has in phrases such as "the intentional fallacy."

Take another example: Proverbs. It would be odd to speak of the authors of the sentence literature that makes up such a large part of this book. Precritical interpreters did so, in that they often thought the author was Solomon, as the book's title implies. But critical opinion may be said to have reacted against this precisely in a nonintentionalist direction, by seeing the individual proverbs, like the individual psalms, as expressions of a widespread aphoristic culture in which it is quite impossible to discover who first uttered a particular saying. If proverbs have meaning, it is not because they are the expression of the ideas of an author, but because they encapsulate the wisdom of many people, perhaps widely diffused in both time and space. Proverbs are the epitome of authorless texts. It has been the achievement of certain modern (and postmodern) approaches to literature to tackle the problem of such texts, where it is not simply incorrect to seek the author's meaning but actually impossible.[12] But to recognize this is, in fact, the crucial *critical* insight—which shows that criticism cannot be equated with a concern for intention.

To complicate, though I hope also to clarify, the picture further, I would refer to my discussion in an article, "Classifying Biblical Criticism."[13] Here I adapted a basic scheme for classifying different styles of literary criticism

10. Martin Noth, *Überlieferungsgeschichte des Pentateuch* (Stuttgart, 1948); ET, *A History of Pentateuchal Traditions* (Englewood Cliffs, NJ: Prentice-Hall, 1972).

11. Martin Noth, *Überlieferungsgeschichtliche Studien I*, Schriften der Königsberger Gelehrten Gesellschaft 18 (1943), 43–266; 2nd ed. Tübingen (1957), 1–110; ET, *The Deuteronomistic History*, Journal for the Study of the Old Testament: Supplement Series 15 (Sheffield: JSOT Press, 1981).

12. See my discussion in *Reading the Old Testament*, 190–97.

13. John Barton, "Classifying Biblical Criticism," *Journal for the Study of the Old Testament* 29 (1984): 19–35.

devised by M. H. Abrams[14] and thus divided biblical study into four modes. Each of these modes is characterized by a concentration (though not an exclusive one) on one of four "coordinates": (1) the external reference of the text, (2) the reader, (3) the text itself, and (4) the author. By this means, it is possible to produce what may be called an analytical history of biblical study, in which one observes that the interest of biblical expositors has shifted from time to time from one coordinate to another.

Much precritical study was interested in (1) what the text refers to: historical events to which it bore witness, theological truths it contained. This trend continues in much conservative biblical scholarship, now often in a somewhat "positivistic" form.[15]

But precritical commentators were also deeply concerned with (2) the relation of the text to the reader, in other words, what the Bible exists to convey to the believer who reads it. This is essentially an "instrumental" view of the text: the text is a vehicle through which God addresses the reader, and one should have regard not primarily to the text considered as of interest in itself, but to the end it is meant to serve. Such a reading resembles what Abrams calls "pragmatic" criticism in the wider literary world—the kind of criticism that asks not what the author meant or what the truths are that the text contains, but rather how far the text edifies and instructs the reader. (Dr. Johnson is the best exemplar of this approach.) "Reader-response criticism" represents a different, and much more recent, slant on an interest in the reader rather than the author, but one that operates with a quite new set of theoretical ideas.

Very recent trends in biblical study have been concerned with (3) the text as it is in itself, in its "finished form." This has been the interest in recent literary interpretation and also in the "canonical approach." In these, though in very different ways, the focus is on the text.

That leaves (4) the author, and on this map of the history of scholarship, concentration on the author comes between the two concerns of precritical interpretation, on the one hand, and the more recent concern with the text itself, on the other. On this way of seeing it, typical critical scholarship has been interested in the author and the author's intentions. The correlative type of criticism in the wider literary world is Romantic literary criticism, with its interest in the author's emotions and state of mind when writing, on literature as "emotion recollected in tranquillity." (Just as this is now very out of date in the literary world, so, it may be argued, is its correlate in the world of biblical

---

14. M. H. Abrams, *The Mirror and the Lamp: Romantic Theory and the Critical Tradition* (New York: Oxford University Press, 1953).

15. Cf. esp. Kenneth A. Kitchen, *On The Reliability of the Old Testament* (Grand Rapids: Eerdmans, 2003).

studies. This is another route to the conclusion that biblical criticism is passé.) So far, this would seem to confirm the hypothesis that intentionalism has been of the essence or the starting point of biblical criticism.

I believe, however, that this is misleading. The shift away from an interest in what the text refers to (what Abrams calls a "referential" idea of literature) or in the importance of the text for the reader ("pragmatic," in Abrams's vocabulary) and toward a concern for the author and his or her intentions is, again, an accidental rather than an inherent part of the establishment of biblical criticism. As part of the background to nineteenth-century biblical scholarship, there seem to me to be two different shifts going on, only one of which can be identified with this turn to the author, and only one of which occurred in the nineteenth century itself.

Undoubtedly one of the most important aspects in which Wellhausen (to take the best-known example) is united with the literary criticism of the late nineteenth century is in his interest in the creative insights of particular biblical authors. The clearest case of this is his high valuation of the prophets—not simply of the prophetic *books*, but of the real prophets as they can be reconstructed by criticism. For him they are lone geniuses, surely conceived in the model of the Romantic hero; the influence of Romanticism on Wellhausen is well documented.

But an important thing to remember is this. Wellhausen could present the prophets as he did—as the high point of the development of religious thinking in ancient Israel—only because he had been able to reconstruct the history of Israel on the basis of his analysis of the Pentateuch, which showed (or claimed to show) that "the prophets preceded the law." And this in turn was possible only because the foundations of pentateuchal criticism had already been laid, in many previous generations, by people who did not share Wellhausen's concern for the intentions of authors, but who worked at a time before Romantic ideas about the genius of authors had appeared on the scene. The shift to a "critical" analysis of the Pentateuch long preceded Wellhausen. But in Wellhausen's predecessors in this critical study of the Pentateuch, the detection of sources was not a question about the intentions of authors but very much a formal procedure, fed by taking seriously the "difficulties in the text" that were discussed in chapter 2. Hobbes, Spinoza, even de Wette were interested not in the *intentions* of J or D, but in what recognizing them implied about the formation of the Pentateuch and hence about its reference to historical events—very much the referential idea of interpretation (no. 1 above). The basic critical impulse that made Wellhausen's view of the prophets possible was thus already in place well before the late nineteenth century.

It is thus implausible to claim that the shift to a concern for "intended" meanings was actually the crucial factor in the move toward a critical approach to the Bible. The shift was in itself certainly very important: after Wellhausen nothing would be the same again in Old Testament studies. But his own keen interest in the intentions of, especially, the prophets, or even of the compilers of JE, is not what makes his scholarship critical. Criticism, in its technical sense, had been under way for two or more centuries before his time.

Indeed, there is no point on the historical analysis driven by Abrams's scheme at which we can mark the emergence of biblical criticism. All four of Abrams's coordinates (or the ones I have based on them) can be pursued critically or noncritically. One may be concerned, for example, with what the text refers to either by treating it as an infallible oracle or by regarding it as a historical source, to be critically evaluated. Some people had moved to the latter position in the eighteenth century; others remain in the first even today. Or one may want to ask how the text is fruitful for the reader either as studied by the critics (the main tendency in modern academic biblical studies) or just as it stands (the usual approach in Bible study groups). Similarly, it is possible to be interested in the intention of the author on a critical basis, as Wellhausen was, or on a noncritical one, as in the writers at whom we shall look next. The critical/noncritical distinction does not cut in at any particular point on Abrams's scheme. That scheme, as I have adapted it, seems to me to remain useful in charting the development of readers' interests in reading the Bible. But it does not solve the question of the essence of *critical* reading.

Thus this discussion leads to the same point we have already reached: criticism can exist without intentionalism. And so, secondly, we turn to the reverse case: noncritical intentionalism. Precritical biblical interpreters often ask about the intentions of the biblical authors.[16] Philo, for example, constantly inquires about what Moses was intending to convey when he wrote this or that portion of the Pentateuch. His assumption that Moses is the author is a noncritical assumption; but asking what Moses meant makes him clearly intentionalist. Augustine asks what John meant or what David, the psalmist, meant by this or that phrase. Two things tend to cloak this from us. One is that the authors whose intentions these commentators were interested in are often not the real authors of the books in question (the Pentateuch is not by Moses, the Fourth Gospel is not by the Beloved Disciple). A second is that most precritical commentators assumed that the statements made in biblical books are true at a literal level, even if (like Origen and many medieval writers) they thought

---

16. Compare Calvin: "Since the only business he [the commentator] has is to lay open the mind of the writer he has set out to explain, the more he leads the reader away from it, the more he deviates from his own purpose and is sure to wander out of bounds" (quoted in Yarchin, *History of Biblical Interpretation*, 184).

the literal level rather unimportant. This means that if the Bible records a particular person as having said certain words, it is assumed without question that
he or she did indeed say them; and this means that in such cases questions
about the *author's* intention do not arise, but only about the intentions of the
purported speaker. Thus Augustine can ask what John meant by the prologue
to his Gospel, since there John speaks *in propria persona*. But he does not ask,
as a modern redaction critic might, what John meant by the discourses he
attributes to Jesus, since for him these were the words of Jesus himself, and the
question was what *Jesus* meant by them, not what *John* meant. In the same way
Philo inquires into Moses' intentions in telling the story as he does,[17] in
reporting the words of God here rather than there in the overall plan of the
Pentateuch, but he does not ask what Moses meant by the divine words themselves, precisely because they are divine words, and the person who had an
intention in uttering them was not Moses, but God. But this does not affect
the point that such commentators were interested in the intention of what
stood in the text. They are precritical intentionalists.

Thus to attempt to find in intentionalism the essence of biblical criticism
fails. There were commentators interested in intentionalism who worked in a
quite uncritical way, treating the "facts" in the biblical text as exactly that,
whether they concerned events or speakers. Equally, there are unimpeachably
critical scholars whose concern with authorial intention has been patchy or
nonexistent. Some would term structuralist/poststructuralist interpreters noncritical, but they clearly belong in the critical camp, yet have been foremost in
dispensing with author's intention as the criterion for finding meaning in texts;
they have been particularly successful in analyzing texts that in the nature of
the case never had authors in the modern sense. Indeed, in the case of many
ancient texts authorship is a misleading category anyway, as many scholars
have pointed out.[18] Yet that does not imply that we cannot talk about the
meaning of such texts—we can and do—nor that such talk is not *critical*.

There is another point to be made about authorial intention, which I
sketched some years ago in an article called "Reading the Bible as Literature:
Two Questions for Biblical Critics."[19] This is that much biblical writing was
produced in a culture that placed less emphasis on the intention of authors in

17. Cf. Philo, *De opificio mundi*, ii.
18. Cf. J. A. Burrow, *Medieval Writers and Their Work: Middle English Literature and Its
Background 1100–1500* (Oxford: Oxford University Press, 1982), and A. J. Minnis, *Medieval
Theory of Authorship: Scholastic Literary Attitudes in the Later Middle Ages* (London: Scolar
Press, 1984).
19. John Barton, "Reading the Bible as Literature: Two Questions for Biblical Critics,"
Journal of Theology and Literature 1 (1987): 135–53.

any case. Ancient authors were often producing something more like a score for performance than a distillation of their thoughts for appropriation, and expected that readers would bring to the text an element of interpretation that went beyond the ideas the author had consciously had. Books were raw material for the reader, rather than encapsulating the thoughts of the author. This means that some forms at least of reader-response criticism are fairer to ancient, including biblical, authors than they would be if applied, for example, to modern discursive texts such as philosophical or scientific writings, and perhaps even novels and poems. As I shall argue in the next section, that does not mean that the exegesis of such works can overlook the historical context in which they were written: indeed, the very recognition that they were not written with intention in the modern sense is itself a historical point about them! But it does mean that an appropriate form of criticism will not be highly intentionalist, perhaps not intentionalist at all.

This can be seen clearly in the case of the psalms. As argued above, form-critical study has convinced most biblical scholars that the psalms are not best read as the expression of the thoughts of an individual, as if they were lyric poems. They are texts that have been used and reused many times, and the attempt to fix an "original" meaning is more or less bound to fail. That does not mean that they fall altogether outside the context in which they came to be and that we should read them as completely free-floating texts, as in some recent "literary" proposals. But it does make the pursuit of the "author's" meaning more or less pointless. And biblical scholars would generally accept this. The form-critical mode of study that has produced such a conclusion belongs to biblical criticism, and scholars who practice it would universally be regarded as biblical critics; it is part of what most people call the historical-critical method. Yet it has implications that are largely anti-intentionalist, since we have in the psalms what C. S. Lewis called "poetry without a poet."[20]

Thus here again a concern for intention fails to be a defining characteristic of a critical approach, though at the same time it contributes another reason for being careful about using the term "*historical*-critical," since a nonintentionalist reading of the psalms somewhat underplays their putative "original" circumstances of composition. Along this line of thought the possibility beckons of some rapprochement between traditional biblical critics and practitioners of newer literary approaches. The two camps may seem opposed when dealing with texts such as the letters of Paul, where biblical critics will insist on trying to discover what Paul intended to convey, whereas

20. See E. M. W. Tillyard and C. S. Lewis, *The Personal Heresy: A Controversy* (London: Oxford University Press, 1939).

a modern literary critic might be interested in the potentiality for meaning of the epistles when cut loose from their historical moorings. But in the case of the psalms, the two are much closer together than is often thought, and some meeting of minds ought to be possible.

THE HISTORICAL SENSE

I have already argued that biblical criticism is not identical with something called the historical-critical method, even though that expression remains in common use and will no doubt continue to do so. A focus on history, or historical methods, is not of the essence of criticism. Yet it is normal to say that the critic is concerned with the text's historical meaning. Often this is expressed in the terminology developed by Krister Stendahl: the critic is concerned with what the text *meant*, whereas the theologian/preacher/ordinary reader is concerned with what it *means*.[21] (The same person may be all of these things at the same time, of course, but there is a conceptual distinction.) In this section we look at what may be meant by the historical sense, and whether Stendahl's formulation does justice to the matter.

On the one hand, biblical criticism has always taken for granted that the meaning a text has is connected with its origins in a particular historical and cultural setting—what some would call its "original" sense, as we saw above. This is most obvious at the level of language. Words are not constant in their meaning across time. To take a simple example, in the novels of Trollope we often find a female character saying that a male friend "made love to her the whole evening." It is crucial in understanding Trollope to realize that in his day this expression meant showing a romantic or sexual interest in someone, not having sexual intercourse with them. Otherwise we shall get a very distorted idea of what happened in Victorian drawing rooms. There are indeed some readers nowadays, working in a psychoanalytic mode, who would argue for hidden meanings of which Trollope himself was unaware.[22] But the kind

---

21. Krister Stendahl, "Biblical Theology, Contemporary," in *The Interpreter's Dictionary of the Bible* (Nashville: Abingdon Press, 1962), 1:418–32; reprinted in *Reading the Bible in the Global Village: Helsinki*, ed. Heikki Räisänen et al. (Atlanta: Society of Biblical Literature, 2000), 67–106.

22. In *The Postmodern Bible*, by The Bible and Culture Collective (New Haven and London: Yale University Press, 1995), 196, we read that psychoanalytic criticism, especially the kind that builds on Lacan, reads texts not for their main "point," but "for what reveals itself unintentionally through slips of the tongue, subtle evasions, audible silences, logical digressions and other such 'accidents' of expression." Umberto Eco firmly rejects any idea that we can interpret texts correctly without regard to the lexical possibilities of the time of writing

of approach that characterizes biblical criticism would be resistant to this suggestion, recognizing that the semantic range of the expression "to make love"
in Trollope's day must be an arbiter of what the text can possibly mean. In that
sense, critics are concerned with a *historical* sense of the text.[23]

What applies at the level of language applies also at the level of discourse—longer units of text than the word or phrase. It matters in what historical context a piece of writing was produced. A biblical example from the
psalms illustrates this well. The psalms often speak of God as existing or
reigning "for ever" (*le'olam*; e.g., Ps. 102:12). Now a real point is being made
if we note the following. Christians (and Jews) have often read this in the
sense that God is eternal, as that idea is conceived by some philosophers: that
God exists outside the constraints of time, that he has his being in a quite
different mode from humans or the material world. But biblical conceptuality is different from this. The idea of eternity in this special philosophical
sense had not yet arisen in the culture that produced the psalms. What the
psalms mean is that God's existence knows no end; however long time
endures, God will still be there. No doubt some interpreters might dispute
this understanding of the matter, but it should be easy to see what kind of
point is being made by it: that there is a gap between the mental world of
ancient Israel and that of a modern (or medieval) philosopher, and that it is
improper to attribute a meaning that would be possible for the latter, to texts
produced in the Old Testament world itself.

This kind of understanding can be relevant even in the textual sphere. Psalm
100 in the Masoretic text says, "It is he that made us, and not we (ourselves)."
This has been highly influential in Christian thought, and can be found in the
metrical version of the psalm sung in many churches: "without our aid he did
us make." Most textual critics, however, think that the correct reading is "it is

---

in discussing Wordsworth's line "a poet cannot but be gay," which, he says, even the most
creative critics do not take to mean what it would mean if written today: "A sensitive and
responsible reader is not obliged to speculate about what happened in the head of
Wordsworth when writing that verse, but has the duty to take into account the state of the
lexical system at the time of Wordsworth" (Umberto Eco with Richard Rorty, Jonathan
Culler, Christine Brooke-Rose, ed. Stefan Collini, *Interpretation and Overinterpretation*
[Cambridge: Cambridge University Press, 1992], 68).

23. Schleiermacher argued that in interpreting any text one must attend to both its
"grammar" and its "rhetoric." By grammar he understands not simply grammar in the nar-
row sense, not even grammar and syntax, but the network of associations and meanings
within which it makes sense. By rhetoric he means the drift of the passage, the way the general resources of the language are employed to convey a particular meaning. (There are some
resemblances to Saussure's distinction between *langue* and *parole*.) See Frank, *Schleiermachers Hermeneutik und Kritik*, 32–33.

he that made us, and we are his" (reading *lo 'anachnu* rather than *lo' 'anachnu*). This reading is attested in some manuscripts and is the Qere. The reason for accepting it is a certain understanding of the thought world that existed when the psalm was produced. If it were a modern text, it might well read "not we ourselves." But if it comes from ancient Israel, it is highly unlikely that it would have this meaning, since the notion that we might have made ourselves would not have arisen and could not have needed rebutting. This is clearly a historical point about the text and its possible meanings, which influences how we reconstruct the psalm's text. Of course the Masoretic version also exists, and also has a meaning, but it is the meaning that was possible in a later period. Whether Christians should use the probable ancient reading or the later Masoretic one is a good question, linked to the issue of which canonical text is authoritative for Christians, and one could easily imagine how a case could be made for adopting the "wrong" reading. My point here is simply that it would need to be acknowledged that the meaning of the wrong reading is not one that could have existed in the time of the text's provenance. This issue has to do with the text's history, and we may therefore speak of its historical sense.

Two texts may bear different senses according to the time of their production, even if they are verbally identical. I illustrated this in my *Reading the Old Testament* from a classic example, Borges's short piece "Pierre Menard, Author of the *Quixote*." Borges imagines a modern author who sets himself the task of writing a new work that will have identically the same wording as Cervantes's *Don Quixote*. He then shows how a given passage of this work will have a different meaning from that which it has in the original *Quixote*, because it has been written against a wholly different intellectual background:

> It is a revelation to compare Menard's *Don Quixote* with Cervantes'. The latter, for example, wrote (part one, chapter nine):
>
>> . . . truth, whose mother is history, rival of time, depository of deeds, witness of the past, exemplar and adviser to the present, and the future's counsellor.
>
> Written in the seventeenth century, written by the 'lay genius' Cervantes, this enumeration is a mere rhetorical praise of history. Menard, on the other hand, writes:
>
>> . . . truth, whose mother is history, rival of time, depository of deeds, witness of the past, exemplar and adviser to the present, and the future's counsellor.
>
> History, the *mother* of truth: the idea is astounding. Menard, a contemporary of William James, does not define history as an inquiry into reality but as its origin. Historical truth, for him, is not what has hap-

pened; it is what we judge to have happened. The final phrases—*exemplar and adviser to the present, and the future's counsellor*—are brazenly pragmatic.[24]

This indicates that meaning is historically bound. Words change their meanings over time, and so do the sentences, paragraphs, even books that contain them. This is incompatible with any notion that a given assemblage of words has a fixed meaning. But it absolutely requires that the provenance of a text should be taken into account—it requires, that is, what biblical scholars call Introduction. We cannot know what the sentence "he made love to me all evening" means, until we know whether it is by Trollope (or another writer of his period) or Martin Amis (or another writer of his). Thus far, we may say that meaning is historically conditioned: what a text means in the eighth century BC is not what it would mean if it were written in the second, or in the twentieth century AD.[25]

On the other hand, however, I am not convinced that the correct way to formulate this point is to say that the text once *meant* X but now *means* Y. We say loosely that Trollope meant by the expression "make love" something different from what we mean by it. But that does not have the consequence that his novels now mean something different from what they meant when they were written. The object of studying the history of the meaning of words is not to establish what Trollope's novels *used to* mean, but what they *do* mean. We can get at this meaning only by some "archaeological" work on the English language. Similarly, with the Psalms we are not searching for what the psalms that speak of God's "eternity" meant, but have now ceased to mean; we are searching for what they actually mean, as opposed to what (on the basis of a faulty understanding of ancient Hebrew conceptuality) they might be thought to mean.

What Stendahl had in mind, in fact, was not that texts change their meaning over time. His discussion arose from his involvement in the movement to ordain women in the Church of Sweden,[26] and what he was concerned to argue

24. J. L. Borges, "Pierre Menard, Author of the Quixote," in *Labyrinths: Selected Stories and Other Writings* (Harmondsworth: Penguin, 1970), 62–71; quotation, 69. Quoted in my *Reading the Old Testament*, 173.

25. This is not in practice denied even by a critic such as Roland Barthes. In analyzing a story by Poe, Barthes takes considerable trouble over the historical context of the text, explaining the background of many things taken for granted in the story; see "Textual Analysis: Poe's 'Valdemar,'" in *Modern Criticism and Theory: A Reader*, 151–172.

26. See Krister Stendahl, "Dethroning Biblical Imperialism in Theology," in *Reading the Bible in the Global Village: Helsinki*, 61–66.

was that though there are Pauline texts that seem clearly to rule this out, they are now to be interpreted in ways compatible with women's ordination. That is, he was contrasting the meaning of the texts with their application—or interpretation, in one sense of this word. By "what the text means" he intended to convey "what the modern implications of the text are"—not a directly semantic question. (This is an attempt, in conformity with the case I have been arguing, to undertake an exegesis of Stendahl's own words on the basis of understanding their provenance.) It is not that the text changes its meaning, but that that meaning is differently evaluated, appropriated, or weighed. This is very inaccurately expressed by the meant/means distinction. The point Stendahl was making was of course a vital and important one, but the way he expressed it can easily mislead one into thinking that texts change their meaning—which is not what he was saying.

The fact that a text's meaning depends on its historical (and social, and intellectual) context affects the issue of what I have called "creative transcription,"[27] as in the example cited above from Borges. A text can in that sense change its meaning over time, but by dint of becoming a new text verbally identical with the original one. This sounds both paradoxical and complicated, but we deal with it daily and with no difficulty at all. We use quotations from the Bible, from Shakespeare, from other works in quite a different sense from what they have within those works, and are perfectly happy to mean by them what *we* mean, not what the texts in question originally meant. If we say that we have escaped "by the skin of our teeth," we are not concerned whether or not this usage corresponds to what Job meant by the expression in Job 19:20—whatever that may be. But it would be odd to say that the text thereby changes its meaning: that *Job* now means something different by "the skin of my teeth" because I use the phrase in my own sense. It is surely better to say that I am using in a particular sense a sequence of words that has a different meaning in the book of Job. The meanings may be related, but are not identical. It is not that Job meant A but now means B; rather, Job means A, but I am using the words that occur in Job to mean B.

The Psalms again provide particular good examples of this by dint of their continuous use over many centuries in Christian and Jewish public liturgy and private devotion. Biblical criticism does not in the least rule out such use. It is common in the monastic tradition of psalm recitation, for example, to adopt one or both of two rather different interpretative devices. One is to generalize the speaker in the Psalms to refer to all human beings, and in that case the ubiquitous "enemies" are taken as those things that are opposed to human

27. See *Reading the Old Testament*, 174.

flourishing: sins and troubles as well as human adversaries. The other is to identify the speaker with Christ, and thus to give every psalm a christological implication. The two approaches can, indeed, be combined, in that Christ can be seen as the very epitome of the one praying in the psalm, the archetypal one who calls out to God for succor. Now there is nothing in biblical criticism that makes such a use of the Psalms in any way illegitimate, though people often think that there is. This is simply a case of "creative transcription": the same words used to convey a different meaning, in many cases not wholly different from the meaning the psalm was composed and transmitted to convey, but in other cases sharply at variance with it.

A liturgical example of such divergence can be illustrated from another text, the use of Wisdom 18:14–15 at Christmas. The text reads:

> For while gentle silence enveloped all things,
> and night in its swift course was now half gone,
> your all-powerful word leapt from heaven, from the royal throne . . .

The church has for many centuries used it to refer to the descent of the Word or Logos to become incarnate in Jesus, as described in John 1:1–18. When the context is examined, it is clear that the original meaning is in reference to the angel who slew the firstborn of Egypt, since the text continues:

> . . . a stern warrior
> carrying the sharp sword of your authentic command,
> and stood and filled all things with death.

Now it does not seem to me appropriate to say that the text in Wisdom once meant to describe the death of the firstborn but now refers to the incarnation. Rather, the text in Wisdom means what it always meant, but Christians have quite legitimately used the form of words found there to create a beautiful text with a quite different reference.[28] Some will believe that God deliberately planted this possibility in the text, so that it could have a messianic significance,

---

28. Umberto Eco similarly distinguishes between *interpreting* a text and *using* it, arguing that use is of course a free-for-all, but that to interpret, one needs to attend to the cultural and linguistic background against which a work was written: see *Interpretation and Overinterpretation*, 68. Elsewhere he argues that a text can become the pretext for any kind of reading, but that we should not call such a reading an interpretation: "Naturally, a text can also be read as an uncommitted stimulus for a personal hallucinatory experience, cutting out levels of meaning, placing upon the expression 'aberrant' codes. As Borges once suggested, why not read the *Odyssey* as written after the *Aeneid* or *The Imitation of Christ* as written by Céline?" (Umberto Eco, *The Role of the Reader: Explorations in the Semiotics of Texts* [London: Hutchinson, 1981], 40).

but even they will not deny that the meaning of the text has to do with the death of the firstborn.

Thus there is truth in saying that biblical criticism is concerned with the historical sense, taking this to be the meaning made possible by the milieu in which a given text was composed and in terms of whose language, conventions, and conceptuality alone it can have any meaning at all. There is also truth in saying that texts, considered as sequences of words and sentences, can be used to convey different meanings in different periods and contexts. This is not well expressed, however, by the meant/means contrast. This contrast implies that the text has no meaning that persists across time: what it meant is simply one of a series of possible meanings. Of course there are many interpreters who believe this, for whom the meaning of a text is simply what it has been taken to mean, so that a critical "reading" is only one—and not in any way a privileged one—among the many meanings that can be found in the text's reception history. Biblical critics are unwise to concede this point by appearing to say, "We study what the text meant, and leave the question about what it means now to you." On the contrary: what the text meant is what it still means. The fact that it can be used as a vehicle for many other meanings does not undermine this.

A major contribution to this point has been made, in my view, by E. D. Hirsch. Hirsch argued, in *Validity in Interpretation*,[29] that we should distinguish between meaning and significance in texts. He was using terminology developed by Gottlob Frege, but in his own way. The significance may vary from one generation to another, but the meaning remains constant throughout. This was taken by many readers at the time to suggest that texts are not open-ended or susceptible of creative rereading, but such was not Hirsch's intention, and he developed this further in two articles published in the early 1980s.[30] There he discusses the fact that much literature has the deliberate intention of being open to future reinterpretation, but that a degree of continuity with what the author meant in writing it is presupposed; it is not endlessly malleable: "It is the nature of textual meaning to embrace many different future fulfilments without thereby being changed."[31] As Hirsch points about, among modern critics Frank Kermode and Paul Ricoeur do not accept the distinction between meaning and significance, but this may be because they fail to see that the orig-

29. E. D. Hirsch Jr., *Validity in Interpretation* (New Haven and London: Yale University Press, 1967).

30. See E. D. Hirsch Jr., "Past Intentions and Present Meanings" (F. W. Bateson Memorial Lecture), *Essays in Criticism* 33 (1984): 79–98; "Meaning and Significance Reinterpreted," *Critical Inquiry* 11 (1984): 202–25.

31. Hirsch, "Meaning and Significance Reinterpreted," 210.

inal meaning can be thus deliberately open to reinterpretation without thereby ceasing to be itself. In Gadamer, by contrast, there is a much more hardline refusal to recognize any distinction between meaning and significance, because the perception of meaning itself is for him so culturally conditioned that no two people "read" the same text. This, Hirsch argues, while appearing to do justice to the plurality of readings of literary texts, ultimately ends in a kind of critical nihilism in which communication between people is impossible. On the contrary, he argues, a given meaning in the text persists over time even when its significance is differently perceived. Most of us assume this in all our reading when we are not consciously reflecting on critical theory: "In most applications of texts, and thus in most of our commentaries about texts, meaning is not interpreted; meaning is assumed."[32]

This is not a plea for a deliberately thin or reductive meaning. A Shakespearean tragedy has its meaning determined by the possible senses that its words could bear in the Elizabethan age.[33] In that context, it may be among the most profound reflections on human life ever penned, and nothing prevents the critic from saying so. There is no denying that there has been a kind of historical criticism that rather deliberately sets its face against discovering profundity in texts, and for which the study of Shakespeare is no more than a matter of technical textual criticism or rather wooden semantics. There is equally no denying that there are biblical scholars whose criticism is also of that kind. But the fact that biblical criticism is historical—in the sense that it concerns itself with biblical texts as products of a specific age in the past—does not mean that it has to be historic*ist*, deliberately opposed to finding depth and significance in the texts it studies, nor that most biblical critics have been of that persuasion.

Such attenuation of meaning is generally what biblical critics are charged with, by those hostile to their enterprise, rather than what they themselves are really seeking. Nearly all biblical critics read the text because they think its

32. Ibid., 215.
33. "New historicist" critics of Shakespeare, like those of the Bible, are strongly committed to the idea that the text must be read in its historical context if it is to speak to the reader today, and oppose the idea common since the advent of the New Criticism that a text has a kind of timeless existence. On New Historicism in Shakespeare, see Louis A. Montrose, "'Shaping Fantasies': Figurations of Gender and Power in Elizabethan Culture," in *A Midsummer Night's Dream*, ed. R. Dutton, New Casebooks (Basingstoke: Macmillan, 1983); on a wider front, see his "Professing the Renaissance: The Poetics and Politics of Culture," in *The New Historicism*, ed. H. Aram Veeser (New York and London: Routledge, 1989); for biblical applications, see Robert Carroll, "Poststructuralist Approaches," in *The Cambridge Companion to Biblical Interpretation*, ed. John Barton (Cambridge: Cambridge University Press, 1998), 50–66.

meanings are profound and important; their technical scholarship is needed to establish the text's meaning because it comes from a remote and obscure past, but it is in the service of establishing the text's meaning, not of reducing that meaning as far as possible to banalities. There is an anticritical rhetoric that talks down what biblical criticism has achieved in this way, and it is very influential at the moment. But biblical criticism has always been concerned with what texts mean, not with what they once meant in some antiquarian sense. When Gerhard von Rad outlined the theology of the Yahwist, for example, he was acting as a biblical critic, for whom the meaning—the theology—was rooted in the age when the Yahwist wrote. J was not for him a free-floating text, capable of taking on new meanings in a new age. Yet the meanings he found in that text were profound, not trivial. There is no reason, of course, why some critics should not concentrate their efforts on the technical skills needed to understand works written in a remote past and in an imperfectly known language. But their work is not the whole of biblical criticism, which has also a strong tradition of seeking meaning in a much deeper sense than this.

It is still worth asking why people are so prone to *think* that biblical criticism is reductionist in effect or even in intention, for many do so think. Students, especially those with a religious commitment, frequently complain that historical criticism takes the Bible away from them (we shall look at this reaction in more detail in chapter 6). Whether intentionally or not, this is the impression that is created, and we may well feel that there is no smoke without fire. Interestingly, students of literature often express an analogous feeling when subjected to "historical criticism" of older texts and wish their teachers would give the texts back to them as aesthetic objects—not at all unlike the way biblical students would like to be given back the Bible as a religious object. The feeling was already caught by J. R. R. Tolkien in his famous lecture on Beowulf.[34] There is no doubt that such critics can have imperialistic designs, or at least can come across as determined to insist that historical questions alone are to be asked in their classes. But this is not the same as choosing to concentrate on such questions for the time being, or because that is where one's competence lies. It is a pity, however, that biblical scholars can sometimes give the impression that they are not interested in the power of the texts they study; it probably represents, in many cases, an anxiety not to seem "committed" religiously while working in the secular environment of a university. Literary critics can easily give students a similar impression by steadfastly concentrating on matters of "scholarship" and

34. See chap. 3, note 26.

ignoring the depth of the texts being studied. But it is an occupational haz-
ard, not to be taken at face value. *Most critics read texts because they love them;
it is just that they do not always say so.*[35]

THE LITERAL SENSE

It is often said that biblical criticism consists in reading the text literally. This
is usually regarded as the most important way it differs from the allegorical
reading common in the Middle Ages and, indeed, in antiquity. Those who have
pointed to Reformation, rather than merely Enlightenment, origins for a critical approach to the Bible have generally drawn attention to the Reformers'
preference for the literal over the allegorical and have argued from that that it
was through their work that a truly critical mode of reading the Bible was
established. Indeed, we shall later see some good reasons to think that biblical
criticism has important roots in the Reformation. But is it precisely in their
opposition to allegory that the Reformers presaged modern biblical criticism?

We begin with some problems about this notion. I argued above that intentionalism cannot be a determining mark of biblical criticism, because it is not
hard to find both nonintentionalist critics and intentionalist noncritics. A similar line of argument may be developed concerning allegory.

First, there are critics who have pursued an allegorical approach or something very like it. This case is urged by James Barr in his "The Literal, the
Allegorical, and Modern Scholarship."[36] Barr suggests that the whole edifice
of biblical theology, which undoubtedly rests on critical investigation of the
Bible, is nonetheless closer to allegory than to a concern with the literal sense
of the text. It is interested in patterns of theological principles that run
through many biblical books, and it concentrates on distilling a unified (or
more or less unified) message from many different texts.[37] Furthermore, the

---

35. Compare the remark of La Bruyère on secular literary criticism, quoted in Jean Steinmann, *Biblical Criticism* (London: Burns & Oates, 1959), 7: "Criticism is such an enjoyable
pastime that its pleasures are liable to rob us of that of being deeply moved by beauty."

36. James Barr, "The Literal, the Allegorical, and Modern Biblical Scholarship," *Journal
for the Study of the Old Testament* 44 (1989): 3–17.

37. This point was already noticed by Franz Overbeck: "All theological exegesis is allegorical, whether secretly or brazenly, or else it is not theological exegesis at all, but merely
a means of getting rid of texts that genuinely theological exegesis strives to retain out of its
religious respect for them" ("Alle theologische Exegese ist allegorisch, verschämt oder
unverschämt, oder sie ist überhaupt keine theologische Exegese mehr, sondern nur das Mit-
tel, Texte, die theologische Exegese in ihrem religiösen Ansehen zu erhalten sich bemüht,
in diesem Sinne loszuwerden") (cited in Smend, "Nachkritische Schriftauslegung," 236).

pattern it discovers is most often conceived along broadly confessional lines—
we shall see this clearly in the case of the Old Testament theologies of both
Eichrodt and von Rad.[38] It is commonly alleged that biblical criticism has been
strongly opposed to allegorical reading,[39] but it may be doubted whether this is
so. The *Heilsgeschichte*, for example, as conceived by von Rad is a conceptual
scheme into which the individual biblical books and utterances can be fitted, and
these are not understood literally but as theologoumena—von Rad was deeply
opposed to what he would perhaps have seen as positivistic attempts to discover
"what really happened." It would be odd to say that von Rad was not a biblical
critic, yet he interprets the Old Testament text in ways highly reminiscent of an
allegorical approach. An even more surprising, and much earlier, case might be
that of de Wette. De Wette is rightly remembered as a historian of ancient Israel.
Yet, as Smend shows, his demonstration that the history recorded in the Old
Testament was not literally true was understood by him as "releasing" it to
become theology: that was how it was most fruitful for the believer.

> He turns against the attempts of Eichhorn and others to reconstruct the
> history of Israel in the most ancient times from the biblical material. In
> his judgment one cannot as a rule recapture kernels of historical truth
> by excluding mythical elements, and then combine them with the help
> of multifarious hypotheses so as to produce a complete picture. The Old
> Testament is trying to convey religion, not history. To try nevertheless
> to extract a history from it, which from the nature of the material can-
> not actually be done, is to act against its own intention. Thus de Wette
> sees no other possibility than for the historian to leave this territory
> aside and let the Old Testament be what it is: a witness to a religion
> which is meant to awaken religion in its readers. . . . Thus his historical
> criticism of the Old Testament is *precisely in its radical character* not at all
> against the Bible; on the contrary, by overturning the historical miscon-
> ception it is meant to clear the way for the correct, aesthetic-religious
> use of the Bible. It places itself at the disposal of theology.[40]

---

38. See below, pp. 165–66.
39. For this, see esp. Louth, *Discerning the Mystery*.
40. "Er wendet sich gegen die Versuche Eichhorns und anderer, aus dem biblischen
Material eine Geschichte des ältesten Israel zu rekonstruieren. Man kann nach seinem Urteil
in der Regel nicht, indem man die mythischen Elemente ausscheidet, historische Kerne
gewinnen, aus deren Verbindung sich dann mit Hilfe mannigfacher Hypothesen ein
Gesamtbild herstellen ließe. Das Alte Testament will Religion bieten, nicht Geschichte.
Man handelt gegen seine Intention, wenn man ihm trotzdem eine Geschichte abgewinnen
will, die man ihm nach der Beschaffenheit des Materials ja auch gar nicht abgewinnen kann.
So sieht de Wette keine andere Möglichkeit als die, daß der Historiker auf dieses Gebiet
verzichtet und das Alte Testament sein läßt, was es ist: Zeugnis einer Religion, dazu bes-
timmt, in den Lesern Religion zu wecken. . . . Seine historische Kritik am Alten Testament
richtet sich damit gerade in ihrer Radikalität keineswegs gegen die Bibel, sondern will im

Barr points out that a normal feature of literalism in Christian discourse has been the affirmation that the text in its literal sense is *true*. This is quite unlike the interpretation of the Bible we find in most modern critical scholarship, where factuality is so far from the center of interest that it is often not even discussed—an aspect of critical approaches often complained of by more conservative Christians. New Testament critics do not tell us whether the resurrection happened; they do not read the story literally, but instead ask questions about the motivation of its compilers or the process by which it was transmitted. In this way modern criticism is far removed from what is usually meant by literalism.

Secondly, and conversely, there are pre-Reformation examples of literal reading which nevertheless do not constitute a critical approach to the Bible in any way that we would recognize today. It has been usual to say that the exegetes of the Antiochene school practiced a far more literal (they would have said "historical") reading of the biblical text than the school of Alexandria. Here, however, we have a full recent discussion by Frances Young, which seriously questions whether Antiochene exegesis was literal in anything like a modern sense. She refers to "the assumption that Antiochene literalism meant something like modern historicism"[41]—that these exegetes felt the same problems as we do in Origenist allegory and wished to oppose it in the name of the literal sense. On the contrary, she writes:

> No Antiochene could have imagined the kind of critical stance of the
> Biblical Theology movement, explicitly locating revelation not in the

---

Gegenteil durch die Widerlegung des historischen Mißverständnisses den Weg für den richtigen, den ästhetisch-religiösen Gebrauch freimachen. Sie stellt sich in den Dienst der Theologie"; see Smend, *Deutsche Alttestamentler in drei Jahrhunderten*, 42–43. Cf. his comments in "Nachkritische Schriftauslegung," 237: "The fact that the biblical writers [in de Wette's view] offer us no history is not only because they cannot do so, but—and for de Wette this is the more essential point—that they have no wish to. Their desire is to present divine action in the world, and to awaken faith in the reader. As de Wette says, they are not after history, but after religion, and it is as religious utterances that what they say should be understood, and in no other way—even leaving aside the general point that the significance of Israel for us does not lie in its history but in its religion." ("Daß die biblischen Schriftsteller keine Historie bieten, liegt nicht nur daran, daß sie es nicht können, sondern auch, und für de Wette ist dieser Punkt der wesentlichere, daran, daß sie es nicht wollen. Sie wollen das göttliche Handeln an der Welt darstellen und den Glauben der Leser wecken. Sie sind, wie de Wette sagt, nicht auf Geschichte aus, sondern auf Religion, und religiös wollen ihre Aussagen verstanden werden, nicht anders, ganz abgesehen davon, daß Israels Bedeutung für uns nicht in seiner Geschichte, sondern in seiner Religion besteht.") As Smend points out, de Wette's heir in this aspect of his work is not (as for the historical reconstruction he carried out) Wellhausen, but Barth.

41. Frances Young, *Biblical Exegesis and the Formation of Christian Culture*, 166.

text of scripture but in the historicity of events behind the text, events to which we only have access by reconstructing them from the texts, treating the texts as documents providing historical data. This is anachronistic, and obscures the proper background of the Antiochenes' protest. For them scripture was the Word of God, an unproblematic account of what had happened which pointed to the truths of Christian dogma.[42]

We shall however need to return to the Antiochenes, for although they do not prefigure modern "literalism," they may be important precursors of critical reading in another sense.[43] Their opposition to Origenist allegory was not necessarily in the interest of a literal meaning,[44] but more often proceeded from a concern that the text should be read as morally and spiritually edifying and should not evaporate into symbols and figures.

There is another example of precritical literalism that is often proposed, but which I would tend to discount. It is sometimes said that the distinction between *peshat* and *derash* in various periods of Jewish exegesis is similar to that between allegory and literalism in Christian exegesis. But Ralph Loewe has argued persuasively that *peshat* in early rabbinic texts does not mean anything like the literal sense of biblical passages; rather, it means "a reading in accordance with the usual interpretation," as opposed to a more far-fetched one that is proposed idiosyncratically by a particular rabbi.[45] David Weiss Halivni has argued that in the Talmud it actually means something like "context" (from its etymological sense, "extension"), so that the principle that "no text can be deprived of its *peshat*"[46] means that texts must not be interpreted without regard to their context.[47] In the Middle Ages *peshat* came to mean something nearer to the literal sense, and it is generally used in that meaning today. But

42. Young, *Biblical Exegesis and the Formation of Christian Culture*, 167.

43. See below, pp. 132–34.

44. Antiochene exegesis frequently applies the Old Testament to Christ, for example, in a way that is certainly not what we should call literal. Theodoret, for example, commenting on Psalm 30, refers the title ("A Psalm. A song at the dedication of the temple") to "the restoration of human nature that Christ the Lord accomplished by accepting death on behalf of us, destroying death and giving hope of resurrection." See Yarchin, *History of Biblical Interpretation*, 83–84, quoting from *Theodoret of Cyrus: Commentary on the Psalms, Psalms 1–72*, Fathers of the Church (Washington, DC: Catholic University of America Press, 2000), 101:187–91.

45. Ralph Loewe, "The 'Plain' Meaning of Scripture in Early Jewish Exegesis," in *Papers of the Institute of Jewish Studies*, ed. J. G. Weiss (Jerusalem: Magnes Press, 1964), 1:140–85.

46. This principle occurs three times in the Babylonian Talmud, at *Shabbat* 63a, and at *Yevamot* 11b and 24a.

47. David Weiss Halivni, *Peshat and Derash: Plain and Applied Meaning in Rabbinic Exegesis* (New York and Oxford: Oxford University Press, 1991). Halivni discusses Loewe's article briefly on 53.

it is still rarely literal in the way that modern critical readings can be literal, being concerned much more with the application of the text to Jewish life— i.e., having a halakic interest—than with penetrating the literal meaning. Halivni comments:

> Our sense and the rabbis' sense of what constitutes simple, literal meaning do not always agree. Their sense of the simple, literal meaning was more inclusive. They felt less committed to our limited sense of peshat, seeing it instead as larger and wider in its scope. To the rabbis, there was less of a distinction between simple and applied meaning with respect to both scope and primacy of peshat than there is to us. . . . Thus the rabbis did not equate peshat with simple, literal meaning as we know it, but with a wider scope of expositions. Indeed, most, if not all of the rebuttals offered (in the *b. Menach.* 65a–66a and parallels) against the Sadducees' interpretation of 'the morrow of the Sabbath' (Lev. 23:15) do not coincide with our sense of what constitutes the simple, literal meaning.[48]

I doubt whether a literal/allegorical distinction does justice to the many readings and uses of the Bible in Judaism.[49]

But where Christian exegetes are concerned, allegorical readings do always exist alongside an ability to perceive the literal sense. The traditional fourfold division of exegesis of course begins with the literal (or "historical") sense, which is always to be established before allegorism can take off. The Reformers may have insisted that only the literal meaning was to be of interest (though this is true only with some qualifications), but in this they were not enthroning a type of meaning that had not been known at all in the Middle Ages, only establishing it as the *sole* legitimate meaning among those conceivable meanings that were already known. Even if we go back to the early allegorizer par excellence, Origen, we do not find there an inability to identify and expound the literal sense, but rather a belief that in many cases the literal sense is not the *true* sense of a given passage. It is when the literal sense is nonsensical or unedifying that we can know for sure that we are being pointed to a deeper, allegorical meaning. But this presupposes that the literal meaning can be established and that it needs to be, in order that its theological inadequacy can

---

48. Ibid., 12.

49. For the *peshat/derash* distinction, see the (oddly named) article by Stephen Garfinkel, "Clearing *Peshat* and *Derash*," in *Hebrew Bible / Old Testament: The History of Its Interpretation*, ed. M. Sæbø (Göttingen: Vandenhoeck & Ruprecht, 1996), I/2:129–34. He suggests that *peshat* means "examining the text on its own terms," as opposed to "appropriating it for changing times," which is *derash*. I am not sure that this, which seems to correspond roughly to my own distinction between exegesis and application, really does justice to the rabbinic material either.

be properly perceived. No one, not even Origen, read the Bible *only* allegorically. Of course what he took to be the literal sense will sometimes strike modern scholars as not the literal sense at all, but that is a different issue.

The difference between ancient and post-Reformation scholars thus lies
not in any lack of ability in the ancient ones to grasp the literal meaning, but
in the respective attitudes to whether it should be affirmed as normative. A
scholar such as Origen was as aware as anyone today of what the literal meaning of the text was; he simply thought this was seldom the meaning that should
be accepted as part of the Christian reader's appropriation of the text as saving truth. In effect he regarded the literal sense as not the true meaning, but
only the apparent meaning—the surface meaning, beneath which the true
sense lay encoded.[50]

From another point of view, it is correct to say that biblical critics tend to
take the text literally, but in a rather restricted sense of the word "literal." We
can see this by considering Genesis 1–2. One of the critical insights here is that
these two chapters contain what are essentially two different stories: one in
which humankind (consisting of both sexes) is created after the animals on the
sixth day, and the other in which humans are there before the animals, and man
before woman. The hypothesis that the two accounts derive from different
writers rests on this observation, which is essentially a matter of noting the literal meaning of the text, and not being willing, for example, to countenance
the idea that the order of events as described is unimportant or trivial. A more
conservative or fundamentalist account has to reorder the two texts in the mind
in such a way that the Genesis 2 account is read as a spelling out of the events
of the sixth day, and desperate measures are needed to account for the discrepancies.[51] In such a case it is the critical reader who is taking the text literally, and the conservative one who is resorting to nonliteral explanations.
The same may be said about the idea that "day" in Genesis 1 designates a very
long period or eon. There is no basis in the text for such an assertion: the days
have a morning and evening, just like the days we experience now, and the passage makes sense as a whole only on that assumption, since it serves to justify

---

50. Something similar might be said of Luther. As R. H. Bainton points out, Luther
"equated the literal sense with the prophetic, and the prophetic meant not a specific
prophecy but the forward reference to Christ implicit and perhaps hidden beneath the
description of some purely contemporary event. This might be called the Christian sense,
as distinguished from the Jewish sense." But if this is so, then, he adds, "the prophetic sense
was really the literal sense." See R. H. Bainton, "The Bible in the Reformation," in *Cambridge History of the Bible* (Cambridge: Cambridge University Press, 1963), 3:1–37; quotations, 25.

51. For the medieval versions of this, see Smalley, *The Study of the Bible in the Middle Ages*,
132–34.

the observance of the weekly Sabbath. Of course the reason why more conservative readers prefer the "strained" interpretation is that it leaves Genesis 1 capable of being true, whereas on the critical reading it is clearly false as a historical account of how the world came to be, which is certainly what it seems to offer. This point was already made by Wellhausen: "The secret root of the manifest preference long shown by historical-critical theology for Gen. i appears to lie in this, that scholars felt themselves responsible for what the Bible says, and therefore liked it to come as little as possible in conflict with general culture."[52] It is interesting that he attributes such concerns to "the historical-critical school," suggesting a sharp change in the use of that term since his day.

This point is thus double-edged. Critical inquiry does often involve taking the biblical text literally, but not taking it to be literally true—a distinction that is perhaps not drawn as clearly as it might be in Barr's article referred to above. In practice, however, critical scholars have varied greatly in the extent to which the literal sense has interested them, and many, having noted, for example, that Genesis affirms a six-day creation, have gone on to argue that this literal sense is not at all what the Bible is trying to communicate to the reader. The message of Genesis 1–2 is identified in most critical commentaries as consisting in the belief that God is indeed the creator, the detail being treated as of secondary importance. Thus in a Hermeneia (Biblischer Kommentar) commentary such as that of Westermann,[53] one would look in vain for any attempt to make interpretative use of the literal seven-day scheme. Instead one finds general theological statements about the creatorship of God and comparisons with other ancient Near Eastern ideas about creation. The literal sense is indeed observed and not denied, but it is not very clearly in focus and certainly not very important. While the six-day scheme is discussed in terms of its historical origins and literary antecedents, in the "Purpose and Thrust" section of the commentary, nothing is made of it.[54]

"Literality" is thus not clearly a marker of a critical approach, though it does sometimes surface within critical readings. For the most part, critical readings are not significantly more literal than traditional ones, and the latter often contain elements of literality in any case. Much the same, incidentally, may be said of conservative readings. These are sometimes literal, as when a commentator defends the real existence of Adam and Eve or affirms that Joshua really did cause the literal walls of Jericho to fall down. At other times, however, as with

52. Wellhausen, *Prolegomena*, 307–8.
53. Claus Westermann, *Genesis 1–11: A Commentary* (London: SPCK, 1984).
54. Ibid., 173–77.

the seven-day scheme in Genesis 1, some conservatives tend to avoid the literal sense and opt instead for a more remote meaning—one that is capable of
being true according to what is now known about the origins of the universe
or at least that does not come into direct conflict with that. (Others, of course,
adhere to the absoluteness of the letter and simply deny the findings of modern science.) Part of the rhetoric of conservatism is, however, often a claim to
accept the Bible literally, a claim that biblical critics very seldom make. One
person's literality is often another person's allegory or metaphor.

Another issue that is seldom addressed when claims are made for or against
literalism is the existence of works whose literal sense is allegorical. If we take
the later chapters of the book of Daniel, it is perfectly clear that the animals
that appear in the various visions are ciphers or symbols standing for various
world powers. To interpret them as literal goats or rams is to mistake the literal sense of the text, which makes it perfectly clear that an allegorical meaning is intended.[55] As Beryl Smalley puts it, "If the 'letter' is defined as the whole
intention of the inspired writer, it makes no difference whether he expresses
himself in plain language or symbolically or metaphorically."[56] The point is
already made explicit by Nicholas of Lyra:

> Because some teachers say the metaphorical sense is the literal sense,
> this must be understood in general, because where there is no sense
> signified by the words, the metaphorical sense is the primary sense and
> thus loosely speaking it is called the literal sense because the literal
> sense exists when no other is there; and to signify this they say the
> metaphorical is included under the literal sense. In this manner of
> speaking I have also called the metaphorical sense literal in many
> places in my writing upon the books of sacred Scripture.[57]

55. Frances Young suggests very helpfully that the important question in patristic exegesis is not whether the text is read literally or allegorically, but what it refers to; in the case of
the animals in Daniel, it was perfectly plain to the Fathers that the referent was the nations
and people for which the animals stand, and they would have regarded this as the plain sense.
See Frances Young, *Biblical Exegesis and the Formation of Christian Culture*, 121. She suggests
that the contrast in the Fathers is often between what would have been seen by rhetoricians
as a distinction between content and style, rather than between literal and allegorical
senses—see, on this, her 129.

56. Smalley, *The Study of the Bible in the Middle Ages*, 300.

57. Nicholas of Lyra, *Postilla*, cited in Yarchin, *History of Biblical Interpretation: A Reader*,
102. Compare Yarchin's comment on the background to Aquinas's theories of textual meaning: "Distinctions between the literal sense and the spiritual sense were not always clear
when, for example, the biblical text itself presented a trope such as a metaphor. Since tropes
are not to be taken literally, what would constitute the literal sense of a metaphor, as distinguished from a spiritual sense that could be derived from it?" (Yarchin, 93–94). It is possible to write a text that has a literal meaning but with a clear intention that it shall be
interpreted allegorically—Dante's *Divine Comedy* is an extended example.

Similar things may be said of claims to have detected the historical meaning of a text. In the case of some texts, a historical reference is not present, and the search for one is wrongheaded. In medieval Jewish exegesis according to the *peshat*, sometimes the aim is to refute Christian christological interpretation, as we see in Rashi's commentary on Psalm 2:1 ("Why do the nations conspire?"). "According to its basic meaning (*lephi mishme'o*) and for a refutation of the Christians," Rashi comments, "it is correct to interpret it as a reference to David himself," going on to say that the reference is to David's wars with the Philistines.[58] A modern psalm commentator would be unlikely to think that the psalm in fact had this historical reference and would more likely refer it to a general context of national peril, since most modern commentators do not think the Psalms were written by David as a comment on particular incidents in his reign. The prophetic reference alleged by traditional Christians (that the text refers to the trials of Jesus by Herod and Pilate, for example) and the literal reference to David are alike in being alien to what the text actually means. What Rashi identifies as the "basic meaning" is not what a critical commentator is likely to see as the "natural" meaning of the text at all, but is a falsely historicizing reading, dictated by polemical concerns.

Or take the Song of Songs. It is normal to say that this makes literal (though poetic) reference to a pair of human lovers, whereas it has been read allegorically in both Judaism and Christianity so as to make it refer to the relation of God to Israel, or the church, or the individual believer. Most people would say that this literalism in interpreting the Song is the fruit of a critical approach, which has supplanted the older allegorical reading. If, however, as argued in a forthcoming monograph, the text was actually written with allegorical intent,[59] then the allegorical sense becomes in a way the literal one, and the interpretation in terms of human love is flawed and can even be accused of reading

58. See *Rashi's Commentary on Psalms, with English Translation, Introduction and Notes by Mayer I. Gruber* (Atlanta: Scholars Press, 1998), ad loc. Some Antiochene exegesis, perhaps sometimes dependent on Jewish models, could also be falsely historicizing. The historical sense in the Antiochenes can mean the historical *reference* of the text, and of course some texts do not have a historical reference but are deliberately allegorical.

59. See Edmée Kingsmill, *The Song of Songs and the Eros of God* (Oxford: Oxford University Press, forthcoming). Frances Young points out that patristic authors who engaged in allegorical exegesis "usually thought that the *hyponoia* was what the author intended. Stoics thought that the original philosophical wisdom was known to Homer, and that he really meant what they thought he meant. Origen believed that the Holy Spirit had clothed the divine *skopos* in the dress of the wording, and that only those who probed for the deeper meaning really understood what the text was about. The Word of God used the conceit of allegory like a well-trained rhetorician!" (Young, *Biblical Exegesis and the Formation of Christian Culture*, 190).

modern concerns into a text that was innocent of them and which really always concerned the divine bridegroom and his human bride, and not human lovers at all. There are, in other words, places where the allegorical reading *is* the literal one. The assertion that biblical criticism prefers always the literal reading is thus true only if we allow "literal" to bear the rather Pickwickian sense just outlined. Most people, to avoid confusion, would probably prefer to say that biblical criticism prefers the "true" or "originally intended" sense of the text in cases such as these—though we have already seen that "original" and "intended" are also slippery terms. Later I shall suggest that the term "the plain sense" is a better one to use in such cases.[60]

Brevard Childs devoted an article to the literal sense in the Festschrift for Walther Zimmerli.[61] He there argues that in the Reformers the literal sense meant the sense that gave the Christian meaning of the text for the reader who was seeking to be formed by Scripture, and was in no way identical with the historical sense, as this has come to be emphasized in historical-critical scholarship. This false identification has, he believes, contributed to the impression that historical criticism is in some way a legitimate extension of Reformation approach to the Bible—an impression that he sees as wholly erroneous. The historical-critical approach is for him an Enlightenment, not a Reformation, method; what the Reformers had in mind by privileging the "literal" sense was something quite different from directing biblical study into historical channels. They were concerned with the way the text should speak to the believer. In a way this is not unlike what Loewe says of the *peshat* (see p. 92): the "plain" meaning in the sense of the meaning accepted in the religious community as edifying and conducive to salvation, not a stripped-down "literal" meaning in the sense of a meaning limited by the original historical context of the text in question.

For Childs, therefore, biblical criticism has not been concerned with (what

60. Halivni (*Peshat and Derash*, 19–20) points to a clear case where rabbinic exegesis interprets literally what the text surely intends metaphorically. Rabbinic tradition, followed by Jewish practice through the ages, takes the injunction in Exod. 13:9 and Deut. 6:8 to wear the commandments on one's forehead to require actual physical objects containing Torah texts (phylacteries). The obvious plain sense of the text, however—what may be called its *peshat*—is metaphorical. "Here," as Halivni comments, "the rabbis deviated from the peshat by being literal." In medieval times the possibility of a metaphorical reading was explored and advocated among others by the Karaites. This is a clear case where *peshat* is not equivalent to literal, except in the special sense just mentioned. It is more akin to the plain sense as we shall go on to define that.

61. Brevard S. Childs, "The Sensus Literalis of Scripture: An Ancient and Modern Problem," in *Beiträge zur Alttestamentlichen Theologie: Festschrift für Walther Zimmerli zum 70. Geburtstag*, ed. H. Donner, R. Hanhart, and R. Smend (Göttingen: Vandenhoeck & Ruprecht, 1977), 80–95.

he calls) the literal sense, because biblical criticism empties out the literal meaning (in his sense of the term) in the interests of a "purely historical" reading. Now I want to disagree with Childs in thinking that biblical criticism has had such a reductionist effect, but I believe he is right on the positive point, that the Reformers used the term *sensus literalis* to signify the full Christian meaning of the text. Certainly the *sensus literalis* did contain (as it had for the Victorines) everything the author had intended, even if that intention had allegorical elements, rather as I have argued above. But it was also understood to include what might now be called a "Christian reading" of the text, in the sense of a deliberately "confessing" mode of interpretation—since the scriptural authors were supposed really to have intended such a meaning.

Similar arguments can be found in an author indebted to Childs, Katherine Greene-McCreight, who maintains that when Augustine spoke of the literal sense of Scripture (as in *De Genesi ad litteram*) or the Reformers spoke of the "plain" sense, they meant the sense as present to a reading conducted by believers and in accordance with the church's rule of faith: "Within the Catholic tradition, a reading can generally be argued to be justifiable, convincing, authoritative and thus 'plain sense' insofar as it abides by the Rule of Faith."[62] She refers to Kathryn Tanner's argument, in conscious dependence on Loewe, that the plain sense is "the familiar, the traditional, and hence authoritative" meaning of a text.[63] She discusses Augustine's treatment of the discrepancy between the six days of creation in Genesis 1 and the single "day" in which God created the world according to Genesis 2:4. Augustine, referring to Sirach 18:1 ("he who lives for ever created all things together"—thus the Latin text: "simul"), argues that the six days of the first account are to be taken not "literally" but allegorically, not referring to a time sequence but to the simultaneous creation of things that are distinct from each other in six categories.[64] This harmonizing account is necessary because Scripture cannot be so interpreted as to speak with a self-contradictory voice (compare the examples of harmonization discussed in chapter 2 above). The whole point is that reading the Bible is a religious activity and must be undertaken in the

62. K. E. Greene-McCreight, *Ad Litteram: How Augustine, Calvin and Barth Read the "Plain Sense" of Genesis 1–3*, Issues in Systematic Theology 5 (New York: Peter Lang, 1999), 6.

63. Ibid., 9–10, referring to Kathryn Tanner, "Theology and the Plain Sense," in *Scriptural Authority and Narrative Interpretation*, ed. G. Green (Philadelphia: Fortress, 1987), 59–78.

64. The question was much discussed in the Middle Ages, with Bede arguing instead that it is the single "day" of Gen. 2:4 that is nonliteral, referring to the whole time period covered by the six days of Gen. 1. The Victorines took the issue further; see the extended discussion of Andrew of St. Victor on this theme in Beryl Smalley, *The Study of the Bible in the Middle Ages*, 132–35.

conviction that a coherent message emerges from the text: "Attention to the flow of the narrative as a seamless whole . . . guides plain sense reading for Augustine."[65] And again:

> There does seem to be a distinction for Augustine between what we will call plain sense and the "letter," because plain sense does not necessarily take the letter *au pied de la lettre* or "literally." This is because plain sense reading is a religious activity, not merely a literary activity alone, and entails basic presuppositions about the text and about God.[66]

Greene-McCreight argues, like some of the other authors influenced by Childs to be discussed later, that such a plain sense reading is the correct model for the church and for biblical scholarship today, as it was also for the Reformers[67] and for Barth. But here our concern is primarily for her historical judgment, which seems to me to be sound, that traditional reading "according to the letter" was not what we would call literal reading. I think myself that to call the type of reading practiced by Augustine "plain sense" is also rather misleading, since this term is better kept for the kind of reading practiced by biblical criticism. But the substance of what she is arguing by using the term seems to me to be true to the evidence. Interpreters such as Augustine (and indeed Calvin, whom she also analyzes) did indeed read Scripture with a prior commitment to the rule of faith, which could overrule apparent discrepancies in the text in the interests of a "holistic" reading. As she puts it, such reading is "Ruled," indicating "a prior 'take' on the subject matter and plot of the Christian story such that the doctrines of creation and redemption are able to be held together."[68]

We may see even more clearly from a passage in *De doctrina christiana* 3:3 how Augustine argued:

> There is that heretical phrasing: *In principio erat Verbum et Verbum erat apud Deum et Deus erat* [John 1:1–2], adopted in order to give another meaning to the next phrase: *Verbum hoc erat in principio apud Deum*; this is a refusal to confess that the Word is God. But this is to be refuted

---

65. Greene-McCreight, *Ad Litteram*, 72.
66. Ibid., 49.
67. The point is made in the case of Luther by Rainer Fischer, *Die Kunst des Bibellesens: Theologische Ästhetik am Beispiel des Schriftverständnisses* (Frankfurt am Main: Peter Lang, 1996), 115: "Wenn Luther im Gegensatz zu Emser den 'buchstäblichen' Sinn zur Grundlage des Bibelverständnisses erklärt, ist damit alles andere als ein positivistischer Literalismus gemeint" ("When Luther opposes Emser by declaring that the 'literal' sense is the basis for understanding the Bible, he means anything but a positivistic literalism").
68. Greene-McCreight, *Ad Litteram*, 22.

by the rule of faith, which prescribes for us the equality of the three divine persons, so that we have to say, *et Deus erat Verbum*; and then add *Hoc erat in principio apud Deum*.[69]

Thus even what we would call the punctuation of a passage is determined not by attention to philological questions (or text-critical ones), but by theological argument. This is, in the terms we have been using, a noncritical way of arguing.[70]

It may then certainly be said that biblical criticism has not been concerned with the literal sense, if we gloss that as Childs does, but with some other sense. It has not been concerned with the plain sense either, if we understand that in the way the term is used by Greene-McCreight. But I would argue that her use of this expression is rather unhelpfully counterintuitive, since it has to be tightly defined as not what the average reader will understand by the term at all, but rather as equivalent to what some modern scholars call a confessing or canonical reading. My own definite preference is to use the term "plain sense" to refer to the sense that biblical criticism is interested in, a sense not colored by any particular prior confessional attachment to the truth of Scripture or its self-coherence. (One consequence of this line of argument, which we will follow up in the next chapter, is that the line connecting modern criticism with the Reformation is less clear than many German Protestant scholars have argued.)

THE PLAIN SENSE

We come at last to the proposal that I should like to make myself: that biblical criticism is concerned with the "plain sense" of the biblical text and that this is not identical with any of the possible senses discussed so far, though at times it may have elements of any or all of them. The term "the plain sense" has been used a great deal in the history of biblical study, often by way of contrast with an allegorical reading, but here I am using it in a particular way that is not directly related to that issue. My thesis will be that biblical criticism, in its quest for this plain sense, is a semantic or linguistic and a literary operation first and foremost, only indirectly concerned with the original, the intended, the historical, or the literal meaning.

---

69. Quoted in Yarchin, *History of Biblical Interpretation*, 69.

70. Augustine's criterion for whether to interpret literally or figuratively is similarly theological rather than literary: "Anything in the divine writings that cannot be referred either to good, honest morals or to the truth of the faith, you must know is said figuratively" (*De doctrina christiana* 3:14; see Yarchin, 71).

Biblical criticism is a semantic operation in that it is concerned with the meaning of words and phrases. As we have seen, words have meaning only in a particular context: a word does not have a timeless meaning that is independent of the historical setting in which it is uttered. To that extent and in that sense biblical criticism is inevitably a historical discipline. One of the most basic functions of criticism is to criticize, not the Bible itself, but people's understanding of the Bible. And one aspect of this is by showing that texts do not mean what they have commonly been taken to mean.

An example would be the vocabulary used in the New Testament to refer to ministerial leaders of the church. When Philippians 1:1 refers to *episkopoi* and *diakonoi*, a biblical critic will point out that these terms do not necessarily mean there what they came to mean in later ecclesiastical practice, bishops and deacons, and hence that this passage cannot be appealed to as a foundation stone for theories of the threefold ministry of later times.[71] Again, much of E. P. Sanders's critique of modern readings of Paul argues that "works" in Paul's vocabulary does not mean "actions through which one tries to establish one's claim on God's favor," as in much traditional Lutheran exegesis, but "actions in which the Torah is kept." What Paul is claiming is that Gentiles can be admitted to the fellowship of God's kingdom without taking on the yoke of the law; he is not suggesting that there is no need for Christians to act morally in general. Thus the term belongs to the Jewish-Gentile issue in the early church, not to later discussions about works righteousness.[72] This is an important point about Paul, but (the relevant point at the moment) it is derived from a critical observation about semantics, the meaning of particular terms at particular times and in particular contexts.

As we have already noted, this does not mean that Philippians *used to* refer to officers different from the later bishops and deacons or that Paul's letters *once* concerned the Jewish-Gentile debate, but that they *now* refer to people and concepts of later times. They may have *relevance* for later times, and any kind of belief in the authority of Scripture implies that they have. But according to a critical approach to the reading of texts, their meaning does not change in the process. The texts mean what they mean, what they have always meant. Otherwise our understanding of basic semantics becomes hopelessly skewed. The point would be readily conceded in the study of most other texts from the past. It is equally true in reading contemporary texts from other cultures,

71. On this, see already my discussion in "Historical-critical Approaches," in *The Cambridge Companion to Biblical Interpretation*, ed. John Barton (Cambridge: Cambridge University Press, 1998), 9–20.
72. See E. P. Sanders, *Paul and Palestinian Judaism: A Comparison of Patterns of Religion* (London: SCM, 1977).

where it is on the whole uncontroversial. There are many similar examples from the differences between American and British English. To "table" a matter means in Britain to raise it at a meeting by circulating a paper about it, but in America to set it aside for the time being (what the British call shelving it). Biblical criticism involves being aware of differences between our usage and the Bible's in just this way.

It is clear to me that this point is a true one, but my object at the moment is simply to indicate that it is central to the operation of criticism. That is, whether or not such an understanding of semantics is correct, this understanding historically has lain at the root of biblical criticism. Such criticism, as I have argued before, in no way rules out the application of the biblical text in the present, but it does not allow the potential application to decide the meaning the text actually has.[73] "Meaning before application" is its watchword, the *subtilitas intelligendi* before the *subtilitas applicandi* in the classic terms.

A modern statement of the necessary divide between exegesis and application can be found in Klaus Berger's work on the hermeneutics of the New Testament.[74] Berger argues that exegesis and application must be separated in the interests of two freedoms: the freedom of the text from the concerns of the interpreter, and the freedom of the interpreter to ask questions not envisaged by the text. There is, he argues, a necessary tension between the historical meaning of the text and the situation in which it is to be applied, and to ignore this tension is to collapse a two-stage process into one. Furthermore, to limit the meaning of the text to what can be applied is to reduce the "richness" of the text, which is open to ever-new applications. In fact, only by respecting the text's otherness can its fruitfulness for the present be safeguarded.

Now some theorists would concede this point at the level of words and phrases, but would argue that identifying meaning at that level is a relatively

---

73. Contrast Fernando Segovia, *Decolonizing Biblical Studies*, 91: "I would eschew any type of formulation that would imply or suggest, no matter how lightly or unintentionally, the presence of a preexisting, independent, and stable meaning in the text, the mind of the author, or the world of the text—formulations along the lines of the meaning 'back then,' being true to the past, or achieving a fuller meaning of the text." It is a well-tried response to this kind of thing, but I believe an entirely justifiable one, to ask whether Segovia would be happy with someone who read his own text by eschewing all those things. I think he would start to complain that he was being misunderstood. But against this degree of critical nihilism, there is not really much one can say. As I argue in chap. 6, it deeply undermines exactly the kind of postcolonial criticism of traditional biblical study that Segovia is engaged in, since it makes it quite impossible ever to *appeal* to the text against its interpreters. The idea of a stable meaning—a meaning which colonial interpreters have signally failed to grasp—ought to be Segovia's best friend.

74. Klaus Berger, *Hermeneutik des Neuen Testaments* (Gütersloh: Mohn, 1988). See the discussion of Berger in Rainer Fischer, *Die Kunst des Bibellesens*, 69–76.

positivistic enterprise. When they talk about the meaning in interpreting texts, they are not thinking of the semantics of individual words, but of the meaning of whole passages or books, in the sense of their resonance and import at a much more profound level. Surely biblical interpretation is more than the kind of operation that produces dictionaries. Indeed it is, but a critical interpretation always retains its link with semantics as just outlined. We might say, in fact, that biblical criticism is also concerned with semantics at a higher level than the word or phrase, that is, with the semantics of whole sentences and passages and books, and maintains that, here too, context and setting cannot be disregarded.

A recent example from a television drama will illustrate the point. In an episode of the series *Sea of Souls*, broadcast in Britain on Saturday, January 8, 2005, one of the characters utters the immortal words, "But everyone bore the brunt of the sabotaged chicken." Now to understand this, we certainly cannot dispense with the semantics of individual words. We need to know what is meant by "chicken" and "sabotage"; we also need to know the meaning of the idiom "bear the brunt of." But this does not materially help in "understanding" the whole sentence. Like a quiz game in which one has to reconstruct questions from their answers, the sentence gives us no clue as to what it could possibly mean in a deeper sense than the purely grammatical. To understand it, we have to know something about the plot of the story. The drama was a supernatural one—or rather one in which the allegedly supernatural played a part—and the protagonists were a team researching the paranormal, who were confronted with various weird events attributed by others to the work of a poltergeist. In the scene in question, the main researcher is listing these events, most of which have affected only one person, but he notes that the whole group in the haunted house has experienced a meal in which a chicken taken from the oven turned out to be studded with cigarette ends. His point is that this cannot be put down to an individual's mistake or hallucination, because all present saw it for themselves. Thus, by contrast, "*everyone* bore the brunt of the sabotaged chicken."

The Bible contains individual sentences which, taken out of context, are every bit as perplexing as this: for instance, "The mystery of lawlessness is already at work, but only until the one who now restrains it is removed" (2 Thess. 2:7). There is no chance of understanding this at anything but a surface level without some knowledge of Paul's eschatology and, indeed, that of his time, and even then its exact reference remains obscure and disputed.[75] But what interpreters agree is that its meaning depends on its context. What

---

75. For a recent discussion, see Paul Metzger, *Katechon: II Thess 2.1–12 im Horizont apoka-lyptischen Denkens* (Berlin: W. de Gruyter, 2005).

its application might be in modern circumstances is very obscure, at least to me, but to find one is not to change its "original" meaning, which remains its meaning.

Take another example, from Psalm 130. This contains a line that, in the version in the *Book of Common Prayer* familiar to Anglicans, reads, "There is mercy with thee, therefore shalt thou be feared." I have heard this expounded as follows: That God is a merciful and forgiving God is very good news for the believer, who can trust that sin will indeed be forgiven. On the other hand, God's forgiveness is not easy, "cheap grace"; it costs the one being forgiven a very great deal, in true penitence, in reformation of his or her life, in confronting the nature and consequences of his or her sin. God is not to be feared as hostile, but is greatly to be feared as the source of forgiveness! Forgiveness is a painful process—no quick fix.

This seems to me spiritually profound, and an excellent and important piece of Christian teaching. That does not mean that it correctly captures the meaning of the psalm. "Fear" in this passage probably does not convey what we should call fear, but respect or reverence, as in the phrase "the fear of the LORD," which is said to be the beginning of wisdom. The sentence does not, within the conceptualities of the Old Testament, convey the idea that God's forgiving mercy should produce fear (terror or dread) in the worshiper, but that it should engender awe and reverence, leading to gratitude and praise.

Of course one may dispute this interpretation and argue that the spiritual reading mentioned before does indeed do justice to the verse. About such matters interpreters differ. But the suggestion that the psalm means something other than what our Christian interpretation of it makes it mean is a classic critical exercise. It does not concern itself with the intentions of the author, the historical circumstances of the psalm's composition, or a literal rather than an allegorical meaning, but simply with the basic semantics of the verse, as understood against the background of the conceptuality one may establish from a wider study of the Hebrew Bible. Its commitment to asking semantic questions is what makes it critical.

The question of meaning can be extended further, from sentences to much lengthier sections or even whole books. It is here, perhaps, that the claims of criticism become most controversial in today's context. The argument of a biblical critic would be that a close reading of a biblical book remains a semantic enterprise and that semantics remains a relevant operation even at this macro level. The text's possibilities for meaning continue to be constrained by the context of its writing—whether or not one insists on "what the author meant," which as we have seen is not inherent in this approach. We may perhaps better speak of the intention of the work, the *intentio operis*, as proposed

by Umberto Eco.[76] In trying to discover what a work means, we are not explor-
ing the inside of its author's mind, but asking about how the assertions that
compose the work cohere with each other to make a comprehensible whole.
Eco asks, "How to prove a conjecture about the *intentio operis*? The only way
is to check it upon the text as a coherent whole."[77]

As an example of this, consider the arguments of James Barr in *The Garden
of Eden and the Hope of Immortality*.[78] Barr there argues that Genesis 2–3 has
been traditionally read in Christianity as an account of the fall, in which the
human race, represented by Adam and Eve, forfeited the immortality it had
previously possessed. This interpretation is present in Wisdom 2:23–24 and
developed by Paul in Romans 5:12. On the contrary, Barr suggests, the story
of the garden of Eden nowhere implies that Adam and Eve were created
immortal. When they are expelled from the garden, this is to prevent the risk
of their *becoming* immortal by eating from the tree of life; and this entails that
they had not been immortal before. What God threatened them with was not
the loss of immortality, which they did not possess in any case, but death, a
penalty that was in the end commuted to hard labor outside the garden. The
story is thus not about how the human race came to fall into mortality, as
implied by Wisdom and Romans.

Now as with any interpretation of a biblical text, it would be possible to dispute this reading, and no doubt many would wish to do so. What is clear, however, is that it rests on an attempt to read these chapters of Genesis in their
own right, without the filter provided by later texts, and to assess what they
mean. The semantic operation here proceeds from the individual words, to
sentences, and up to the whole passage. The words are given their normal
sense in Hebrew: "die," for example, is understood as meaning "die," rather
than "forfeit immortality" or "live an impoverished life."[79] If one wished to
dispute this, one would have to find compelling evidence that the word here
bears some special sense. The sentences into which these words fit are similarly interpreted as normal Hebrew sentences: for example, "lest [the man] put
forth his hand and take also of the tree of life, and eat, and live for ever" (Gen.
3:22 RSV) is taken to be a possible event that God is taking steps to prevent,
since that is what is implied by "lest" (Hebrew *pen*). And the whole passage is
accordingly given an interpretation that allows the individual words and sen-

76. See Umberto Eco, *Lector in fabula: La cooperazione interpretativa nei testi narrativi*
(Milan: Tascabili Bompiani, 1979).

77. *Interpretation and Overinterpretation*, 65.

78. James Barr, *The Garden of Eden and the Hope of Immortality: The Read-Tuckwell Lectures
for 1990* (London: SCM, 1992).

79. See further on this Barr's article "Is God a Liar? (Genesis 2–3)—and Related Matters," *Journal of Theological Studies* 57 (2006): 1–22.

tences to be meaningful and does not twist or strain them to yield a different sense. Thus Barr tries to establish what I would call the plain sense of the garden of Eden story. If his interpretation is mistaken, that will have to be shown by the same methods—not, for example, argued on the basis that since it contradicts Paul (to some extent), there must be something wrong with it. Barr's is a critical reading because it accepts the semantic constraints of the language in which the passage is written. (There is, we may note again, nothing particularly *historical*-critical about this reading, which says nothing about when the passage was written or whether it is composed from several different sources. It is, in the current jargon, a synchronic reading, simply taking the story as it stands.)

One may go even further and ask critically about the meaning of each testament, or even of the whole Bible, though the resulting reading is likely to be extremely vague. One recent example, however, may be found in the work of R. Kendall Soulen.[80] Soulen argues that Christianity has construed the Old Testament as containing the first two steps in a four-stage history of universal providence, consisting of creation, fall, redemption through Christ, and final consummation. This scheme can be found in almost all Christian theologians down the ages, including, in the twentieth century, Barth and Rahner. But, he argues, this actually falsifies the natural shape and progression of the Old Testament story. Jewish readers have of course long maintained that the story of Adam and Eve is not a "fall" story, and that Adam should be regarded in a much more positive light, just as he is, for example, by Ben Sira (Sir. 49:16, "above every other created living being was Adam"). For a Jewish reader, the Hebrew Bible is not about the creation followed by the fall of the human race, but about God's providential guidance of Israel. If it is open-ended, that is not because it requires completion through the work of Christ to reverse the results of the fall, but because it leads into the subsequent history of the Jewish people. From this perspective, Christians have placed a straitjacket on the text and attributed to it a meaning that is not its true meaning. The Jewish reading is to be preferred, and Christians ought to revisit their own scheme of things and change it accordingly.

In this line of argument, there is some sense that Christians owe it to Jews to adopt a Jewish reading of the Hebrew Bible, partly because it is truly theirs, so they should make the rules for reading it, and partly on the grounds that it is high time to make some reparation for centuries of supersessionism, in which salvation in Christ replaces God's covenant with the Jewish people. Both of these may be fair points, though they are also disputable; but neither has any particular connection with biblical criticism. But alongside them there is

---

80. R. Kendall Soulen, *The God of Israel and Christian Theology* (Minneapolis: Fortress Press, 1996).

also an argument that the Jewish reading does better justice to the contours of the biblical text. The plain sense of the Hebrew Bible, Soulen would argue, is better conveyed by the Jewish interpretation of it as concerned with the providential history of the people of Israel—to which the primeval history in Genesis 1–11 is a kind of prologue—than by the Christian sense that creation and fall provide the key and the entire subsequent history is little more than comment on that, or merely provides a matrix for the prophetic promises of the coming of Christ. Whether this is so or not, it is clearly a critical argument in the sense we have been using the term.

The point about Genesis 1–11 as a prologue rather than as setting the theme of the Old Testament was indeed already made by Gerhard von Rad in his Genesis commentary,[81] and he consistently maintained that the Old Testament was about the *Heilsgeschichte*, rather than about creation and fall, arguing similarly in the case of Deutero-Isaiah, where on the face of it the creation is a central element.[82] This interpretation arises from an attempt to read the text as a whole and to judge the balance between its various components. The fact that this is part of what would now be called a holistic reading does not affect this point: holistic readings can also be critical. What constitutes it as critical is that it asks about the sense the text makes if it is read without a constraining framework of expectations.[83] We recall again Werner H. Schmidt's point that (if criticism is understood in its more hostile sense) biblical criticism is not so much criticism of the Bible as criticism of the Bible's interpreters in the light of the witness of the text itself. In this the plain sense of the text is the essential weapon. Compare the comment of Philip Davies: "The question to be asked is whether the reader can tell a difference between what the text says (or might say) and what the Jewish and Christian interpretative traditions have decided that it says (or should say)."[84]

81. Gerhard von Rad, *Genesis: A Commentary* (London: SCM, 1961, 2nd ed. 1972); translated from *Das Erste Buch Mose, Genesis* (Göttingen: Vandenhoeck & Ruprecht, 1956).

82. See Gerhard von Rad, "The Theological Problem of the Old Testament Doctrine of Creation," in *The Problem of the Hexateuch and Other Essays* (Edinburgh: Oliver & Boyd, 1966), 131–43; trans. from *Gesammelte Studien zum Alten Testament* (Munich: Kaiser Verlag, 1936).

83. Here I differ, as will be made clearer in chapter 6, from Francis Watson, *Text and Truth: Redefining Biblical Theology* (Edinburgh: T. & T. Clark, 1997), 123. Watson rightly opposes a positivistic approach to what he calls the literal sense of the Bible, but sees as the correct alternative to this an application of the text within the framework of a canonical context. I am arguing for freedom from a constraining canonical context.

84. Philip R. Davies, *Whose Bible Is It Anyway?* (Sheffield: Sheffield Academic Press, 1995), 12–13. Cf. also Krister Stendahl, "The Bible as a Classic and the Bible as Holy Scripture," *Journal of Biblical Literature* 103 (1984): 3–10. On 8–9, he argues that biblical criticism appeals to the original meaning against later (mis)readings. Cf. also Gerhard Ebeling, "The Bible as a Document of the University," in *The Bible as a Document of the University*, ed. Hans

I spoke earlier of the importance of genre recognition in biblical criticism.[85] This may be seen as part of the quest for the plain sense. Until we know what kind of text we are dealing with, we cannot complete the semantic operation of understanding its meaning. If we take the sentence I quoted above from a television drama, "But everyone bore the brunt of the sabotaged chicken," this would mean something quite different if it appeared in a cookery program—though this may be hard to imagine. Within the Bible, sentences in Wisdom books such as Proverbs may similarly bear a different sense from the one they would have if they appeared in a law code. A good example of this is the previously cited verse in Proverbs 26:4–5: "Do not answer fools according to their folly, or you will be a fool yourself. Answer fools according to their folly, or they will be wise in their own eyes." If this were a piece of law, it would plainly be contradictory; but as a pair of proverbs it perfectly captures the dilemma of dealing with fools. As observed earlier, there is a rabbinic discussion of it as in fact a contradiction, which exegetical skill is used to dispel: the argument runs that it depends on whether the fool is occupying himself with words of Torah or merely human words.[86] This betrays a failure to grasp the genre of the text and may be called precritical. Critical scholarship requires attention to the type of text being studied. What is its plain sense will depend on that.[87] The point is well made by J. A. Burrow:

Dieter Betz (Chico, CA: Scholars Press, 1981), 5–23; see esp. 13: "The student of the Bible must rigorously and uncompromisingly determine what the authors of the Biblical books really did say. The student of the Bible must in no way know from prior external sources what those authors said or should have said."

85. Compare my comments already in *Reading the Old Testament*, 8–19. There is a good deal about the importance of genre in E. D. Hirsch Jr., *The Aims of Interpretation* (Chicago and London: University of Chicago Press, 1976). Hirsch uses the useful phrase "corrigible schemata" for genres, signaling that they are frameworks for reading and yet can be corrected in the light of further investigation of the text being read. Genre is also given a prominent place in Kevin J. Vanhoozer, *Is There a Meaning in This Text?* (Leicester: Apollos, 1998), 336–50.

86. Babylonian Talmud, *Shabbat* 30b; see above, p. 21.

87. A good example of a failure to address genre questions can be found in the debate between Luther and Jacob Masson, known by his Latin name Latomus, about Luther's article "Every Good Work Is Sin" (*Omne opus bonum est peccatum*). Luther's argument was that, because sin remains in the human person even after baptism, everything a person does, even when it is fully righteous, remains tainted with sinfulness and the effects of the fall. Hence every human work, not just those that are overtly evil, falls under God's judgment. The saving good news of the gospel is that God nevertheless has mercy. Though even the good we do is evil in his eyes, yet he loves us and pardons us and makes us righteous in Jesus Christ, so that a believer is *simul iustus et peccator*, at the same time just and a sinner. Luther justifies this position by reference to a particular Old Testament text, Isa. 64:5–12, with its line "all our righteous deeds are like a filthy cloth." The two disputants then get locked into a debate about how far this text really implies the complete depravity of the human person, but neither stops to consider that the text is a lament rather than a dogmatic statement, which

We may see genre as one manifestation—the prime manifestation in literature—of a principle which governs all human communication, and indeed all perception. At its most fundamental, the principle simply states that perception involves identification. The very act of seeing or hearing, insofar as it is not purely physiological, is itself an act of interpretation. We decide what sort of thing we are seeing or hearing; and that identification in turn governs what we see or hear. . . . Linguistic communication employs this principle at several different levels. At the level of whole utterances—which is where the question of genre chiefly arises—speakers and writers construct utterances which can be recognized and construed by readers and listeners as utterances of a certain *kind*. Each of these kinds has characteristics which native speakers readily learn to respond to as signals of a certain sort of meaning—the sort of meaning appropriate to a command, a road sign, a sonnet, a summons, or a joke, or a riddle.[88]

A rather clear example of this point may be seen in apocalyptic texts such as Daniel 7–12. All readers see that this text is allegorical, with animals standing for human beings: the text has always been read in such a way. In this case an allegorical meaning is the text's plain sense, and a "literal" reading misses the point. The question whether a given text is allegorical in meaning cannot always be readily solved, and there are many examples of texts that have been allegorically interpreted when they are not, in fact, allegories; almost the whole of the Bible has been allegorized at some time. But where the text is an allegory and has always been one, the allegorical meaning is the plain meaning. This point was raised above in the section on the literal sense, where we saw that literality is inappropriate in the case of allegorical texts. Of course one could make this point by saying that the allegorical sense is the literal sense in such cases, but that would be confusing; it would be better to call the allegorical sense here the text's plain meaning, as suggested above.

Another complication is raised by texts that are ironic. The classic case is Jonathan Swift's biting satire *A Modest Proposal*, in which he proposed that the solution to the Irish famine was for parents to eat their own children.[89] The aim was to shock the English reader into realizing just how dire things in Ireland were, not, of course, seriously to propose cannibalism. It is notoriously

might, for example, result in its using hyperbole. See *Luther's Works*, ed. Jaroslav Pelikan (Philadelphia: Fortress Press, 1955–86), 32:172–73; trans. George Lindbeck.

88. J. A. Burrow, *Medieval Writers and Their Work: Middle English Literature and Its Background 1100–1500* (Oxford: Oxford University Press, 1982), 56.

89. Jonathan Swift, *A Modest Proposal for Preventing the Children of Poor People from Being a Burden to Their Parents or the Country, and for Making Them Beneficial to the Country* (London, 3rd ed. 1730); reprinted in Jonathan Swift, *A Modest Proposal and Other Sceptical Works* (New York: Dover, 1995).

difficult to discover by what means we recognize irony in texts, but we certainly often succeed in doing so; it is akin to recognizing metaphor. But to fail to register it when it is present is to miss the plain sense of the text, which is again not to be equated with its literal sense, as this example shows. Just how plain this meaning in Swift's pamphlet was is shown by the number of readers who successfully decoded it as an attack on the English, rejecting the literal sense as clearly not what the text intended. There may be examples of irony in the Bible, though the cultural gap that separates us from it makes it difficult to be certain.[90] Some would argue, however, that Ecclesiastes is an example of an ironic text that uses sayings originally making positive points about human life to undermine the wisdom enterprise and so lead to skepticism or even despair.[91] Whether this is in fact so or not, we recognize the question as a genuine one. If it could be shown that Ecclesiastes does indeed work in this way, then we would be able to accept the ironic sense as the plain sense of the text.

In the case of a text from as ancient and remote a culture as the Bible, we shall sometimes be unable to identify a book's genre and shall to that extent be unable to arrive at a fully satisfactory understanding of its meaning. This is one of the problems in Gospel criticism. Are the Gospels biographies, mere collections of sayings and incidents indicating a "wisdom" origin, kerygmatic works belonging to the world of preaching, or what?[92] Commentators have been unable to come to a certain conclusion about this, and consequently the question of the Gospels' plain sense remains unresolved. "Plain," after all, does not mean "obvious."[93] What I wish to emphasize at the moment is simply that such questions belong to critical scholarship, a claim I suppose no one would deny. Where such questions are asked, we have at least inchoately a critical attitude.

Finally, recognizing the plain sense of a word, a sentence, a passage, or a book is not the same as restating that sense in one's own words. Exegesis is

---

90. Erasmus found irony in Jesus' words to the sleeping disciples in the Garden of Gethsemane, "Sleep on now, and take your rest," as also in Elijah's taunts to the prophets of Baal on Mount Carmel; cf. the comments of Louis Bouyer, "Erasmus in Relation to the Medieval Biblical Tradition," in *Cambridge History of the Bible*, 2:502.

91. See, for example, Benjamin L. Berger, "Qoheleth and the Exigencies of the Absurd," *Biblical Interpretation* 9 (2001): 141–79; Carolyn J. Sharp, "Ironic Representation, Authorial Voice, and Meaning in Qohelet," *Biblical Interpretation* 12 (2004): 37–68; and Izak J. J. Spangenberg, "Irony in the Book of Qoheleth," *Journal for the Study of the Old Testament* 72 (1996): 57–69. I am grateful to Melissa Jackson for putting me on to these articles.

92. For a full discussion, see Richard Burridge, *What Are the Gospels? A Comparison with Graeco-Roman Biography* (Cambridge: Cambridge University Press, 1992).

93. Even when Luther emphasizes the "clarity" of the Bible, he does not mean that its meaning is always apparent at once. See the discussion in my *People of the Book? The Authority of the Bible in Christianity* (London: SPCK, 1988), 85.

often understood to mean "drawing out" the meaning of a biblical text, that is, telling a reader what it means. Hence the coinage eisegesis, used to convey the sense of reading in one's own meaning to the text. Biblical criticism has certainly been opposed to this latter practice, but the contrast between exegesis and eisegesis is not a happy way of expressing the point. In origin, an exegete was not someone who drew out the meanings of texts, but a guide to a sacred place, who *led the visitor out* to see it and explain it, a kind of tour guide. This is a better image for exegesis than the sense of extracting meaning from a text. One of the objections sometimes leveled by literary critics at traditional exegesis is that it is flat, unimaginative, and positivistic. Few would deny that this is sometimes the case. But such flatness is not inherent in exegesis, by contrast with a literary or theological interpretation. The exegete's task is to help the reader to understand the text, not to bring out and restate the meaning in such a way that the text is evacuated of its content and replaced with the exegete's interpretation,[94] but to lead the reader *into* the text to appreciate what it has to say and to communicate. In a sense, therefore (though this usage would be confusing now), the true exegete is an eisegete, someone who brings the reader into the text's inner sanctum. Biblical criticism so understood is much closer to modern literary approaches than is often thought. Compare the words of F. R. Leavis: "[The critic's] first concern is to enter into possession of the given poem . . . in its concrete fullness, and his constant concern is never to lose his completeness of possession, but rather to increase it."[95]

To confuse restatement of meaning with the understanding of it is to confuse, in Schleiermacher's terms, the *subtilitas intelligendi* with the *subtilitas explicandi*. These are two stages, however closely they often go together, just as the *subtilitas applicandi* represents a further stage still. As Schleiermacher pointed out,[96] as soon as one restates a text's meaning, one has produced a new text, which is then subject to all the hermeneutical constraints of any other text: the reader has to try and discover its plain sense, and to understand how it is articulated.[97] The act of understanding itself precedes the act of restatement, and this precludes the possibility of replacing the text with our own interpretation

94. Valentine Cunningham, *Reading after Theory* (Oxford: Blackwell, 2002), 73, comments, "Who ever really thought the poem was a container of items for a clean and simple extraction job?" The idea, he argues, is a straw man.

95. F. R. Leavis, "Literary Criticism and Philosophy: A Reply," *Scrutiny* 6 (1937): 1; cited with approval in David Daiches, *Critical Approaches to Literature* (London and New York: Longman, 2nd ed. 1981), 296.

96. Cf. below, p. 176.

97. Is it wrong to see here an anticipation of Derridean *différance*, the endless deferral of our grasp of textual meaning?

of it, as in the common but misleading translation model of hermeneutics. Our aim as critics is not to translate the text (either literally or metaphorically) into our own terms, but to get inside it and understand it from within. Translation of either kind is a subsequent stage. The task of exegetes is not to replace the text, but to help the reader to share the understanding of it that they have themselves achieved. In this, biblical criticism is in precisely the same position as literary criticism; both are servants of the text, not its masters, and both are concerned to help the reader discover the plain sense.

Does an attachment to the plain sense rule out any polyvalence in texts? It may sound as though I have been saying that there is always just one meaning in a text, that texts cannot signify in a plural way. Here there is a balance to be struck. Some literary theorists have taken to expounding the idea that texts can have infinite meanings, and indeed that there is no such thing as fixity in textual meaning. They have done so by way of reaction to a supposed emphasis on univocality among older critics. But this emphasis is a straw man; traditional critics have seldom espoused the view that there is one single meaning in texts that is *the* meaning. Classic texts such as the Bible lend themselves to reading and rereading precisely because there is always more to be found in them; they answer not one question, but a plethora of questions. But they do so, I would argue, through what they can possibly mean, given the constraints of convention, genre, time, semantics; they cannot mean simply anything you like. Valentine Cunningham expresses the two sides of this point with great energy:

> To be sure, the fact that strong texts—the timocracy—can stand many reading approaches and will yield to many and varied hermeneutic squeezes, is what sustains the classics of literature, keeps them in their front rank as classics. A great part of what defines The Classic is its potential for much rereading. The big ones are indeed copious with meaning, plurivalent, great cornucopiae of hermeneutic possibility, plenipotentious sites of meaning, *grands magasins* for the eager literary shopper.[98]

But he goes on to point out how literary critics have spoken as though this were somehow a new insight made possible only by Theory (as postmodern literary theory is now sometimes called), and continues:

> (Some of the temporary excitement, as if reading were now being licensed to enter utterly new territory, was clearly misguided. I don't know anywhere in the whole history of reading where the single monodic reading, the monovalent text, have been seriously maintained as ideals and achievements, except perhaps among certain

---

98. Cunningham, *Reading after Theory*, 79.

upholders of certain sacred texts such as *The Book of Mormon*, among Soviet Realist critics [of] the 1930s, and in the dystopia of Swift's Houyhnhnms in *Gulliver's Travels.* . . .) Univalence is another of Theory's throng of straw men.[99]

Now much reading of the Bible, as Cunningham goes on to show, has been highly profligate with meaning and really has seemed (since long before Theory) to operate on the principle that you can make this text mean anything you like. Against that, biblical critics utter a denial: no, there are some things the text cannot mean. As sane readers of any text know, a text that can mean anything means nothing, and biblical criticism stands against treating the Bible as a kind of endless palimpsest on which we are free to inscribe our own meaning. I have tried to chart some of the ways in which it does this. The danger that then impends is that I shall be heard as saying that biblical criticism authoritatively closes down the text's possibilities for meaning and reduces it to a single thin voice without harmony or polyphony. And this would be a mistake in the opposite direction. Umberto Eco gets the balance right: "I accept the statement that a text can have many senses. I refuse the statement that a text can have every sense." "It is not true that everything goes."[100]

What does "go" then? Biblical texts are for the most part resonant texts, not to be treated as workaday texts like recipes or instructions on operating household equipment. Recognizing this is indeed part of the genre recognition that is central to reading any text. Many Old Testament texts in particular are poetic in character and do not have a simple and straightforward sense that can be restated in prosaic language. This is why I stressed that the exegete's task is not to extract the meaning from the text, but to conduct the reader on a guided tour of it, considering the many strands of meaning such a text may contain. The plain sense of most biblical texts, like the plain sense of a Shakespearean tragedy, has depth and subtlety: "plain" does not mean "elementary."[101]

99. Ibid., 80.

100. *Interpretation and Overinterpretation*, 141 and 144; cited in Cunningham, *Reading after Theory*, 85. Eco makes the point in more detail on 23, commenting on the reception of his earlier book *The Open Work* (Cambridge MA: Harvard University Press, 1989; from *Opera aperta*, 1962): "In that book I advocated the active role of the interpreter in the reading of texts endowed with aesthetic value. When those pages were written, my readers mainly focussed on the open side of the whole business, underestimating the fact that the open-ended reading I was supporting was an activity elicited by (and aiming at interpreting) a work. . . . I have the impression that, in the course of the last decades, the rights of the interpreters have been overstressed."

101. At the other extreme, critical reading makes it possible to recognize some texts as meaningless or at least very odd—nullivalent, we might say. Of course a piece of utter nonsense may make sense if it is, for example, reported in a novel as the direct speech of someone suffering from a speech disorder.

The point may be illustrated from Psalm 84. This is generally regarded by commentators as a pilgrim psalm, possibly intended to be sung during a pilgrimage to Jerusalem, possibly meant as a later reflection on a completed pilgrimage: in the first case, the "I" may stand for the community of those on the pilgrimage; in the second, it may be literal. In verse 6 there is a reference to the valley of Baca. This location is unknown but seems to mean "valley of balsam trees," by implication a dry place presenting the pilgrims with a physical challenge. But both Jewish and Christian tradition have seen in the word "Baca" a play on the word "weeping" (*bokeh*): this psalm, indeed, is the source of the description of the world as a vale of tears. The psalm thus evokes in many readers a sense of the misery and transience of this world, by contrast with the world in which God dwells and toward which the whole of human life can be seen as a pilgrimage. Beyond the literal reference to a trudge through the hills and valleys of Palestine on the way to Jerusalem, there are hints of the greater pilgrimage that is life itself. Thus, for example, Artur Weiser:

> The poet characterizes the fatiguing journey of the pilgrims from the foreign country to Jerusalem with all the strains and dangers it involved as passing through the valley of tears (cf. Ps. 23.4; Hos. 2.15) which the pilgrims transform into a place of springs. . . . By virtue of that divine power the believer is able to endure and overcome troubles and dangers. . . . The impossible and the improbable is here made possible and real: affliction is transformed into joy, hardship into rejoicing, weakness into strength.[102]

Marvin Tate comments in a similar vein:

> The transformation of the Valley of Baca into an oasis (v. 7) is indeed "a classic statement of the faith which dares to dig blessing out of hardships" (Kidner, II, 305). J. Levenson (*Sinai and Zion: An Entry into the Jewish Bible* [Minneapolis: Winston, 1985], 177–78) writes of this same verse: "it implies a kind of natural/spiritual transformation: *Natural* in that a valley becomes a mountain, Zion, and *spiritual* in that the ascent somehow enables the worshippers to make the water of tears into springs."[103]

Now there is a kind of flat-footed belief in the plain sense that would rule out this evocation of wider horizons and insist that the psalm means only the

---

102. Artur Weiser, *The Psalms: A Commentary* (London: SCM, 1962), 567.

103. Marvin E. Tate, *Psalms 51–100*, Word Bible Commentary (Dallas: Word Books, 1990), 362. The reference to "Kidner" is to Derek Kidner, *Psalms 73–150: A Commentary on Books III–V of the Psalms* (Leicester: Inter-Varsity Press, 1975).

physical place, the valley of Baca.[104] Against such an interpretation a reader with any literary sensibilities is likely to protest that a powerful and resonant text is being reduced to the humdrum. This is exactly the kind of thing that biblical critics are generally suspected of doing. My own reaction, on the other hand, would be to say that such more prosaically minded scholars are here failing to identify the plain sense of the text. As a poem, the psalm can be expected to point beyond its own literal meaning, to have further layers or textures that a bare literalism will fail to grasp. This is another reason why I cannot accept the identification of biblical criticism with literalism: in the case of a text such as this psalm, the literal meaning is not the full, and therefore not the true, meaning of the text. To refuse to see the resonances in the word "Baca" is a *failure* in criticism, of the same order as a failure to see that animals in Daniel are symbolic or metaphorical.[105] That some critics have tin ears in this way is undoubtedly the case, but their criticism is to that extent bad criticism. Biblical criticism, however historical, is a form of literary criticism, as I have argued a number of times.[106]

Thus the plain sense can well contain within itself possibilities for finding layers of meaning well beyond the literal, and biblical critics need no more be under a self-denying ordinance that would rule this out than are their colleagues in the study of other branches of literature. To acknowledge this is far from making biblical study a free-for-all of the kind deplored by Cunningham. There is responsible criticism, and there is irresponsible criticism, and knowing the difference is part of the skill of the good critic. Exegetes' guided tours of the text will involve noticing many blooms that are not part of its literal content, but also being able to distinguish them from the weeds that come only from their own imaginations.

---

104. But a trawl of many modern commentaries on the Psalms has failed to discover any in which the resonance of the verse is in fact denied, contrary to what might be suspected by opponents of biblical criticism. The sole exception is Mitchell Dahood (*Psalms II—51–100*, Anchor Bible [New York: Doubleday, 1968]), who eliminates the reference altogether by emendation and thus translates, "May he cause brooks to flow in the valley, turn it into a spring; with a crash may the Raingiver cover it all with pools!" (reading *bibbika'* for *habbaka'*).

105. Compare the discussion above, pp. 96–97.

106. See above, pp. 19, 59–60, and compare F. W. Dobbs-Allsop, "Rethinking Historical Criticism," *Biblical Interpretation* 7 (1999): 235–71.

5

The Origins of Biblical Criticism

There are many histories of biblical criticism, and my aim in this book is not to provide another.[1] My purpose is analytical rather than historical: to ask what are the *defining marks* of a critical approach to the Bible. But in doing this, it is essential to say something about the intellectual pedigree of biblical criticism as we encounter it today, and this inevitably involves taking a position on questions of origin.

There is, however, a measure of circularity here. The sources of biblical criticism have been identified with reference to how it is defined, so that, for example, the use of the expression "the historical-critical method" naturally leads scholars to ask about the origins of modern historical modes of inquiry, and to find in them the roots of the work done by biblical critics. H.-J. Kraus's standard history is actually called *History of Historical-Critical Research on the Old Testament*.[2] But this in turn encourages the reader to think that history has indeed been the primary concern of biblical critics. Whereas if, as I have argued, this is not the case, then the search for the roots of biblical criticism might need to start in a different place.

---

1. See, for example, Ludwig Diestel, *Geschichte des Alten Testaments in der christlichen Kirche* (Jena: Hermann Dufft, 1869); T. K. Cheyne, *Founders of Old Testament Criticism* (London: Methuen, 1893); Emil G. Kraeling, *The Old Testament since the Reformation* (London: Lutterworth, 1955); W. G. Kümmel, *The New Testament: The History of the Investigation of Its Problems* (London: SCM, 1973); Hans-Joachim Kraus, *Geschichte der historisch-kritischen Erforschung des Alten Testaments* (Neukirchen-Vluyn: Neukirchener Verlag, 3rd ed. 1982); Robert M. Grant with David Tracy, *A Short History of the Interpretation of the Bible* (London: SCM, 1984).

2. *Geschichte der historisch-kritischen Erforschung des Alten Testaments.*

THE TRADITIONAL EXPLANATION: ENLIGHTENMENT AND REFORMATION ROOTS OF HISTORICAL CRITICISM

At all events, the traditional presentation of the matter is at present that biblical criticism as we know it is first and foremost a product of the Enlightenment.[3] This can also be expressed by saying that it is "modern," in the technical sense of that term in which it does not mean "of the present" but "the product of an agenda dictated by 'modernity'"—part of the attempt to establish objective truth through reason and without respect to tradition that is often described nowadays as "the Enlightenment project."[4] Those who see biblical criticism as the enemy of a wholesome appropriation of the Bible often accuse it of having sold out to the Enlightenment, and so turned its back on the idea that the Bible belongs to the church and the believer. It is thus possible for essentially conservative scholars to make some common cause with those who would call themselves postmodern, since both are opposed—though for different reasons—to the "modern" work of traditional biblical critics.

The association of biblical criticism with the Enlightenment is almost too common to need illustration, surfacing even in book titles, as with H. Graf Reventlow's *The Authority of the Bible and the Rise of the Modern World*, in German *Bibelautorität und Geist der Moderne*—more literally "the authority of the Bible and the spirit of modernity."[5] Others use the term *Neuzeit*, which equally refers to post-Enlightenment thinking. Thus Gerhard Ebeling can write, "In its engagement with the past and the interpretation of its sources it [sc. the historical method] cannot simply set aside the understanding of reality as discovered *by the spirit of the modern world*. Consequently it is closely linked with the progress of academic disciplines and with the development of philosophy"[6]

---

3. Cf. W. Baird, "New Testament Criticism," in *Anchor Bible Dictionary*, ed. David Noel Freedman (New York and London: Doubleday, 1992), 1:730–36: "Modern biblical criticism began in the period of the Enlightenment" (730).

4. It is not implied that biblical criticism is part of modernism as that term is understood in literary, artistic, or musical circles.

5. H. Graf Reventlow, *Bibelautorität und Geist der Moderne: Die Bedeutung des Bibelverständnisses für die geistesgeschichtliche und politische Entwicklung in England von der Reformation bis zur Aufklärung* (Göttingen: Vandenhoeck & Ruprecht, 1980); ET, *The Authority of the Bible and the Rise of the Modern World* (London: SCM, 1984).

6. "Sie kann bei der Beschäftigung mit der Vergangenheit und bei der Interpretation von deren Quellen nicht einfach des Wirklichkeitsverständnisses beiseite setzen, wie es *der Geist der Neuzeit* gewonnen hat. Sie ist darum eng verkoppelt mit dem Fortschritt der Wissenschaften und mit der Entwicklung der Philosophie" (G. Ebeling, "Bedeutung der historisch-kritischen Methode," *Zeitschrift für Theologie und Kirche* 47 [1950]: 1ff.; ET, "The Significance of the Critical Historical Method for Church and Theology in Protestantism,"

(my italics). There is no one who can plausibly count as the founder of biblical criticism, but various figures more or less affected by Enlightenment ideas tend to be cited as among the earliest. Klaus Scholder lists F. C. Baur (proposed by H. Liebing in an article written to celebrate the hundredth anniversary of Baur's death[7]—but surely Baur is far too late for this accolade); Semler (according to Hornig)[8]; and Richard Simon (Kraus's candidate). Another possible "first true critic" would be Spinoza, especially preferred by those who see criticism as originating in hostility to the Bible and the church. Reventlow has drawn attention, too, to the importance of the English Deists, easily overlooked by German scholars who tend to think of biblical criticism as originating in the German-speaking world and to ignore its anticipations in Britain, where, it may be said, the Enlightenment arrived somewhat earlier.[9] Scholder himself suggests that more useful than the quest for a first exponent is the recognition that criticism depends on a certain intellectual style. For him, we may talk of biblical criticism when philosophy (in a broad sense) calls the tune and asks the questions, rather than (as in seventeenth-century Germany) it is theology that is dominant, with all that that implies of the dominance of the Bible as an authoritative text. Like Reventlow, Scholder sees the loosening of biblical authority as intimately bound up with the rise of criticism.[10] Someone like Simon is for him a symptom rather than a cause of the great shift toward historical criticism, which lies "in that intellectual process at whose end there stands the dethronement of the Bible as the authoritative source of all human knowledge and understanding."[11]

For Scholder, most of the early critics are a symptom rather than a cause of

---

in his *Word and Faith* [London: SCM, 1963], 17–61). (*Word and Faith* is a translation of *Wort und Glaube* [Tübingen: Mohr Siebeck, 1960].) The article is cited in Klaus Scholder, *Ursprünge und Probleme der Bibelkritik im 17. Jahrhundert (Ein Beitrag zur Entstehung der historisch-kritischen Theologie)*, Forschungen zur Geschichte und Lehre des Protestantismus 10:33 (Munich, 1966), 8; ET, *The Birth of Modern Critical Theology* (London: SCM; Philadelphia: Trinity Press International, 1990).

7. H. Liebing, "Historisch-kritische Theologie: Zum 100. Todestag F. C. Baurs am 2.12.1960," *Zeitschrift für Theologie und Kirche* 57 (1960): 303.

8. Gottfried Hornig, *Die Anfänge der historisch-kritischen Theologie: J. S. Semlers Schriftverständnis und seine Stellung zu Luther*, Forschungen zur systematischen Theologie und Religionsphilosophie 8 (Göttingen: Vandenhoeck & Ruprecht, 1961).

9. This point is made well by Scholder, op. cit., 9–14.

10. It is generally supposed that it was Spinoza's hostility to the authority of the Bible that made possible his rational criticism of it; cf. Leo Strauss, *Die Religionskritik Spinozas als Grundlage seiner Bibelwissenschaft: Untersuchungen zu Spinozas theologisch-politischem Traktat* (Berlin: Akademie-Verlag, 1930).

11. "In jenem geistigen Prozeß, an dessen Ende die Entthronung der Bibel als der autoritativen Quelle aller menschlichen Kenntnis und Erkenntnis steht" (ibid., 14).

the great shift toward historical criticism. We shall see that the reduction of
biblical authority is certainly a factor in the growth of criticism. However, it is
worth noting a caution given by Reinhart Kosellek, who stresses that criticism
was not in origin hostile to the Bible:

> The terms *critique* and 'criticism' (and also 'criticks') established them-
> selves in the seventeenth century. What was meant by them was the
> art of objective evaluation—particularly of ancient texts, but also of lit-
> erature and art, as well as of nations and individuals. The term was ini-
> tially used by the Humanists; it incorporated the meaning of
> judgement and learned scholarship, and when the philological
> approach was expanded to Holy Scripture, this process too was called
> 'criticism'. One could be critical and Christian; the critical non-
> believer was set apart by the sobriquet 'criticaster'.
>   Criticism still stood in the service of the religious parties. When in
> 1678 Richard Simon published his *Histoire Critique du Vieux Testament*
> he used the term 'critique', a term previously used only by 'personnes
> scavantes', to describe his reading of the Bible. He owed both the term
> and the method to Capelle, who in 1650, in his *Critica sacra*, had made
> a comparative philological study of the original text and translations
> of the Old Testament.[12]

Furthermore, most of those who have written histories of biblical criticism—unlike its opponents, to be discussed in chapter 6—have regarded the
move to Enlightenment values as a positive force in biblical study. Rowan
Greer (who takes the opposite view), writing on biblical interpretation in the
early church, contrasts the church's exegesis based on the rule of faith with
modern "scientific" methods and takes it for granted that modern biblical critics think these methods superior to those in use by the Fathers—a belief he is
himself anxious to reject:

> It is tempting to contrast late antique with modern exegesis by regard-
> ing the first as subjective and eisegetical and the second as objective
> and exegetical in the proper sense. There is, of course, some truth in
> putting the issue this way, but doing so blocks a correct understand-
> ing of patristic exegesis by assuming that a perspective *largely the prod-
> uct of the nineteenth-century Enlightenment is alone defensible*.[13]

The nineteenth century is a bit late for the Enlightenment, but the idea he is
objecting to would be widely shared by writers on the history of biblical crit-

---

12. Reinhart Kosellek, *Critique and Crisis: Enlightenment and the Pathogenesis of Modern
Society* (Oxford, New York, and Hamburg: Berg, 1988), 105; trans. of *Kritik und Krise. Eine
Studie zur Pathogenese der bürgerlichen Welt* (Freiburg and Munich: Karl Alber, 1959).
13. James L. Kugel and Rowan A. Greer, *Early Biblical Interpretation* (Philadelphia: Westminster Press, 1986), part 2: "The Christian Bible and Its Interpretation," 177, my italics.

icism: that it is essentially an application of Enlightenment values to the biblical text, a rational, "objective" approach that sets itself against traditional
ecclesiastical readings. And this for most such writers is a good thing.

It is a good thing because it combines the Enlightenment with the Reformation, which was equally an attempt to read the Bible without the filter provided by the authority of the church. Ebeling also argues this in his essay in
defense of "the historical-critical method."[14] For him, and for many German
Protestant scholars, biblical criticism is a true child of the Reformers, because
it enables readers to make up their own minds about the meaning of Scripture,
rather than accepting existing readings on authority.[15] This point is not, I
think, seen clearly enough by some contemporary (mainly English-speaking)
Protestant critics of the biblical-critical enterprise:[16] they see the rationalism
but not the zeal to free the Bible from an ecclesiastical stranglehold. Probably they feel that the stranglehold was real enough in the sixteenth century,
when it was represented by the Catholic Church, but that now roles are
reversed, and biblical study has become so secular there is a need to fight for

14. Gerhard Ebeling, "The Significance of the Critical Historical Method for Church
and Theology in Protestantism." See 55: "I venture to assert that the Protestantism of the
nineteenth century, by deciding in principle for the critical historical method, maintained
and confirmed . . . the decision of the Reformers in the sixteenth century. That of course is
not to say that wherever in the history of modern Protestant theology the motto of the critical historical method has been most loudly proclaimed and most radically applied, there
men have also really been nearest to the Reformation in every respect. But what it certainly
does mean is, that wherever they made way for the critical historical method and, however grievous their errors, took it seriously as their task, there, if certainly often in a very
paradoxical way, they were really asserting the fundamental principle of the Reformers in
the intellectual situation of the modern age." Cf. also Ebeling, "The Bible as a Document
of the University," 10: "Supported by the goals and achievements of Humanism, Luther placed
the Bible in the center of studies. Now, however, the Bible was interpreted according to its
original languages, so that its own *modus loquendi* was brought out in contrast to its scholastic misrepresentation"; also Wolfhart Pannenberg, "The Crisis of the Scripture Principle,"
in *Basic Questions in Theology* (London: SCM, 1970), 1:1–14. This is a translation of *Grundfragen systematischer Theologie* (Göttingen: Vandenhoeck & Ruprecht, 1967); the essay in
question has a complicated history, which is outlined on p. 1 in the English edition.
15. To this sometimes added the argument that biblical criticism in its more negative
conclusions enshrines the principle of justification by faith *alone*, taken to mean "without the
aid of historical proof." This idea was especially developed by Rudolf Bultmann, who maintained that the unprovable character of the details of the life of Jesus, for example, precisely
illustrated the truth that faith does not depend on knowledge. But I think, with Smend, that
it is hard to trace back to the Reformers any idea that *sola fide* requires or justifies a lack of
concern for historical factuality in the Gospel narratives; rather, it is the Reformation's commitment to the criticism of tradition that leads in the direction of historical criticism. See
Smend, "Nachkritische Schriftauslegung," 241.
16. On whom see chapter 6 below.

the churches to have any say at all in how the Bible is interpreted. I shall suggest that this is a misreading of the current situation, but it does help to explain why Anglo-American biblical scholars tend to see biblical criticism not as a tool of liberation from ecclesiastical authority, but instead as a tool of enslavement to the scholarly "guild."

Certainly there is something in the picture of the Reformation as one, at least, of the parents of biblical criticism. Once one insists on reading the Bible in its natural sense and not allowing oneself to be told by someone else what it means, one is simultaneously reading it critically and reading it in a potentially Protestant way, insofar as Catholicism insists on the authority of the church to tell one how to read it. One may question whether Catholicism is obliged to take this line, and of course recent Catholic documents on biblical study have been much more open to biblical criticism: I think especially of the report *The Interpretation of the Bible in the Church*, presented to Pope John Paul II on April 23, 1993, by the Pontifical Biblical Institute.[17] Most Catholic biblical scholars today do not feel inhibited in accepting and using the results of biblical criticism, and in contributing to it themselves. There is also a chicken-and-egg question here, about whether the Reformation was a response to a new way of reading the Bible or the main cause of it. Did Luther, for example, read Romans as teaching a doctrine at variance with what he understood the usual Catholic doctrine to be because he was already thinking in a reformational way, or was it the reading that helped to turn him into a Reformer? This is the kind of question hard to solve by any amount of empirical evidence, since the two processes may be simultaneous, and even people's own perceptions of how they come to a change of mind seldom tell the whole story. Certainly there is a historical connection between the Reformation and biblical criticism; on this, German scholars are surely right, whether or not the connection is an inherent one.

But if, with a good many modern Protestant scholars in the English-speaking world, one is broadly in favor of the Reformation and broadly against the Enlightenment, then the nexus between the two to be seen in biblical criticism becomes something of a problem. On the whole, it is the Reformation side that tends to be downplayed. The Reformation provided many of the impulses toward a critical reading of the Bible, but once these got into the hands of Enlightenment thinkers, they became exaggerated and took the Bible away from the churches, it is thought. In effect, the freedom of inquiry that Reformers encouraged had never been intended to lead to an exegetical free-for-all, and certainly not to the skeptical spirit in which someone such as Spinoza would

17. *The Interpretation of the Bible in the Church* (Rome: Libreria editrice vaticana, 1993).

come to read the Bible. The historical-critical method, it would be argued, develops reformational freedom in the direction of positivism and destructive criticism, a development Luther or Calvin would never have owned.

AN ALTERNATIVE APPROACH

What I have written so far has been written on the assumption that historians of biblical criticism have been correct in identifying its distinctive marks, and has presented various theories about where these derive from. Indeed, however one defines biblical criticism, it is correct to detect in it strains of thought that derive from both the Enlightenment and the Reformation, though against current tendencies in the English-speaking world I would personally place rather more weight on the Reformation strand than is common, following in this more closely a German tradition. But in previous chapters I have argued in detail that the equation of biblical criticism with historical-critical method is in important respects unsatisfactory. I should like to ask, therefore, how it might affect our account of the intellectual roots of biblical criticism if we follow the kind of revisionist definition that has emerged from the discussion in this book so far.

I have argued that the association of biblical criticism with history and with historical methods has been important and that especially in the nineteenth century it became dominant. To deny this would be absurd. Yet the connection with history, for all its importance, has emerged as essentially contingent. History has been a considerable part of what some biblical critics have been interested in, but it is not part of the definition of biblical criticism. We have seen that the *defining* marks of biblical criticism do not include an interest in history, but come down to three features, which are linked in a logical chain.

First, biblical criticism is concerned with semantics and is to that extent a literary/philological discipline, rather than first and foremost a historical discipline. It approaches the question of meaning in the biblical text in exactly the same way as readers look for meaning in any other texts, by studying the state of the language at the time of writing and seeking to enter into the meaning of the text as illuminated by such study. (I stressed that "entering into" meaning is a better metaphor than that of "extracting" meaning.)

Second, semantics does not operate only at the level of words or even sentences; there is a macrosemantics of whole texts. In understanding a whole text, however, one is confronted—and this is the second mark of criticism—with questions of genre. What kind of text is this, and what questions does it make sense to pose to it? Meaning depends not only on historical context but also on generic context. Establishing the genre of a text and reading it appropriately is, even more obviously than basic semantics, a literary procedure, and it involves entirely nonpositivistic traits such as empathy and openness.

The third factor is that such a reading can be attempted only if the reader is not constrained by prior convictions about the text's meaning, drawn from an interpretative tradition. Where the biblical text is concerned, this entails that one cannot read the text properly if one knows in advance what it is bound to turn out to mean—because the church or some other tradition of interpretation (which *includes* the scholarly guild) claims to know already. A rider to this is that the reading will be inhibited if it is believed that whatever meaning emerges from studying the text is bound to be true in some way (whether literally or figuratively or theologically) that can be established from some other source of information. In theory, one might believe that the Bible will always turn out to be true and still practice biblical criticism—skepticism about the truth of Scripture is by no means built into the critical impulse. But those who think everything in the Bible is true (in some sense) usually have an idea already of what the truth is and believe that the Bible will turn out to conform to it—and that is not compatible with biblical criticism as received down the years. Criticism, as we have already seen, needs to treat the meaning of a text and its truth as two stages in inquiry, and cannot legitimately collapse them into one.[18]

Now if we ask about the intellectual pedigree of criticism conceived in this way, we may not get the same answers as those who ask about the origins of the historical-critical method, though the answers will not be wholly different. What we are looking for is essentially a source for philological, literary-critical, and noncommittal approaches to texts; and the Renaissance is a more obvious candidate than either the Enlightenment or the Reformation.[19] Biblical criticism may be called a *humanist* investigation of texts. Even where there is a deep theological concern for the biblical text, it may be seen as evidence of a Renaissance insistence on pristine meanings, rather than of a Protestant opposition to authority. (Of course Protestantism can itself be seen as the indirect product of a cultural Renaissance.) Reventlow indeed makes this point himself:

> It was not so much Calvinist theology (its teaching on predestination, say) that was the real impulse behind Puritan activity, with its criticism of the Church and the demand for reform which it directed to the Church. It was, rather, the humanist call *ad fontes*, the idea of

---

18. On this point, see further below, pp. 158–64.

19. Cf. J. C. O'Neill, "Biblical Criticism," in *Anchor Bible Dictionary*, ed. David Noel Freedman (New York and London: Doubleday, 1992), 1:725–30: "The foundations of modern biblical criticism were laid in the Renaissance with the recovery of Greek and the editing and printing of ancient sources" (726).

a reshaping of the Church according to its pure original form, which was to be found embodied in the Bible, and especially in the New Testament.[20]

The Renaissance roots of biblical criticism become particularly clear, however, when we remember that some of its founding figures were not Protestants at all, but Catholics. Here the work of Patrick Lambe is particularly significant. The attitude that predisposes to criticism, he points out, is a belief that "truth and authority truly can be 'found' rather than dictated,"[21] and this idea occurs in many thinkers who are children of the Renaissance, including many Catholics in the seventeeth century. Whether we call Richard Simon *the* first biblical critic or not, he was certainly in the vanguard of the critical movement, with the publication of his *Histoire critique du Vieux Testament* in 1678.[22] The motivation behind Simon's work, as later behind that of Astruc, was not to belittle the Bible in the manner of Enlightenment figures such as Voltaire, nor to use it as the basis on which to reform the church, as for the Reformers, but to examine it as an ancient document, in much the same spirit as Renaissance figures had examined the works of classical antiquity.

Against Reventlow, Lambe argues that Simon's work was not an application of the avowedly skeptical principles of Spinoza, but a relatively theory-free attempt to discover how the Old Testament had in fact developed. His theory has, as Kraus pointed out, an extraordinarily modern flavor in that he accounted for the growth of Old Testament literature by postulating a succession of scribes who transmitted an ever-growing tradition—anticipating traditio-historical criticism by some centuries. It was quite deliberately an attempt to take the Tridentine notion of Catholic tradition as an analogy for the development of the Old Testament, and Simon saw Old Testament tradition, like that of the church, as divinely inspired.[23] Each of the generations

20. "Nicht so sehr die calvinistische Theologie, etwa die Prädestinationslehre, war der eigentliche Antrieb der puritanischen Aktivität, ihrer Kritik an der Kirche und der Forderung auf Reform, die sie an sie richteten. Vielmehr war es der humanistische Ruf ad fontes, die Idee einer Wiederherstellung der Kirche nach dem reinen Urbild, das man in der Bibel, vor allem dem Neuen Testament, verkörpert fand" (Reventlow, *Bibelautorität und Geist der Moderne*, 173). Cf. also Quirinius Breen, *John Calvin: A Study in French Humanism* (Grand Rapids: Eerdmans, 1931).

21. P. J. Lambe, "Critics and Skeptics in the Seventeenth-Century Republic of Letters," *Harvard Theological Review* 81 (1988): 271–96; quotation, 290.

22. See the brief discussion of Simon in J. Steinmann, *Biblical Criticism* (London: Burns & Oates, 1959), 46–48. There is a fuller discussion in Kraus, *Geschichte der historisch-kritischen Erforschung des Alten Testaments*, 59–64.

23. Cf. David Weiss Halivni, *Revelation Restored: Divine Writ and Critical Responses*, Radical Traditions: Theology in a Postcritical Key (London: SCM, 2001).

of scribes had prophetic inspiration; hence, although they changed the original deposit that God delivered to Moses, they did so under the influence of
the Holy Spirit.

Nothing could have been further from Simon's intentions than to attack
the Bible, even though the way he chose to defend it struck the Catholic
authorities (in the person of Bossuet) as heretical. Simon's theories owe
nothing to Protestantism and are hardly to be seen as any kind of anticipation of the Enlightenment. They had, indeed, a consciously *anti*-Protestant
intention, though this did him no good in the eyes of Bossuet: by showing
the dynamically changing nature of the Bible and its lack of fixity, he sought
to argue that the church could therefore never be content with *sola scriptura*
as its basis, but needed the authority of the magisterium. There was no skeptical or freethinking agenda at all in Simon's intentions; he conceived his
studies as standing loyally within Catholic teaching and as a potential bul-
wark against rising Protestantism. Rational inquiry into the scriptural text,
read as one would read any other ancient document, would show that Protestant theories about Scripture were untenable; such was Simon's line of
thought.[24] If he really was a great founder of biblical criticism, then the interpretation of criticism as a mixture of the Reformation and the Enlightenment
needs serious revision.

One sees the desire to treat the Bible like other ancient sources also in a
later critic such as Lowth, who tried to show that the Bible is as interesting as
the classics and could be studied in the same way. Lowth begins his lectures
On the Sacred Poetry of the Hebrews[25] by tackling the problem that readers of
the Bible do not find it as interesting or as well expressed as the classics, and
tries through his elucidation of the techniques of Hebrew poetry to show that
it is not *inferior* to classical works. The intellectual background is not a high
evaluation of the Bible that has to be cut down to size, but a low evaluation of
it, at least from a literary point of view, that needs to be corrected by showing
that it is, if I may put it this way, not just divine revelation but also good literature.[26] This proceeds from a humanistic approach to the scriptural texts that
harks back to Erasmus, rather than from a Protestant commitment to the texts
as uniquely authoritative.

24. Cf. Kosellek, *Critique and Crisis*.
25. For a translation, see Robert Lowth, *On the Sacred Poetry of the Hebrews* (London:
Routledge/Thoemmes Press, 1997).
26. Thus "it is not my intention to expound to the student of theology the oracles of
Divine truth, but to recommend to the notice of the youth who is addicted to politer sciences, and studious of the elegance of composition, some of the first and choicest specimens
of poetic taste" (Lowth, 36).

This is biblical criticism as secular criticism applied to the Bible, the negation of any "special hermeneutic"; and it has its roots primarily in the Renaissance. Scholder[27] notes that the Socinian catechism partakes of this same spirit when it lays down that one must consider the historical background and the *Tendenz* of each biblical book, just as with any other book;[28] though the Catechism moves back to more familiar Christian ground with its other principles, such as the need to compare text with text, and the interpretation of what is obscure in the light of what is clear.[29] Nevertheless this document clearly reflects the basically rational (not necessarily rationalistic!) basis of biblical criticism. Naturally enough the catechism defends the authenticity of all the biblical books; but it allows that rational considerations could in principle challenge this, "cum Author sit suspectus" ("when the author is suspect"), or "cum apparet alicunde, librum esse corruptum" ("when it appears that the book is corrupted"), or "cum testimonia supersunt idonea, quae fidem libro derogant" ("when there are suitable testimonies that call the reliability of the book into question").[30] Similarly, Reventlow makes the point that in such a scholar as Hobbes clearly humanist concerns are to be found ("all Hobbes' basic theological utterances are typically humanistic"[31]). Like Erasmus, Hobbes regards biblical interpretation not as the prerogative of the individual reader but as belonging to kings and clergy, yet in practice he applies to the Bible the same critical criteria as to any other text and is, of course, the source of a number of critical ideas that still operate in much biblical study, such as the Josianic date of Deuteronomy. Similarly, Locke argued that though everything in the Bible comes from God and is to be believed implicitly, one needs to apply to it the same ways of understanding the text that one would use with any other work.[32]

27. Scholder, *Ursprünge und Probleme*, 47–48.

28. "Ut primum diligenter animadvertatur loci scopus, ac caeterae circumstantiae, quemadmodum in omnium scriptorum dictis interpretandis fieri debet"; see *Catechesis Ecclesiarum Polonicarum (1609)* (Irenopoli, 1659), 16.

29. "Deinde ut diligens instituatur collatio phrasum ac sententiarum similium, earumque clariorum; praeterea, ut ad sententias, quae in sacris literis clarissime sunt expositae, tamquam ad principia quaedam obscuriorum locorum exigatur interpretatio, nec quicquam admittatur, quod ab illis dissideat. Denique ne quid statuatur, quod ipsi sanae rationi repugnant, seu contradictionem involvat" (ibid., 16).

30. Ibid., 2.

31. "Alle theologischen Grundaussagen Hobbes' sind typisch humanistisch" (Reventlow, *Bibelautorität*, 368).

32. See H. Graf Reventlow, *Epochen der Bibelauslegung IV: Von der Aufklärung bis zum 20. Jahrhundert* (Munich: C. H. Beck, 2001), 66. Reventlow shows that Toland adopts the same principle: "Für die Deutung der Schrift gelten keine anderen Regeln als für alle anderen Bücher" ("For determining the meaning of Scripture no rules apply other than those that apply to all other books"), 75.

Erasmus already anticipates a number of later developments that may be regarded as critical. He stresses, for example, that in every passage of the Bible "it happens that not a little light is thrown on the understanding of the sense of Scripture if we weigh up not only what is said, but also by whom it is said, to whom it is said, in what words it is said, at what time, and on what occasion; what precedes, and what follows."[33] Thus context is crucial for understanding the text. He points out that the same word can have different meanings in different contexts and that one must attend to the whole drift of a passage, not atomize it: "thus Paul sometimes uses the word 'flesh' to signify family or blood relations, sometimes the human being as such; sometimes the grosser part of the person, or of some other thing is called 'flesh'; at times he calls the affections of man that lead toward vice, 'flesh.' He often calls 'body' that which consists of the members, but sometimes 'body' signifies the same as 'flesh.'"[34] As Louis Bouyer comments, "He insists on the danger of taking words in a sense they may well have in classical Greek, but which is not the same in which they are used in the New Testament."[35] This recognition that words change their meaning and that their sense depends on how they are used in context is a feature of the concern for semantics that we have seen lying at the heart of a truly critical approach, and it is already there in Erasmus.[36]

It can also be found in the text that is regarded by many as the very first example of historical criticism, Lorenzo Valla's discourse proving the forged character of the so-called Donation of Constantine, where the most telling arguments are those from linguistic usage. For example, according to the Donation, clergy are to be referred to as "patricians and consuls," but this usage reflects a much later date than that alleged for the document.[37]

33. "Accedit hinc quoque lucis non nihil ad intelligendum scripturae sensum, si perpendamus non modo quid dicatur, verumtamen a quo dicatur, cui dicatur, quibus verbis dicatur, quo tempore, qua occasione, quid praecedat, quid consequatur" (Erasmus, *Ratio seu Methodus compendio perveniendi ad veram theologiam*).

34. "Sic Paulus alias carnem vocat cognates aut sanguinis affinitatem: alias totum hominem carnem appellat: nonnumquam crassior hominis, aut alterius cuiuspiam rei par, caro dicitur: interdum affectum hominis ad vitia solicitantem, carnem appellat: item corpus saepe vocat, quod ex membris constat: aliquando corpus idem illi valet, quod caro" (ibid.).

35. Louis Bouyer, "Erasmus in Relation to the Medieval Biblical Tradition," in *Cambridge History of the Bible* (Cambridge: Cambridge University Press, 1963), 2:504.

36. And made explicit much later by Johann Jakob Wettstein; cf. Reventlow, *Epochen der Bibelauslegung IV*, 86: "Es wird . . . eine neutrale, allgemein-profane Hermeneutik gefordert" ("What is demanded is a neutral, ordinary, nonreligious hermeneutic").

37. Lorenzo Valla, *De falso credita et ementita Constantinii donatione declamatio*, xiii; cf. the discussion in Umberto Eco, *The Limits of Interpretation* (Bloomington and Indianapolis: Indiana University Press, 1990), 195. For the text, see Christopher B. Coleman, *The Treatise of Lorenzo Valla on the Donation of Constantine* (Toronto: University of Toronto Press in association with the Renaissance Society of America Press, 1993).

Awareness of the importance of genre is a recurring feature of Renaissance approaches to literature.[38] It can be illustrated nicely from a well-known passage of Sir Philip Sidney in which he recognizes the nature of "poetry" (imaginative literature) as different from that of philosophical or scientific discourse. The passage is a response to the (Platonic) accusation that poets are liars:

> Of all writers under the sun the poet is the least liar, and, though he would, as a poet can scarcely be a liar. The astronomer, with his cousin the geometrician, can hardly escape, when they take upon them to measure the height of the stars. How often, think you, do the physicians lie, when they aver things good for sicknesses, which afterwards send Charon a great number of souls drowned in a potion before they come to his ferry? And no less of the rest, which take upon them to affirm. Now for the poet, he nothing affirms, and therefore never lieth. For, as I take it, to lie is to affirm that to be true which is false; so as the other artists, and especially the historian, affirming many things, can, in the cloudy knowledge of mankind, hardly escape from many lies. But the poet (as I said before) never affirmeth. . . . And therefore, though he recount things not true, yet because he telleth them not for true, he lieth not—without we will say that Nathan lied in his speech . . . to David;[39] which as a wicked man durst scarce say, so I think none so simple would say that Aesop lied in the tales of his beasts; for who thinks that Aesop writ it for actually true were well worthy to have his name chronicled among the beasts he writeth of.[40]

One finds this realization already in so early a biblical critic as Matthias Flacius Illyricus (1520–75), who remarks that in reading a text one must decide "whether it deals with a narrative or history, a piece of teaching or instruction, a text offering consolation or an accusation, the description of something, or a speech or something similar."[41] It is also in evidence in the great Anglican Reformer of the end of the sixteenth century, Richard Hooker. When Hooker

---

38. For a discussion, see Baxter Hathaway, *The Age of Criticism: The Late Renaissance in Italy* (Ithaca, NY: Cornell University Press, 1962), 38; and A. F. Kinney, *Continental Humanist Poetics: Studies in Erasmus, Castiglione, Marguerite de Navarre, Rabelais, and Cervantes* (Amherst: University of Massachusetts Press, 1989).

39. The reference is to Nathan's parable of the ewe lamb, 2 Sam. 12:1–4.

40. Sir Philip Sidney, *The Defence of Poesy* (1579), cited here from *Sir Philip Sidney: Selected Writings*, ed. Richard Dutton (Manchester: Carcanet Press, 1987), 129–30.

41. Quoted above, p. 23, from Reventlow, *Epochen der Bibelauslegung IV: Von der Aufklärung bis zum 20. Jahrhundert*, 21. Reventlow comments, "It is remarkable to note that study of forms is by no means a modern invention, but at least as a postulate can already be encountered here!" ("Es ist bemerkenswert festzustellen, daß Gattungsforschung keineswegs eine moderne Erfindung ist, sondern, zumindest als Postulat, schon hier anzutreffen ist!") Dilthey regarded Flacius as one of the principal founders of modern biblical criticism, "the

complains about his Puritan opponents' use of the Bible, he frequently suggests that they ignore genre distinctions. Thus in a passage where he is contesting the argument that nothing may be done in church that is not expressly
commanded in the Bible—against the position of the Church of England,
which was that things might be done that seemed reasonable, provided they
were not scripturally forbidden—he argues as follows:

> That which they took for an oracle, being sifted, was repelled. True it is
> concerning the Word of God, whether it be by misconstruction of the
> sense, or by falsification of the words, wittingly to endeavour that any
> thing may seem divine which is not, or any thing not seem which is, were
> plainly to abuse and even to falsify divine evidence; which injury offered
> but unto men, is most worthily counted heinous. Which point I wish
> they did well observe, with whom nothing is more familiar than to plead
> in these causes, the Law of God, the Word of the Lord; who notwith
> standing, when they come to allege what Word and what Law they
> mean, their common ordinary practice is, to quote *by-speeches in some his
> torical narration or other*, and to urge them as if they were written in most
> exact form of Law. What is to add to the Law of God, if this be not?
> When that which the Word of God doth but deliver historically, we con
> strue without any warrant, as if it were legally meant, and so urge it fur
> ther than we can prove it was intended; do we not add to the Laws of
> God, and make them in number seem more than they are?[42]

What is historical in form should not be treated as if it were legal: that is a clear
recognition of generic distinctions in the Bible.

ANCIENT BIBLICAL CRITICISM

But—to go a stage further back—the Renaissance was consciously an attempt
to return to older sources, a rediscovery of the heritage of the classical and
postclassical world. Its literary principles were not in every case its own; many
derived from reading classical authors. This may suggest to us that the roots
of biblical criticism, if it is indeed connected with the Renaissance, in fact go
deeper still into the past. From Aristotle's *Poetics* onward, critics had been
aware of issues of style, genre, and context. Thus Aristotle objects to describing all compositions in verse as poetry, saying that "Homer and Empedocles

---

first to use methodically the help to be gained from context, aim, proportion and the consistency of individual parts or links in determining the definite meaning of passages" ("The
Development of Hermeneutics," in *Dilthey: Selected Writings*, edited, translated, and introduced by H. P. Rickman [Cambridge: Cambridge University Press, 1976], 254, trans. from
vol. 5 of the *Gesammelte Schriften* [Leipzig: B. G. Teubner, 1914]).

42. Richard Hooker, *Of the Laws of Ecclesiastical Polity*, 3.5; my italics.

have nothing in common except their metre, so the latter had better be called a scientific writer, not a poet, if we are to use 'poet' of the former."[43] Classical treatises on rhetoric are concerned with the ability to construct, and so also to recognize, a coherent argument with a meaningful drift, which is a decisive factor in critical reading.

Staying within the Christian world, we might point to two works in antiquity that anticipate critical insights: Julius Africanus's letter to Origen, and Jerome's *De viris illustribus*. In both we find a number of features that modern scholars have long regarded as anticipations of biblical criticism, but which they have tended to be unwilling to see as fully critical, probably because of a belief that criticism proper arrived only with the Enlightenment.

Critical reasoning was clearly present in Africanus's arguments.[44] His discussion of Susanna points to several difficulties in thinking the text an original part of the book of Daniel:

- Daniel is there presented as an inspired prophet, receiving direct revelations from God, whereas in the rest of the book he is informed through visions.
- The style is different in the two cases.
- The puns in the story work in Greek but not in Hebrew, which implies that the book is not a translation from the Hebrew (or Aramaic), as is the rest of Daniel.
- The work is not present in the Bibles of Jews, who accept only the Hebrew and Aramaic portions of Daniel.
- The story is historically implausible because it attributes to the exiles in Babylonia conditions that cannot have applied—possession of grand gardens, for example. (Ironically, Africanus appeals for evidence of what conditions were like to the book of Tobit, apparently not knowing that it, too, was of doubtful canonicity.) He also argues that Jewish courts would not have had the authority to pass the death sentence.
- The story is ridiculous and thus unworthy of a place in Scripture.

The arguments adduced by Africanus are a mixture of literary and historical points. The appeals to language, style, the evidence from paranomasia, the absurdity of the story, and the different conception of inspiration may be called literary ones; they show that Susanna is not the same kind of book as Daniel and must have a different origin. The argument that the conditions in which the exiles are portrayed as living do not fit the period in which the story is set is a piece of historical reasoning. All are just the kinds of argument employed by modern biblical critics.

43. Aristotle, *Poetics*, 1447b.
44. See Origen, *La lettre à Africanus sur l'histoire de Suzanne*, Sources Chrétiennes 302 (Paris: Editions du Cerf, 1983), 469–578.

Jerome's *De viris illustribus* contains fewer examples of critical reasoning, but style is again cited as a criterion in his discussion of Hebrews, which, he says, cannot be by Paul because its style is different from that of the other epistles—again, a literary argument.

Rather than saying that these are unusual *precursors* of biblical criticism among precritical commentators, it seems to me better to acknowledge that biblical criticism as we now know it genuinely does go back into the remote past. However, criticism was often neutralized, and its insights ignored or discouraged, because of a commitment to the religious authority of the biblical text. Thus Origen does not for the most part counter Africanus's objections to Susanna on their merits, but argues that the acceptance of the work by the church overrules them—even though elsewhere he accepts the validity at least of the argument from style as valid in deciding whether or not Hebrews is by Paul. He also accepts that the literary point about the inherent merit of the story is potentially valid, though he tries to show that it is in fact no more ridiculous than the story of Solomon and the two prostitutes, and therefore may well stand in Scripture.

Even this one example is sufficient to show that neither the Enlightenment, nor the Reformation, nor even the Renaissance was a *necessary* precondition of such questions arising in the mind of an acute reader. It is thus impossible to argue that criticism became possible only through the establishment of Enlightenment values; it was already in existence in ancient times. There certainly is a link with the loosening of biblical authority, as is argued by Reventlow, because belief in this authority can have the effect of blocking critical awareness. Africanus's argument about the spuriousness of Susanna is possible only because Susanna was marginal in the canon, indeed in dispute between Jews and Christians. Had the book in question been 1 Kings, say, it is unlikely that his critical questioning would have got off the ground. But the questioning is in itself based on purely rational considerations that did not need the Enlightenment for their discovery. The Enlightenment perhaps did release critical awareness to an extent that had not been in evidence earlier, but it did not create such awareness in itself.

It may also be possible to find genuine anticipations of modern biblical criticism in the Antiochene school of biblical interpretation. It has been traditional to say that the Antiochenes practiced a literal interpretation, as opposed to the characteristically allegorical approach of the Alexandrian school and that in *this* respect they are precursors of historical criticism; but this, as we saw with the help of Frances Young, is only partially true.[45] But what we do

45. See above, pp. 91–92.

find in the Antiochenes is an interest in genre and a concern for the intentions and purposes of the author and for the overall sense of works, rather than for meaning contained in individual verses; they thus avoided the atomization frequently encountered in other patristic and rabbinic exegesis. Such is what they generally mean by the text's "historical" sense—the sense it had in its original context and in its overall thrust, rather than necessarily any reference to historical events. William Yarchin in his very useful reader on the history of biblical interpretation suggests that this is evidence of their dependence on "ancient rhetorical hermeneutics," and that would certainly be my impression.[46] Rhetoric taught readers how to understand the flow and drift of an author's work, just as it taught speakers how to structure their works so as to draw the reader (or rather listener) along their line of argument. The Antiochenes are indebted to this kind of hermeneutical practice and theory. Young argues this point at length, suggesting that

> Origen was happy to decode symbols without worrying about textual or narrative coherence, and the symbols were tokens. . . . This meant the wording of the text found its significance in jots and tittles over-exegeted, rather than in context and flow. The Antiochenes sought a different kind of relationship between wording and content, style and meaning. The narrative sequence and flow of argument mattered. The text was not a pretext for something else.[47]

> So neither literalism as such, nor an interest in historicity as such, stimulated the Antiochene reaction against Origenist allegory, but rather a different approach to finding meaning in literature which had its background in the educational system of the Graeco-Roman world. Perhaps we could say that it was not 'allegory' as such that they objected to; for allegory was a standard figure of speech, and, if the text carried some indication of its presence, even allegory could be

46. Yarchin, *History of Biblical Interpretation: A Reader* (Peabody, MA: Hendrickson, 2004), 77: "True to the ideals of ancient rhetorical hermeneutics, the concern for 'history' among the Antiochenes had more to do with respecting narrative integrity and rightly understanding the biblical author's intent than with historicity in the strictly modern sense." See also Frances M. Young, "The Rhetorical Schools and Their Influence on Patristic Exegesis," in *The Making of Orthodoxy: Essays in Honour of Henry Chadwick*, ed. Rowan Williams (Cambridge: Cambridge University Press, 1989), 182–99.

47. Frances Young, *Biblical Exegesis and the Formation of Christian Culture*, 184. The contrast between this and allegorizing reading is a contrast between interpretations that do and do not attend to the context of the passage being interpreted; cf. James Barr, "The Literal, the Allegorical, and Modern Biblical Scholarship," 14: "Ancient and medieval allegory is, in very large measure, *de-contextualizing*, and in two ways: firstly, in that it works from very small pieces of text . . . and interprets them in ways that are irreconcilable with the context within the books; secondly, that it uproots them from the culture in which they have meaning."

allowed. What they resisted was the type of allegory that destroyed textual coherence.[48]

Young argues that the background of the Antiochene approach lies in ancient training in rhetoric: Libanius, the teacher of both Theodore of Mopsuestia and John Chrysostom, may be an important figure in mediating this to these Christian writers. Antiochene exegesis is thus importantly close to the secular norms of its day:

> Summary and paraphrase are persistent techniques used by the Antiochenes to bring out the gist of the argument and the *hypothesis* usually includes this, together with circumstantial introductory material. This technique ensures the context and thrust were not lost under the mass of detailed commentary. Like school exegetes, they sought to discern the underlying idea dressed up in the words and style of the text. They often show concern with the *akolouthia*, or sequence, of argument or story. They also discussed genre and the particular literary characteristics of, for example, prophecy.[49]

Thus the Antiochenes are not so very important for their insistence on the literal or historical sense of Scripture—the role in which they have long been cast. As we saw in an earlier chapter, these trends are apparent only to a very limited degree. But they may be important for their interest in genre, in style, in the way an argument flows. In these respects they can more truly be hailed as forerunners of a critical approach to the text, indeed as exemplars of it.[50]

Where genre is concerned, the ancient church in general was not entirely

48. Young, *Biblical Exegesis and the Formation of Christian Culture*, 176. Compare my remarks above on cases where the allegorical sense is the "literal" sense, pp. 96–97.

49. Ibid., 172. On Antiochene exegesis, see also Dimitri Z. Zaharopoulos, *Theodore of Mopsuestia on the Bible: A Study of His Old Testament Exegesis* (New York: Paulist Press, 1989), who stresses the Antiochenes' insistence on *internal* evidence for their critical conclusions; thus Theodore rejected the psalm titles as incompatible with the contents of the psalms themselves, and argued that it was clear that Job was a postexilic work, not by Moses, as was the prevailing opinion. Cf. also Robert C. Hill, *Reading the Old Testament in Antioch*, The Bible in Ancient Christianity 3 (Leiden: Brill, 2005).

50. Rudolf Bultmann's 1912 Habilitationsschrift in Marburg was on Theodore of Mopsuestia: *Die Exegese des Theodor von Mopsuestia* (Stuttgart: Kohlhammer, 1984). He stressed Theodore's attachment to the "plain sense": "He uses Scripture, not as a treasure-trove of dogmatic or historical information, nor as material with which he can show off his learning and exercise his art, nor again in order to dispute about it or to preach it; his aim is to let the text speak clearly, and it is to this goal that he subordinates everything he has to say" ("Er benutzt die Schrift nicht als Fundgrube dogmatischer oder historischer Kenntnisse, ebensowenig als Stoff, seine Gelehrsamkeit zu zeigen und seine Kunst zu üben, oder auch darüber zu disputieren oder zu predigen. Er will den Text zum deutlichen Reden bringen, und diesem Zweck ordnet sich alles, was er zu sagen hat, unter") (40). Bultmann also noted

precritical anyway. The Jewish division of the Old Testament canon into Torah, Prophets, and Writings seems to show rather little in the way of genre recognition. The distinction between Torah and Former Prophets in particular does not pay attention to generic questions, since both are narrative works, but is concerned more with the level of inspiration. The Torah is thought of as a direct revelation through Moses, the Prophets as the result of a somewhat lower level inspiration, and the Writings, according to some, as primarily human works. But the Christian division of the canon, which though more informal than the Jewish one is fairly standard in older manuscripts, is into historical, Wisdom, and prophetic books, and this does seem to reflect an awareness of genre distinctions. All the narrative books are lumped together, even though in the Hebrew canon they appear in all three divisions, on the basis that they recount history. Josephus, interestingly, seems to attest a similar way of organizing the sacred books—if not physically, then at least in the mind—though in a traditional Jewish way he does make a distinction between what is by Moses and what is by lesser prophets. But awareness of genre is certainly present in his thinking.[51]

The effect of seeing the matter in this way is that the distinction between critical and precritical scholarship begins to look shaky, to be replaced by a distinction between critical and noncritical that is not essentially a matter of chronology. Attention to semantics, awareness of genre questions, and the ability to consider the text with questions of truth bracketed out—all these were in evidence long before any period that could possibly be called modern, even if they were not reflected on as questions of theory. It remains true that it was not until the Renaissance that they emerged into the foreground.

CONCLUSION

To conclude: if we define biblical criticism differently from the received opinion, according to which it is the application of the historical-critical method to the Bible, and instead stress its attention to the meaning of words and the

---

Theodore's attention to genre: "Part of an investigation of Theodore's explanation of the form of the Scriptures is the question how he grasped *the forms of Scripture as a whole*, and its literary genres" ("Zur Untersuchung der Erklärung Theodors der Form der Schriften gehört endlich die Frage, wie er *die Formen der Schrift als ganzer*, ihre literarischen Gattungen aufgefaßt hat") (64), distinguishing *species prophetica, traditio historiarum*, and *demonstrativa admonitio*.

51. See Josephus, *Contra Apionem*, 1:37–43, who speaks of "the laws," "the traditional histories," and "hymns to God and precepts for the conduct of human life."

genre of the texts that are composed of them, then we are likely to see it as having a pedigree less exclusively indebted to the Enlightenment than is generally supposed. The flowering of biblical criticism is certainly a modern phenomenon, but its roots lie deeper than most people think. The rationality it applies to the biblical text is not simply an Enlightenment rational*ism*, but a use of reason that was already available in the ancient world and was extended in Europe at the Renaissance. The link with Protestantism, though historically obvious, is essentially a historical accident; biblical criticism is not in origin a Protestant pursuit, though Protestants were mainly responsible for its modern development.

6

Biblical Criticism and Religious Belief

To anyone uninitiated in the jargon of biblical studies, biblical criticism sounds like an attack on the Bible. There has been a persistent tendency among those who are initiated to think that this is not so far from the truth. The contention may be that any critical approach to the Bible must reflect an underlying hostility to the Bible, or perhaps to the religions (Judaism and Christianity) whose Scriptures it is. Or it may be, more subtly, that biblical critics damage the Bible even when their intentions are not hostile. A common complaint is that the critics have "taken the Bible away from the church" and that some means needs to be found of reconnecting them. In this chapter we shall examine a range of opinions that share this general sense of wariness or hostility toward the work of "the critics."

CRITICISM PERCEIVED AS HOSTILE

Some of what has been practiced under the banner of biblical criticism has undoubtedly been hostile, in both intention and effect, not only to the Bible itself but also to theology. One may think of the work of Reimarus, or in our own day of Gerd Lüdemann. But more often the hostility has been perceived rather than intended—though a scholar might be correctly perceived as hostile in effect, even though not in intention. One cannot, in any case, resolve the question whether biblical criticism is hostile toward the Bible by counting heads or by anecdote, as if the idea could be refuted merely by pointing to critics who happened not to be anti-Bible in their thinking; the question is one about the nature of biblical criticism, not about the personalities of the critics. To put it another way, critics may not *feel* hostile, but the effect of their work may still be hostile to the Bible.

Christopher Rowland argues that historical criticism has been exclusively focused on the original sense and that this has sundered the Bible from believing communities:

> I believe that so damaging has been a one-sided preoccupation with original meaning, as given us by historical-critical 'experts', that a real question arises about the proper place of historical criticism. In many circles in modern times it has been at least implicitly assumed that interpreting the Bible was about recovering its original meaning, hence the misleading idea arose that those with skills in recovering the original meaning have the key to biblical interpretation as a whole. It is vital to distinguish between the study of the Bible in the 'Academy' and the interpretation of scripture within the faith community. The two are related but they are not the same. Historical criticism has had some seriously undermining effects on the functioning of the Bible as scripture. Through being placed within its original setting, the Bible for many loses its immediate religious impact, and is in danger of becoming just another ancient text. . . . The focus on analysis and on the parts at the expense of the whole erodes a sense of the coherence of scripture. Within ministerial training biblical studies can become a process of alienation rather than integration, threatening to rob ordinands of the very scripture which nurtured their faith and their sense of vocation. In these and similar ways, the functioning of scripture can be undermined and stultified.[1]

There is a real and urgent concern here that biblical study is taking the Bible away from the church.

Modern biblical criticism may indeed be said to have begun under a cloud of suspicion in this respect. One of the earliest scholars whom all modern writers recognize as "critical" is Richard Simon, who published his *Histoire critique du Vieux Testament* in 1678. (We have already discussed the claim that Simon is the founder of biblical criticism, as maintained by Kraus.) Simon's work was promptly suppressed in France and survives only because it was subsequently published in the Low Countries. Simon's object was at least partly to confound Protestants by showing that the Old Testament contained such contradictions that it could not serve as the sole basis for faith; hence the magisterium of the Catholic Church was needed, if the Christian faith was to be securely founded. But Simon's work was construed as an attack on that church's Scriptures, and thus as attacking at its foundations the very structure it was intended to shore up. It therefore fell under suspicion and was declared heterodox, and this set the tone for the attitude of church authorities (Protes-

---

1. Christopher Rowland, "Criteria in Using the Bible?" in a study pack for a course on "The Bible: Its Use and Influence" in the Oxford theology faculty.

tant as well as Catholic) toward the critical investigation of the Bible from then on. As Patrick Lambe puts it,

> Because the first essays in biblical criticism were interpreted in terms of the issue of authority—as exemplified by the case of Richard Simon—the practice of criticism became polemicized, and more attention was paid to the polemic than to the proper aim of criticism, understanding. The ecclesiastical authorities in the seventeenth century interpreted the work of Simon as an attack upon their authority and exercised their authority in order to suppress his book. Simon's success in having his books published abroad and smuggled into France itself conformed to the established pattern, for it was an overt challenge to the authority which had attempted to impose itself. Biblical criticism came to be seen by the world as a glamorous and revolutionary enterprise.[2]

In subsequent centuries criticism continued to be seen by many as revolutionary, but the glamour soon wore off. In the nineteenth century a critical approach to the Bible established itself firmly in the world of German universities, but in the churches it continued to be suspect. Criticism was eventually accepted by most academic theologians, but in every generation it had its detractors, who regarded it as a secularizing, rationalistic, and faithless undertaking.

Kierkegaard's attack on the biblical critics is well known. He himself regarded expounding Scripture as a central part of theology, but not in a critical spirit. As Richard Bauckham puts it:

> Kierkegaard is not an exegete, at least in the modern sense. He makes his contribution at a stage of interpretation and appropriation of the biblical texts which lies beyond the historical exegesis practiced by modern commentators. It makes no sense to ask where his reading of James ends and his own creative thinking begins. . . . An example like Kierkegaard's should make biblical scholars a little more modest than they often are about the importance and the limits of what they do, especially when they are tempted to speak as though they have the meaning and the effect of the text in their professional control.[3]

The later nineteenth century was also not without its dramas, however. Wellhausen gave up his chair in the theology faculty at Greifswald, not because he himself thought he was damaging the Bible, but because he knew he was

---

2. Patrick J. Lambe, "Biblical Criticism and Censorship in Ancien Régime France: The Case of Richard Simon," *Harvard Theological Review* 78 (1985): 149–77; quotation, 175.

3. Richard Bauckham, *James: Wisdom of James, Disciple of Jesus the Sage* (New York: Routledge, 1999), 161.

seen as doing so by many in the Lutheran churches.[4] William Robertson Smith, his Scottish supporter, fared worse and was deprived of his chair in the Free Church college in Aberdeen. Even the very modest acknowledgment of biblical criticism in the collection *Lux Mundi*[5] seemed to many English church leaders dangerously damaging to the credibility of the Bible as the foundation document of the Christian faith. In Oxford, Edward Bouverie Pusey, for fifty-four years Regius Professor of Hebrew (1828–82), strove with all his power to keep back the tide of biblical criticism flowing in from Germany—even though it was, in truth, in England that much of the movement had begun a couple of centuries earlier. Though Pusey had studied in Germany as a young man, he came to believe that German scholarship had led students of the Bible into unorthodox and faithless positions, and he was, for example, a strong defender of such matters as the historicity of the book of Jonah.[6] Through the work of

4. Wellhausen did not by any means strike all who studied with him as antireligious. Here is a testimony from someone who heard him lecture in Marburg: "This man had such a rich inner life, and when he came in to lecture he showed a certain degree of embarrassment in spite of his quite laddish appearance. He immediately captivated us with his brilliant, free delivery (he spoke without any notes), and also through the religious power and the theological depth and clarity of the thoughts he drew from the word of Scripture. He lectured on Job with such a strong sense of being inwardly moved, that we in the audience (who were few enough!) received a deep impression that the man standing before us was one whose desire was not simply to practice exegesis, but to bear witness to the truth of the word of revelation—the word which breaks the one who thirsts for God's word, in order to draw him into God's grace. So great was this personal impression, and so glad were we of the knowledge which Wellhausen's exegesis of Job, with its religious emphasis, imparted to us, that we were happy to make allowances for the labor of detailed philological work that we also had to complete, and which the master never let us off: he had an eye for the smallest linguistic irregularities in the text" ("Dieser innerlich so reiche Mann, in dessen Auftreten bei allem Burschikosen etwas von Befangenheit lag, fesselte gleich sehr durch die glänzende freie Darstellung—er sprach ohne jedes Manuskript—wie durch die religiöse Kraft und die theologische Tiefe und Klarheit der Gedanken, die er aus dem Schriftwort erhob. Er las über Hiob mit so starker innerer Bewegung, daß wir wenigen Zuhörer unter dem tiefen Eindruck standen, es stehe da einer vor uns, der nicht bloß Exegese treiben, sondern der Zeugnis ablegen will von der Wahrheit des Offenbarungswortes, das den nach Gottes Liebe dürstenden Menschen zerbricht, um ihn in seine Gnade zu ziehen. Über die Größe dieses persönlichen Eindrucks und über die Erkenntnis, die uns Wellhausens religiös betonte Exegese des Hiob eintrug, nahmen wir die Mühsal der philologischen Kleinarbeit, die dabei zu leisten war, und die uns der Meister mit dem Scharfblick für die kleinsten sprachlichen Unebenheiten des Textes nicht erließ, gern in Kauf" (Willy Staerk, "Willy Staerk," in *Die Religion der Gegenwart in Selbstdarstellungen*, ed. Erich Stange, 5 vols. [Leipzig: F. Meiner, 1929], 5:159–206; quotation, 168; quoted in Rudolf Smend, *Julius Wellhausen: Ein Bahnbrecher in drei Disziplinen* [Munich: Carl Friedrich von Siemens Stiftung, 2006], 45.

5. *Lux Mundi: A Series of Studies in the Religion of the Incarnation*, ed. Charles Gore (London: John Murray, 1889).

6. See the discussion in Yvonne Sherwood, *A Biblical Text and Its Afterlives: The Survival of Jonah in Western Culture* (Cambridge: Cambridge University Press, 2000), 45–48.

Pusey's successor, S. R. Driver, pentateuchal criticism in the style of Wellhausen was finally widely accepted in England, some time after it had become relatively respectable in Germany. But comparable study of the Gospels continued (and continues) to encounter hostility within the churches, as it had in the 1830s in the case of D. F. Strauss. One may think of reactions in the British and American churches to the work of Rudolf Bultmann in the middle of the twentieth century.

Nowhere in the world is biblical criticism uncontroversial. The Catholic Church—paradoxically, in view of its reaction to Simon—has now embraced critical approaches perhaps more wholeheartedly than any other Christian confession. But within Protestant circles Kierkegaard's ghost lingers, calling in question the very possibility of a truly critical approach to the Bible on the part of a true believer. After this brief historical retrospect, we turn to some of these contemporary reactions to the work of biblical critics.

THE NEED FOR A THEOLOGICAL HERMENEUTIC

The world of academic theology today contains few figures who are simply hostile to biblical criticism as such or who regard it as proceeding from a complete, faithless rejection of scriptural authority. Attitudes are more nuanced than that. At the same time, there is a powerful lobby that canvasses the view that biblical criticism has been an extremely mixed blessing—distancing the Bible from the churches and from religious believers. What is needed, it is urged, is a more theological style of biblical study, starting from an overtly confessional position and acknowledging that these books are the church's Scriptures, not a playground for scholars. Biblical criticism, so it is said, may be legitimate as far as it goes (though not all would concede even that), but it is hopelessly inadequate as a total approach to the Bible. It has a false self-image as an objective and unprejudiced approach, wholly at variance with its actual practice, which betrays a deep commitment to "the Enlightenment project" of rationalism and religious skepticism, and is often rooted in white, Western, middle-class values. It fragments the text in order to get back to its supposed original sources, rather than interpreting what lies before us—which, after all, is the text that church and synagogue have committed to us to interpret. In short, biblical criticism as we have known it is bankrupt and marked by hostility to the very text—the Bible—that it should be serving, for the sake of the church's faith.

This charge is obviously a complex one, in which one may detect several strands. Some of these have already concerned us, for example, the "false objectivity" of critics and attachment to the values of the Enlightenment, and the "fragmenting" of the text in place of reading the "final form." Here we shall deal with the charge of hostility to faith commitment. There are at the moment at least two proposals that try to reverse these alleged shortcomings in biblical criticism by developing a theological hermeneutic in which criticism's hostility to a theological reading of the text is replaced with a committed (sometimes called a "confessional" or "confessing") approach. These may be called the canonical approach, which is an attempt to reclaim the Bible as the church's book, and "advocacy" readings, in which the Bible is to be read as an instrument of human liberation as against the oppressive character of traditional biblical criticism.

Reclaiming the Bible for the Church

A first response to the alleged hostility of biblical criticism to the Bible as a book of faith can take as a shorthand designation the title of a collection of essays edited by Carl Braaten and Robert W. Jenson, *Reclaiming the Bible for the Church*.[7] The authors claim that in the hands of the critics the Bible has ceased to be the church's book and has been set on the same level as any other piece of writing from the past.

> The historical-critical method was originally devised and welcomed as the great emancipator of the Bible from ecclesiastical dogma and blind faith. Some practitioners of the method now sense that the Bible may meanwhile have become its victim. Questions of every conceivable kind have been put to the biblical texts, but for many in the church—pastors, teachers, and laity—the Bible seems to have lost its voice. Can the Bible still speak to the church in an age of critical historical awareness? Or better, does God continue to speak his Word through the Bible as a whole?[8]

> To a large degree the distorting effects of this social shift can be observed in a variety of secular interpretations, interpretations that are often removed from the faith and practice of those communities who worship Christ as Lord within a trinitarian theology and ecclesiology. What lies at the core of many of these nontrinitarian hermeneutical enterprises is an epistemological monism that assumes that historical knowledge is omniscient and that it determines theological truth.[9]

---

7. *Reclaiming the Bible for the Church*, ed. Carl E. Braaten and Robert W. Jenson (Grand Rapids: Eerdmans, 1995; Edinburgh: T. & T. Clark, 1996).

8. Carl E. Braaten and Robert W. Jenson, "Introduction: Gospel, Church, and Scripture," in *Reclaiming the Bible for the Church*, ix–xii; quotation, ix–x.

9. Karl P. Donfried, "Alien Hermeneutics and the Misappropriation of Scripture," in *Reclaiming the Bible for the Church*, 19–45; quotation, 20.

In all this, the sense is that there is a problem or crisis in the interpretation of the Bible. This problem is the Bible's perceived irrelevance to Christian life and thought; the cause is thought to lie in the procedures that distance the Bible from the community of faith through an insistence on studying it "critically," that is, according to rationalistic or secularist norms of inquiry. Scholars in the study are out of touch, it is suggested, with preachers in the pulpit and congregations in the pew, because they deliberately look away from the Bible's religious claims in order to subject it to analysis. The solution to the crisis lies with a willing return to seeing the Bible as the church's book and reading it by a deliberately theological hermeneutic.

It is crucial for supporters of traditional biblical criticism to be aware, not only of the intellectual arguments here, but also of the existential and emotional force of what is felt by those who perceive biblical criticism as marginalizing them because it has come to be seen as the province of experts detached from the church's life. This is well caught by Timothy Gorringe in a paper prompted by E. P. Sanders's book *Jesus and Judaism*:

> The bundle of documents which we call 'Scripture' were . . . written from faith to faith . . . Faith is a community word: it only pertains to the individual as it first pertains to the community. The project for the reform of the heart of Christianity, which is what Christology is, in no matter how lowly a form it is conceived, is then not the affair of an individual's study but an affair of the community. The community's awareness grows through debate and discussion and in this the person with the charism of scholarship has his or her part to play. What is that? It is not, what the academic situation so easily suggests, that of teacher to pupil, imparter of knowledge to the ignorant. There is a great deal more to reading Scripture than historical knowledge and on many counts the person with that charism is on all fours with, or in debt to, others without it. The Argentine theologian Enrique Dussell frequently reminds us, and we cannot be too frequently reminded, that a very great proportion of today's church lives under the cross and that the martyrs of the past thirty years exceed the number of those who died in the whole of the first three centuries of the church's life. These people died and are dying for the truth of the gospel, because they believed that the Lord of life was crucified alongside them and rose to give them hope. . . . Now exegesis, I suggest, involves, beyond scholarship, an experiential or existential element which involves the readiness to lay one's life on the line in this way.[10]

One response to this kind of challenge can be found in the work of Brevard Childs, who proposes a "canonical approach" to biblical interpretation. We

---

10. Timothy J. Gorringe, "Pride and Prejudice," unpublished paper circa 1985.

quoted above his argument that the interpreter of the Bible should not confront the biblical text as if it were a newly discovered document lying in the
ground in the form of "inert sherds," but should recognize it as a living work
that has been and remains important for at least two communities of faith, Jewish and Christian. Traditional criticism, as Childs sees it, involves steadfastly
looking away from the ecclesial context of the Bible and treating it as if it were,
say, one of the Dead Sea Scrolls, evidence for religious thought in one particular period and place. A properly theological reading of the Bible, by contrast,
would treat it just as it stands as the vehicle of a living faith. It would not be
focused on the parts from which the Bible is made up—and especially not on
alleged underlying sources such as J, E, D, and P (or indeed Q)—but on the
Bible as a finished product, for that is the Bible the modern church and synagogue have inherited.

Childs's case may be summed up by saying that biblical interpreters need to
adopt a theological hermeneutic in reading Scripture. Biblical criticism as we
have grown used to it brackets out the theological truth or falsehood of the
text while it seeks its meaning, and only then—if at all—asks about its relevance to faith.[11] For Childs, if we begin by ignoring the religious claims of the
Bible, we shall find it ever more difficult to reconnect with them after the work
of criticism is done. He writes:

> The modern hermeneutical impasse which has found itself unable
> successfully to bridge the gap between the past and the present, has
> arisen in large measure from its disregard of the canonical shaping.
> The usual critical method of biblical exegesis is, first, to seek to
> restore an original historical setting by stripping away those very ele-
> ments which constitute the canonical shape. Little wonder that once
> the biblical text has been securely anchored in the historical past by
> 'decanonizing' it, the interpreter has difficulty applying it to the mod-
> ern religious context.[12]

---

11. This principle is clearly stated by Spinoza, *Tractatus theologico-politicus*, chapter 7, "Of
the Interpretation of Scripture": "I term a passage obscure or clear according to the degree
of difficulty with which the meaning can be elicited from the context, and not according to
the degree of difficulty with which its truth can be perceived by reason. For the point at issue
is merely the meaning of the texts, not their truth. I would go further: in seeking the meaning of Scripture we should take every precaution against the undue influence, not only of
our own prejudices, but of our faculty of reason in so far as that is based on the principles of
natural cognition. In order to avoid confusion between true meaning and truth of fact, the
former must be sought simply from linguistic usage" (trans. Samuel Shirley [New York: E.
J. Brill, 1989]; quoted in Yarchin, *History of Biblical Interpretation*, 200).

12. *Introduction to the Old Testament as Scripture*, 79; cf. *Biblical Theology in Crisis* (Philadelphia: Fortress Press, 1970), 141–42; "'Interpretation in Faith': The Theological Responsibility of an Old Testament Commentary," *Interpretation* 18 (1964): 432–49, esp. 437–44.

Thus for Childs the interpretative process does not consist of two stages—*first* ask what the text means or how it came to be, and *then* ask what it has to say to the modern believer—but only one. This single, unitary approach asks what the text means in the context of the whole canon, that is, what it has to say to the theologically attuned reader. As soon as we concede that questions of meaning are to be settled *before* asking about what traditional terminology calls application, we have already sold the pass. For any meaning so discovered will by definition be merely historical, not properly theological, and from it there is no route open to a contemporary appreciation of the depths of the text.

Childs's ideas have been developed in various ways in the United States by Gerald Sheppard and in Britain by Christopher Seitz (himself an American), Walter Moberly, and Francis Watson, though the last operates at considerably more distance from Childs than the other two, at least as I read him.

All these scholars begin from the position that biblical criticism has been reductionist and positivistic in its approach to the biblical text. All believe that there is a pressing need to reintegrate it with the wider theological task and that this is best achieved by attending to the text in its present (or final) form, as the form in which the church has canonized it. Here are some representative quotations.

> [The first challenge for Old Testament studies is] the cultivation of a proper respect—reverence is not too strong a term—for what an honor it is to read this literature at all. When the Old Testament requires jacket blurbs, snazzy new translations every other week, and maybe even snazzy lectures to match, we need to stop and ask whether the problem is in or behind the text or in us. The basic challenge of the Old Testament is not historical distance, overcome by historical-critical tools, or existential disorientation, overcome by a hermeneutics of assent or suspicion. The Old Testament tells a particular story about a particular people and their particular God, who [*sic*] in Christ we confess as our God, his Father and our own, the Holy One of Israel. We have been read into a will, a first will and testament, by Christ. If we do not approach the literature with this basic stance—of estrangement overcome, of an inclusion properly called "adoption"—historical-critical methods or a hermeneutics of assent will still stand outside and fail to grasp that God is reading us, not we him.[13]

The rule of faith was formulated in the early Church concurrently with the process of canonical recognition and compilation. The purpose of the rule of faith, which was in due course summarized in the creeds, is to guide readers so that they may discern that truth of God in Christ

---

13. Christopher R. Seitz, *Word without End: The Old Testament as Abiding Theological Witness* (Grand Rapids: Eerdmans, 1998), 11.

to which the Church, through its scripture, bears witness. In an historic Christian understanding, formation of canon, rule of faith, and creeds are mutually related and integral to the quest of recognizing truth about God. In general terms, guidelines such as a rule of faith embodies are obviously integral to the health of the never-ending dialectic between an authoritative text and a community which seeks to conduct itself in the light of that text.[14]

How then might a rule of faith be understood? It sets the biblical text within the context of the continuing life of the Christian Church where the one God and humanity are definitively understood in relation to Jesus Christ. In this context there is a constant interplay between the biblical text and those doctrinal, ethical, and spiritual formulations which seek to spell out its implications. The concerns in this are at least twofold. On the one hand, the initial concern is not so much to explain the Bible at all (in senses familiar to philologist or historian) as to preserve its reality as authoritative and canonical for subsequent generations, so that engagement with the God of whom it speaks, and the transformation of human life which it envisages, remain enduring possibilities; that is, to say 'God is here'. On the other hand, the interest is not so much the history of ideas and religious practices (though this remains an important critical control) as the necessities of hermeneutics and theology proper, that is, the question of what is necessary to enable succeeding generations of faithful, or would-be faithful, readers to penetrate and grasp the meaning and significance of the biblical text; that is, to say 'God is here' in such a way that the words can be rightly understood without lapse into idolatry, literalism, bad history, manipulation, or the numerous other pitfalls into which faith may stumble. It is when the Christian community fails sufficiently to grasp the implications of its own foundational texts that a rule of faith changes role from guide to inquisitor.[15]

Seitz and Moberly are alike in seeing a definite role for biblical criticism as a check on "uncritical" reading ("idolatry, literalism, bad history, manipulation"), but also in thinking that the true role of the biblical interpreter is to move beyond criticism—or rather, to *begin* not with criticism, but with a commitment to the Bible as divine communication with the Christian community. The meaning discovered in Scripture should be "ruled," to use again Greene-McCreight's terminology, or "confessing," as Moberly calls it; not neutral or detached, but engaged and connected with Christian faith.

14. R. W. L. Moberly, *The Bible, Theology, and Faith: A Study of Abraham and Jesus* (Cambridge: Cambridge University Press, 2000), 42–43.
    15. Ibid., 43.

It could be thought that this does not conflict with biblical criticism. One might argue that criticism delivers the plain sense, but that readers are entirely free then to go on and use the text in other ways, including a confessing use to illustrate or commend the Christian faith—rather as in the example cited above of the liturgical use of a text from the Wisdom of Solomon to bring out a theme of Christmas.[16] But clearly both Seitz and Moberly mean more than this. They argue that the "ruled" reading of Scripture provides an access to its *true* meaning, the meaning that a responsible interpreter should feel constrained to adopt. Their position is not compatible with a pluralistic approach in which one may use the Bible for any purposes one likes, including critical ones, but rather makes claims to normativity. And in that respect it comes into genuine conflict with a critical approach, if a critical approach is as I have proposed.

Francis Watson puts forward a somewhat more complex line of thinking. In *Text and Truth* and *Text, Church and World*[17] he argues that historical criticism has indeed mistreated the Bible, ignoring its character as Holy Scripture, and thus far he stands on the same ground as Seitz and Moberly. He speaks of Old Testament theology as a "Christian theological enterprise" and is very cool toward any idea of "neutrality" in reading the Bible. However, at the same time he defends against Childs the idea that the biblical text has a "literal sense" that is to be linked to authorial intention, and he sees this intention as crucial to the establishment of the text's meaning. But such authorial meaning must always be interpreted in relation to what he calls the "center," which I take to mean the overall intention of Scripture, something like Childs's "canonical intention." For him the essential way in which biblical interpretation should be distinguished from secular criticism is that it attends to the fact that God has "communicative intentions" too. Thus he writes:

> The *literal sense* of the biblical texts comprises (*i*) verbal meaning, (*ii*) illocutionary and perlocutionary force, and (*iii*) the relation to the centre. As communicative actions, the texts seek to convey a meaning in order to evoke a particular response. To concern oneself with the literal sense is therefore to reflect on 'application' as well as on verbal meaning, for without this dimension the texts are no longer understood as communicative actions. The criteria by which scriptural communicative actions are assessed derive from God's definitive communicative action in the incarnation of the Word.[18]

16. See above, p. 85.

17. Francis Watson, *Text, Church and World: Biblical Interpretation in Theological Perspective* (Edinburgh: T. & T. Clark, 1994).

18. Francis Watson, *Text and Truth: Redefining Biblical Theology* (Edinburgh: T. & T. Clark, 1997), 123. "Attention to the center" seems reminiscent of Augustine's principle

This is a "literal" sense in a rather special sense of that term: it means what God literally intends to communicate through the scriptural text. As such, it certainly belongs to a reading which Moberly would call "confessing."

In *Text, Church and World* Watson applies this principle to how we should approach the stories of Jesus in the Gospels. He is against the "quest of the historical Jesus," arguing that the attempt to reconstruct what lies behind the text is reductionist. Yet at the same time he opposes any idea that the story of Jesus is simply a textual construct with no extratextual reference or that the task of the Christian theologian is to think only "intratextually" about the person of Jesus, as (he argues) is implied by Lindbeck and others of his persuasion.[19] The text of the Gospels, he thinks, does not *construct* the story of Jesus, but *mediates* it. It really refers to realities in the external world, but we cannot have any unmediated access to those realities. Thus we are enclosed in the world of the text, yet we can know (by faith?) that that world corresponds to the real world. What we cannot do is to check up on such correspondence by stepping outside what is mediated by the text, as historical critics try to do. The Jesus the Christian worships is a real person who actually existed, but our only access to him is through a textual representation of his story that is not to be subjected to historical criticism.

It is clear that the writers surveyed here have been considerably influenced by the ideas of Karl Barth:

> The idea we have to set our face against is one which has become very much at home in theology in connection with modern historicism. It is the idea that our concern in reading, understanding, and expounding the Bible can and indeed should be to pass over the biblical texts and attain to some facts lying *behind* the texts. Then, it is believed, we should recognize revelation as lying in these facts—whose factuality is now firmly established independently of the texts themselves![20]

---

that exegesis should be determined by attention to the rule of faith; on this, see the discussion above, pp. 99–101.

19. See George Lindbeck, *The Nature of Doctrine: Religion and Theology in a Postliberal Age* (London: SPCK, 1984).

20. "Die Vorstellung, gegen die wir uns abzugrenzen haben, ist die im Zusammenhang mit dem modernen Historismus in der Theologie weithin heimisch gewordene, als könne und müsse es beim Lesen, Verstehen und Auslegen der Bibel darum gehen, über die biblischen Texte hinaus zu den irgendwo *hinter* den Texten stehenden Tatsachen vorzustoßen, um dann in diesen (in ihrer Tatsächlichkeit nun auch abhängig von den Texten feststehenden!) Tatsachen als solchen die Offenbarung zu erkennen" (Karl Barth, *Die Kirchliche Dogmatik I: Die Lehre vom Worte Gottes*, 2 [Zollikon-Zurich: Evangelischer Verlag, 1932], 545–46; translated as *Church Dogmatics* I/2 [Edinburgh: T. & T. Clark, 1956]).

The mistake, Barth argues, lies in "reading the biblical canon differently from how it wishes to be read and, indeed—this is a point of convergence—can be read."[21] What biblical interpreters should have done is as follows:

> Theology, at least, and particularly a historical theology, one specially addressed to the biblical texts, should (let us be open about this) have had the tact and the taste to acknowledge how inextricable is the link between form and content in biblical texts, which cannot fail to be clear to it. Then it should have shrunk from the temptation to pose the inquisitive question about what may stand behind the text, and have turned with that much more attention, exactitude, and love to the texts as such.[22]

Barth foresees, or at least hopes to see, a day when biblical scholars will turn from fragments to the interpretation of the whole once more:

> If only . . . the exegesis of the canonical Scriptures as such—a connected exposition of Genesis, of the book of Isaiah, of the Gospel of Matthew, and so on, in the form and extent in which they now exist—could be recognized and freshly engaged with as in the end the *only* possible goal of biblical studies.[23]

This hope has certainly been fulfilled in recent scholarship. There is now a wealth of material reflecting on whole books of the Bible. In the study of Isaiah, there has been nothing less than a revolution, with those who still prefer to study First, Second, and Third Isaiah, rather than the book as a finished whole, somewhat in retreat before "holistic" interpretations that claim to respect the contours of the canonical book of Isaiah.[24] In that sense, though

---

21. "Den biblischen Kanon anders zu lesen, als er selber gelesen sein will und als er—denn das fällt hier zusammen—gelesen werden kann" (ibid., 546).

22. "Mindestens die Theologie, und zwar auch und gerade die historische, die speziell den biblischen Texten zugewandte Theologie hätte—sagen wir einmal: den Takt und Geschmack haben müssen, angesichts der Verklammerung von Form und Inhalt der biblischen Texte, um die sie doch wissen mußte, vor jener Versuchung zurückzuweichen, die neugierige Frage nach dem, was hinter dem Text stehen möchte, zu unterlassen und sich dafür mit so mehr Aufmerksamkeit, Genauigkeit und Liebe den Texten als solchen zuzuwenden" (ibid., 547).

23. "Ob . . . die Exegese der kanonischen Schrift als solcher, also die zusammenhängende Auslegung des Genesis, des Jesaja-Buches, des Matthäusevangeliums usw. in ihren nun einmal vorliegenden Bestand und Umfang als das schließlich *allein* mögliche Ziel der biblischen Wissenschaft wieder anerkannt und neu in Angriff genommen werden wird" (ibid).

24. See, for example, Edgar W. Conrad, *Reading Isaiah*, Overtures to Biblical Theology 27 (Minneapolis: Fortress Press, 1991); David Carr, "Reading for Unity in Isaiah," *Journal for the Study of the Old Testament* 57 (1993): 61–80; Brevard S. Childs, *The Struggle to Understand Isaiah as Christian Scripture* (Grand Rapids: Eerdmans, 2004). The movement was

there may not be so many scholars who are card-carrying canonical critics, the general atmosphere in biblical studies has changed markedly (at least in the English-speaking world) in the direction suggested by Childs. And this is largely true at a theological as well as a literary level; those who practice holistic exegesis of the texts are frequently influenced by the theological conviction that in doing so they are honoring the text as part of Scripture, not simply reading it as a finished product for reasons of literary criticism. (There is also a holistic movement that proceeds from literary causes, as seen, for example, in the work of Robert Alter, and the two approaches sometimes make common cause. But much holistic exegesis certainly has a theological agenda.) A holistic approach, respecting the text as we have it, is thus felt to undo the damage wrought by traditional biblical criticism.

"Advocacy" Interpretation

Gorringe's passionate advocacy on behalf of the vast majority of Christians, whom biblical scholars can easily ignore as they chat contentedly to each other in their ivory towers, leads naturally to a second element in the indictment against biblical criticism: that it is the preserve of a small coterie of people in the rich Western world, trying to legislate for how the vast mass of humanity ought to read the Bible. *Reading the Bible in the Global Village: Helsinki* and *Decolonizing Biblical Studies*[25] are two recent studies that sum up in their titles what their authors think is wrong with traditional Western biblical criticism. Not only has such criticism detached the Bible from believing communities; it has also appropriated it for a particular group, namely, white, male, Western scholars (what Elisabeth Schüssler Fiorenza refers to as "the malestream"). It is the norms of these people that operate when the Bible is read "critically."

Such has been the argument of many who favor what are sometimes called "advocacy" readings of the Bible, from a liberationist or feminist perspective, or from the standpoint of someone who belongs to a nontraditional

---

anticipated by Northrop Frye in *Anatomy of Criticism* (Princeton, NJ: Princeton University Press, 1957), 56: "The Book of Isaiah can be analyzed into a mass of separate oracles, with three major foci, so to speak, one mainly pre-exilic, one exilic and one post-exilic. The 'higher critics' of the Bible are not literary critics, and we have to make the suggestion ourselves that the Book of Isaiah is in fact the unity it has always been traditionally taken to be, a unity not of authorship but of theme, and that theme in epitome the theme of the Bible as a whole, as the parable of Israel lost, captive, and redeemed."

25. Fernando F. Segovia, *Decolonizing Biblical Studies: A View from the Margins* (Maryknoll, NY: Orbis Books, 2000).

community so far as critical biblical interpretation is concerned (i.e., a *majority* community from all other perspectives!). The point is made well by R. S. Sugirtharajah:

> I would like to make it clear that my attitude toward historical criticism is one of an ambivalence. On the one hand, I would like to affirm the historical method, and I can see its benefits, but on the other, I can see its damaging effects when it is transferred to other parts of the world and especially when it is used to conquer and subjugate other people's texts and stories and cultures. . . . Though historical criticism was liberative particularly to the Western, white and middle classes, it had a shackling and enslaving impact on women, blacks and people of other cultures, as the recent exegetical works of these groups have manifestly demonstrated.[26]

Biblical criticism, it is alleged, has worked with a false self-image of objectivity and unprejudiced detachment, when in fact it has represented the interests of first-world scholars, rather than of people in the developing world, and of men rather than women. The interpretations to which it has led have been slanted.

The charge being leveled against biblical critics is not simply that they have come to the wrong conclusions by the use of methods that might be, in themselves, perfectly acceptable in more skillful hands. It is that the methods themselves are fatally flawed. The whole ideal of objectivity, of simply reading what is "actually there" in the text, deceives. In reality what is being practiced is "eisegesis," reading one's own attitudes into the text, thereby doing violence to it and turning it into a vehicle for violence itself—violence against the oppressed, whether the poor or women or some other minority (actually majority!) community. The charge is a grave one, not to be set aside by pleading that no such effect was intended, for good intentions are not enough to excuse lamentable blindness to the effects of one's actions. This attack on biblical criticism as the academic world of biblical scholarship has received it is not to be ignored with a superior smile.

POSTCRITICAL INTERPRETATION

We have spoken so far as though attacks on biblical criticism came mostly from outside the community of critical scholarship, from those who feel themselves alienated from it and wish to see it reformed or abolished. This is only partly

---

26. R. S. Sugirtharajah, "Critics, Tools and the Global Arena," in *Reading the Bible in the Global Village: Helsinki*, 49–60; quotation, 49 and 52.

true in the case of the canonical approach, for Childs and those who have followed him are themselves no mean critical scholars, able to hold their own in
any critical discussion, even though they have come to feel out of sympathy
with much of the work their colleagues engage in. It is more obviously true of
those calling for the Bible to be given back to the church, who are mostly working in areas of theology other than biblical studies and who are impatient with
the critics' apparent inability or unwillingness to free the Bible to speak in
places where real theology is done, whether that is the pulpit or the local community of faith. It is most true of advocacy interpreters, though many of them
as a matter of fact come out of a training in traditional criticism but have taken
up the cause of those (the vast majority of the human race) who do not.

Be that as it may, there has long been a tradition of protest at the allegedly
numbing or desiccating effect of biblical criticism, from deep within the critical community itself. Even more than the canonical approach, the so-called
biblical theology movement in Anglo-American biblical studies after the Second World War proceeded from within critical scholarship and represented a
sense of disillusionment that this kind of scholarship had not delivered any
great benefits; the vast labor of the mountain of biblical critics had brought
forth only a tiny theological mouse. Criticism had not been, to use the German expression, *ergiebig*, productive. This could be illustrated from the writings of many biblical theologians in Britain and North America in these years,
but perhaps it is more telling to cite two of the most influential writers in the
German tradition, where criticism is felt by many to be most at home.

Walter Eichrodt, in his great *Theology of the Old Testament*, written before
the war but highly influential in the postwar years, states his aim explicitly in
terms of moving beyond historical criticism:

> It is high time that the tyranny of historicism in OT studies was bro-
> ken and the proper approach to our task re-discovered. This is no new
> problem, certainly, but it is one that needs to be solved anew in every
> epoch of knowledge—*the problem of how to understand the realm of OT
> belief in its structural unity and how, by examining on the one hand its reli-
> gious environment and on the other its essential coherence with the NT, to
> illuminate its profoundest meaning.*[27]

27. "In der Tat ist es hohe Zeit, daß auf dem Gebiet des Alten Testaments einmal mit der
Alleinherrschaft des Historismus gebrochen und der Weg zurückgefunden wird zu der alten
und in jeder wissenschaftlichen Epoche neu zu lösenden *Aufgabe, die alttestamentliche
Glaubenswelt in ihrer strukturellen Einheit zu begreifen und unter Berücksichtigung ihrer
religiösen Umwelt einerseits, ihres Wesenszusammenhanges mit dem Neuen Testament andererseits
in ihrem tiefsten Sinngehalt zu deuten*" (Walter Eichrodt, *Theologie des Alten Testaments*, 1:4;
Eichrodt's emphasis). For the complicated history of Eichrodt's *Theology* and its translation,
see the bibliography.

Criticism is not invalid for him, it is true; but on its own it represents a poor substitute for a proper theological engagement with Scripture.

The other scholar who should be mentioned here is Gerhard von Rad, author of the other great *Old Testament Theology* of the twentieth century. Like Eichrodt, von Rad was a fully convinced biblical critic, who assumed the results of previous criticism (sources of the Pentateuch and so on) in his own work but consistently sought to move biblical study into areas he thought more productive, that is, theological areas. How far-reaching his criticism of biblical criticism was is well summed up by Manfred Oeming, who draws close parallels with von Rad's Heidelberg contemporary Hans-Georg Gadamer. Oeming draws out six points on which von Rad, like Gadamer, criticized historical criticism:[28]

1. The historical-critical method is significant and necessary, but no more than preliminary to a full understanding of texts: "An approach to the texts through method should, it may be conceded, not be abolished or bypassed; but a grasp of the full truth of the tradition transcends any merely methodical approach."[29] This is reminiscent in many ways of Childs, who also argues that historical-critical method is needed, yet that it fails to deliver more than the most rudimentary help to the interpreter who is looking for the theological significance of the text.
2. The interpreter's assumptions (which for von Rad means his or her Christian beliefs) are a perfectly proper, indeed necessary, part of the interpretation of the text.
3. The meaning of a text is linked strongly to how it has been read in the past (its *Wirkungsgeschichte*). This is an issue we have not touched on so far, but it will become important in our discussion later.
4. Interpretation needs to focus on the tradition within which the text stands, not treating the text as an isolated entity.
5. The process of the transmission of texts across time acts as a filter, allowing the best elements to persist: thus the final form of a text has a special status as against earlier stages in its growth. This, again, unites von Rad to the ideas of Childs and disposes him too to be interested in the texts as they stand, rather than in hypothetical earlier components or sources.
6. Historical reconstruction on the basis of the text is always somewhat dubious: "Establishing historically what happened misses the point of the claim of truth which tradition poses to the reader's present."[30] This reminds one

---

28. Manfred Oeming, *Gesamtbiblische Theologien der Gegenwart* (Stuttgart: Kohlhammer, 1985), 42–44. A seventh point of contact with Gadamer—a shared Humboldtian philosophy of language, according to which language determines thought—is important but not relevant in the present context.

29. "Der methodische Zugang zu den Texten soll zwar nicht abgeschafft oder übersprungen werden, aber eine Erfassung der vollen Wahrheit der Tradition transzendiert bloß methodischen Zugriff" (ibid., 42).

30. "Die historische Konstatierung dessen, was gewesen ist, verfehlt den Wahrheitsanspruch, den die Tradition an die jeweilige Gegenwart stellt" (ibid.).

of Barth's opinion, cited above, that we should not always be striving to get *behind* the text but should read it as it is. The "reconstructive" side of historical criticism may produce historically interesting results, but it does not contribute to theological *Ergiebigkeit*.

None of this prevented von Rad from being himself a biblical critic, who often delved beneath the text's surface and who was quite prepared to talk of sources and of historical development underlying the text. But it does align him with some of the movements we have been discussing, in suggesting a certain distancing from biblical criticism, at least as he understood it. The first readers of his great Genesis commentary felt that here was a breath of fresh air, in which the older arguments about the exact delineation of sources gave way to a theological evaluation of the finished text; in that, von Rad certainly anticipated both the canonical approach and some of the newer literary approaches to reading biblical texts. And in the process he made an implicit or explicit criticism of criticism.

At the same time, one should be careful in recruiting von Rad to the post-critical cause. While he could strongly affirm the need to move beyond analysis to synthesis, he was not happy with any attempt to interpret the Bible as though the analysis had never happened. Against W. Vischer's assertion that we should simply read "what is there" ("was da steht") in the Old Testament, von Rad commented:

> Well, what is there is a text that owes its form to the coming together of very diverse sources. Let us pose the question quite sharply: when is it justified for a theological interpretation of the Old Testament to ignore such a conspicuous complexity in the text? Surely it is obvious that this can be legitimate only if the redactional combination of sources does not only mark a rounding-off from a literary-historical point of view but also theologically contains a witness to faith which transcends the actuality of the witnesses taken in their separate forms. It is this that Vischer absolutely needed to demonstrate if he wanted to receive the confidence of scrupulous readers faced with such a literary unification. But so long as we remain unable to see a witness which is topical for us in the chaotic final form of the Pentateuch, but can see only garbled redactional work, then theology is obliged to take the greatest interest in surveying as exactly as possible the theological profile of the individual sources.[31]

31. "Nun, es steht da ein Text, der seine Gestalt dem Zusammenschluß von sehr verschiedenen Quellen verdankt. Stellen wir einmal die Frage ganz scharf: Wann dürfte eine theologische Auslegung des Alten Testaments die Tatsache einer derart auffallenden Komplexität des Textes unberücksichtigt lassen? Doch offenbar nur dann, wenn dieser redaktionelle Zusammenschluß der Quellen nicht nur literargeschichtlich einen Abschluß

As Smend remarks, Vischer's position would probably be more acceptable to many nowadays, with the canonical approach widely appreciated, than it was in the 1930s (when it might have struck the reader as almost fundamentalist in character).

While all this demonstrates that the canonical approach is in some ways not so new as it is sometimes thought to be, it also shows that there was perceived to be a certain vulnerability in biblical criticism already in the early 1960s (von Rad) and indeed even in the 1930s (Eichrodt). It was seen as flawed, in that it apparently did not allow any place to theological interpretation but kept the reader of the Bible in a kind of arid scholasticism. For Barth, the trouble with biblical criticism was that it was not critical enough: it criticized the text but was unable to criticize itself and to see where its own blind spots lay. "For me the historical critics need to be more critical!"[32] What was needed was, as Smend calls it, a postcritical interpretation of the Bible.[33] And on that, all of the writers we have been surveying would probably agree.

Biblical criticism may have been needed in the past, they would perhaps say, in order to challenge interpretations that had hardened under the dead hand of ecclesiastical authority. But to persist with it now—when the threat comes instead from the excessive liberty of the modern world, with its secularism and wild chasing after ever-new opinions—is to elevate what was a necessary corrective into an eternal principle. Indeed, historical criticism has by now itself hardened into a form of domination from which we need emancipating once again! It is time to move on. This is argued very neatly by Jürgen Ebach:

> The historical-critical method of exegesis originally came in to destroy illegitimate relationships of dominance whose claim to legitimacy

---

bedeutet, sondern auch theologisch ein Glaubenszeugnis enthält, das die Aktualität der Glaubenszeugnisse in ihrer Sonderung überbietet. Diesen Beweis hätte Vischer unbedingt führen müssen, wenn er bei einer solchen literarischen Vereinerleiung sich das Vertrauen gewissenhafter Leser erhalten wolle. Solange wir aber in der unförmigen Jetztgestalt des Pentateuch nicht das letztaktuelle Zeugnis zu sehen vermögen, sondern entstellende Redaktorenarbeit, solange muß der Theologe das höchste Interesse daran haben, das theologische Profil der Einzelquellen möglichst genau zu übersehen" (*Theologische Bibliothek* 14 [1935]: 249ff.; cited in Smend, *Deutsche Alttestamentler*, 237–38.)

32. "Kritischer müßten mir die Historisch-Kritischen sein!" (Karl Barth, *Römerbrief* [Zurich: Theologischer Verlag, 1919], x; trans. as *The Epistle to the Romans* [2nd ed., London: Oxford University Press, 1933, from 6th German ed.]; quoted in Rudolf Smend, "Nachkritische Schriftauslegung," in *Parrhesia. Karl Barth zum 80. Geburtstag*, ed. E. Busch, J. Fangmeier, and M. Geiger [Zurich: EVZ-Verlag, 1966], 215–37; also in Smend, *Die Mitte des Alten Testaments* [Munich: Kaiser Verlag, 1986], 212–32; and in Smend, *Bibel und Wissenschaft* [Tübingen: Mohr Siebeck, 2004], 230–35; quotation, *Bibel und Wissenschaft*, 231).

33. Rudolf Smend, "Nachkritische Schriftauslegung."

rested on an ahistorical (or suprahistorical) and uncritical interpretation of texts—biblical texts above all. Historical-critical exegesis pursued the *re*construction of the originally intended sense of a (biblical)
text, and this sprang from a critical interest in examining a meaning
that was currently alleged to have been intended[34] all along. . . . The
historical-critical method owes its rise and its triumph to the Enlightenment, and to the Enlightenment's interest in criticizing ideology and
furthering emancipation. But thereby it participates in the "dialectic of
the Enlightenment"—the conversion of emancipation into a fresh ideology, of freedom into domination, of illumination into obfuscation. A
method that when left unexamined proved to be more persnickety
than critical came to be concerned with its own self-affirmation. The
historical-critical method arose in order to criticize rigorously the
plausibility-system of ecclesiastical domination that existed in the Middle Ages and lasted well into modern times, but it became itself the
theological sport of a dominant academic system, contributing to that
system's cleansing of itself from subjective forms of appropriation and
modes of living. The historical-critical method arose in order to
deploy historical reconstruction against the tendency of ecclesiastical
hermeneutics to use biblical texts to construct stable systems, but
it proved able to turn into an instrument for removing the basis of a
critical-constructive appropriation of biblical texts through the very
means of historical *re*construction.[35]

---

34. On the "intended" sense, see chapter 4 above, pp. 71–80.

35. "Die historisch-kritische Methode der Exegese trat einst an, illegitime Herrschaftsver-
hältnisse zu destruieren, deren Geltungsanspruch auf einer un- bzw. übergeschichtlichen und
unkritischen Interpretation von—vor allem biblischen—Texten basierte. Historisch-kritische
Exegese verfolgte die *Re*konstruktion des einst gemeinten Sinnes eines (biblischen) Textes aus
dem kritischen Interesse an der Überprüfung eines gegenwärtig für immer schon gemeinten
ausgegebenen Sinnes. . . . Die historisch-kritische Methode verdankt ihre Entstehung und
ihren Siegeszug der Aufklärung und ihrem ideologiekritischen, emanzipatorischen Interesse.
Doch hat sie damit teil an der 'Dialektik der Aufklärung', dem Umschlag von Emanzipation
in Ideologie, von Befreiung in Herrschaft, von Erhellung in Verdunkelung. Selbst affirmativ
wurde eine Methode, die sich unhinterfragt weiter verdrossen als kritisch bezeichnet. Angetreten, das mittelalterliche und weit in die Neuzeit reichende Plausibilitätssystem kirchlicher
Herrschaft wissenschaftlich zu kritisieren, ist die historisch-kritische Methode selbst zur theologischen Spielart eines herrschenden Wissenschaftssystems geworden, an dessen Selb-
streinigung von subjektiven Aneignungsformen, von Lebenspraxis sie Anteil hat. Angetreten,
historische Rekonstruktion gegen systemstabilisierende kirchliche Hermeneutik biblischer
Texte zu wenden, konnte historisch-kritische Exegese selbst zu einem Instrument werden, mit
dem vermittels historischer *Re*konstruktion kritisch-konstruktiven Aneignungswesen biblischer Texte der Boden entzogen werden soll" (Jürgen Ebach, *Ursprung und Ziel: Erinnerte
Zukunft und erhoffte Vergangenheit. Exegesen, Reflexionen, Geschichten* [Neukirchen-Vluyn:
Neukirchener Verlag, 1986], 49–50). Cf. the comments of Paul S. Minear, *The Bible and the
Historian: Breaking the Silence about God in Biblical Studies* (Nashville: Abingdon Press, 2002),
35: he argues that the publication of Ernesti's *Institutio Interpretis* "was a new weapon in 'the
battle with stark orthodoxy,' a battle that had to be won before other advances could be made.
This weapon effectively liberated scholars, widened the areas open to research, and produced

An important theme in the call for postcritical interpretation is the need for a "second naiveté." The first naiveté in biblical study is a simple, precritical acceptance of what is in the Bible as "gospel truth," and more or less all the writers we have discussed are agreed that that is no longer available to anyone practicing scholarly study of the Bible. Biblical criticism puts an end to that naiveté. But Barth argued powerfully that there was a need, after criticism, to become naive again, in the sense of recapturing the openness and wonder in the presence of the text that had characterized precritical reading. Smend shows how Emil Brunner defended Barth against the accusation that his *Commentary on Romans* was "naive" in the ordinary sense of the word, as though it simply ignored academic study of Paul in his context and accepted him as an authority figure. Yet Barth did believe that naiveté could be recaptured postcritically:

> One certainly cannot call Barth's position naive "in the vulgar sense."
> Even so, it is possible to understand it as a form of naiveté. . . . Barth
> himself used the concept to refer to two periods in the reading of
> Scripture, the periods before and after historical criticism. Before crit-
> icism it was possible to be *still* naive in one's reading of Scripture. Crit-
> icism put an end to naiveté, but not forever; rather, there is a
> postcritical era, in which the Bible can *again* be read naively. Barth's
> own exegesis of Scripture represents this *third* era, not—as one might
> suppose if one was unaware of the fact that this third era existed as a
> separate entity—the first. Criticism does not lie before but behind it.[36]

Here is an expression of the point in Barth's own words:

---

vast alterations in the reconception of biblical history. Today, however, that rebellion has become a new 'establishment,' with its own restrictive axioms. A 'union card' is now virtually limited to scholars who have been professionally trained to apply objective methods and to restrict their conclusions to data which can be verified by those methods." Barth made a similar point: the historical-critical approach to the Bible is now a given for all scholars, he argued, and there is no need to keep on pushing at an open door; it is time to move on. See the comments in Smend, "Nachkritische Schriftauslegung," 232–33. This was in Barth's *Das Wort Gottes und die Theologie* (Munich: Kaiser Verlag, 1925), 76. My own perception is that, eighty years later, the door is still not open for all who study the Bible, and biblical criticism is now by no means accepted so unproblematically as Barth was able to assume then.

36. "Naiv 'im vulgären Sinn' kann man Barths Position in der Tat nicht nennen. Trotzdem läßt sie sich als Naivität verstehen. . . . Barth selbst hat den Ausdruck auf zwei Perioden der Lektüre der Schrift angewandt, nämlich die vor der historischen Kritik und die nach ihr. Vor der Kritik ließ sich die Schrift *noch* naiv lesen. Die Kritik hat der Naivität ein Ende gemacht, aber nicht für immer; es gibt vielmehr eine nachkritische Epoche, in der die Schrift *wieder* naiv gelesen werden kann. Die Barthsche Schriftauslegung repräsentiert diese dritte Epoche, nicht, wie man in Unkenntnis der Tatsache, daß diese dritte Epoche überhaupt etwas für sich ist, anzunehmen pflegt, die erste. Sie hat die Kritik nicht vor, sondern hinter sich" (Smend, "Nachkritische Schriftauslegung," 233).

> In reading the biblical histories one may of course ask about those dis-
> tinctions [sc. between what can be historically proved and what has the
> character either of saga or of conscious invention], and even make
> them, hypothetically. But in that case one will be withdrawing from
> the kerygmatic sense in which the stories are told—the more so, the
> more one makes these distinctions, and the more decisive they become
> in the exposition. To be true to the kerygmatic sense one must either
> *not yet* have asked about these distinctions, or, having once asked them,
> must ask them *no longer*—one must read the histories naively, either
> *still* or *once again*, in their unity and wholeness. It is then that the his-
> tories communicate what they are trying to communicate, and not
> otherwise! . . . After one has made such distinctions, one must put the
> stories back together again, and read the whole as a whole, as it pre-
> sents itself in the text, with an examined, critical naiveté.[37]

The idea of a second naiveté has been extensively developed by Paul Ricoeur,
to describe the point at which we start to attend to the text as something that
addresses us.[38] But we will return to Ricoeur later, since his espousal of second
naiveté does not at all have a polemical thrust against biblical criticism, but
sees this as an essential precondition.

TWO STAGES IN CRITICAL READING

The arguments against traditional biblical criticism outlined above are highly
complex and often passionately felt. They add up to an indictment of what are
called critical approaches as essentially hostile to the text, or at least to its
appropriation by readers who expect to be challenged, nourished, or inspired
by it. I have tried to present this case as persuasively as possible and not to distort it, but it will be apparent that I do not share it myself. What may be said

---

37. "Man kann selbstverständlich auch bei der Lektüre der biblischen Historien nach
jenen Unterscheidungen fragen, sie auch hypothetisch vollziehen. Nur eben deren keryg-
matischem Sinn, in welchem sie erzählt sind, wird man auch dann—je bestimmter man sie
vollzieht und je maßgebender man sie für die Erklärung werden läßt, um so sicherer—
entziehen. Um ihm gerecht zu werden, muß man nach jeden Unterscheidungen entweder
noch nicht gefragt haben oder, nachdem man nach ihnen gefragt hat, *nicht* mehr fragen, muß
man diese Historien *noch* oder *wieder* naiv, in ihrer Einheit und Ganzheit, lesen. Dann sagen
sie nämlich, was sie sagen wollen—sonst nicht! . . . Man wird dann jene Unterscheidungen,
nachdem man sie gemacht hat, wieder zurückstellen und das Ganze (in so geprüfter, kritischer Naivität!) als Ganzes lesen, wie es sich im Text darbietet" (Barth, *Die Kirchliche Dogmatik* IV/2 [1955], 541–42.

38. See the discussion of Ricoeur's "second naiveté" in Anthony C. Thiselton, *New Horizons in Hermeneutics: The Theory and Practice of Transforming Biblical Reading* (London:
HarperCollins, 1992), 344–78, esp. 360–61.

in response, by way of a defense of biblical criticism against the charge that it diminishes the Bible?

The heart of the matter is this. Assimilating any text, the Bible included, is a two-stage operation. The first stage is a perception of the text's meaning; the second, an evaluation of that meaning in relation to what one already believes to be the case. (This may or may not lead to a third stage in which one's beliefs about what is the case are changed, but that is not the point at the moment.) This operation cannot be collapsed into a single process, in which meaning is perceived and evaluated at one and the same time and by the same operation.

The point can be illustrated from feminist criticism of the Bible. It is common for feminist critics to argue that traditional, largely male interpreters have read the Bible in ways that are demeaning to women. And this is very likely the case. But this may mean two quite different things.

First, it may mean that the texts are indeed misogynistic, as many would argue is the case with the "prophetic pornography" in Ezekiel 16 and 23, or with Hosea's "disciplining" of his wife in Hosea 2. The complaint then is that male scholars, while reporting correctly on what the text has to say, have not stated their own revulsion at it or, worse, have actually connived with it as though what it says were quite acceptable.

Alternatively, what may be meant is that male scholars have read misogynistic attitudes into the Bible when they are not there in the text.[39] An example, actually from within the Bible itself, might be the argument in 1 Timothy 2:14 that it was not Adam who was deceived in the garden of Eden, but Eve, who misled him. One might very well argue that this is a misreading of Genesis 3, in which it is perfectly clear that both Adam and Eve are deceived: the misogynistic writer of 1 Timothy has decided, against the text, to heap all the blame on the woman.[40]

39. This tends to be the line taken by Phyllis Trible. She argues, for example, that some translations have suppressed imagery of God parenting or giving birth that is actually there in the text. Thus the Jerusalem Bible rendered Deut. 32:18, "You forgot the Rock who begot you, unmindful of the God who *fathered* you," whereas the RSV had more correctly preserved an image of giving birth: "You were unmindful of the Rock that begot you, and you forgot the God who *gave you birth*" (see *God and the Rhetoric of Sexuality* [Philadelphia: Fortress Press, 1978], 62 and 70n9).

40. There is a similar dichotomy in feminist readings of Shakespeare. Some critics argue that Shakespeare is incorrigibly misogynistic and that the critic should say so; others that for his time Shakespeare had quite "advanced" views on women and that many of the plays subtly subvert male dominance. The latter may sometimes arise from "a refusal to admit that Shakespeare could write a play as sexist as this [*The Taming of the Shrew*] appears to be" (Sean McEvoy, *Shakespeare: The Basics* [London and New York: Routledge, 2000], 131); this is quite similar to the tendency of some biblical scholars to explain away misogyny in the biblical text, out of a similar feeling that the Bible could not have got it so badly wrong! The *Winter's Tale*

Indeed, probably very often both things are true: scholars rightly perceive that there are some biblical texts that express hostility to women, and are by that so encouraged in their own misogyny that they then read the same hostility even into texts that do not express it.

But this whole line of reasoning breaks down, it seems to me, if we cannot distinguish between establishing the sense of the text and evaluating it. To take the first case just presented, it makes sense to reproach male scholars for not dissociating themselves from misogynistic texts only if those texts are indeed misogynistic. About this, there may of course be debate—some feminists think the Bible is deplorably misogynistic, others that it has only been read so. But suppose the Bible really does contain misogynistic passages (which I must say seems to me to be the case); then one can deplore this only if one is first allowed to say that the passages are actually there. One must be able, irrespective of one's own attitude, to recognize that there are places where the Bible is hostile to women. Otherwise the argument can never get off the ground. I am sure that feminists are right in thinking that many male scholars in the past did not notice misogyny in the text because they were not sensitized to it. But to say that is precisely to say that the texts were there and had that meaning all along.

To take the second case, where male scholars are accused of reading misogyny into the text—heightening the role of Eve, as is done in 1 Timothy, or overlooking the strong women in much of the Old Testament (Rebekah, Deborah, Abigail, for example)—this again makes sense only if the deplorable male attitudes can be compared with the evidence of the text itself. "Reading in" implies seeing what is not there, or distorting what is there because of some prejudice. Again, it seems to me true that scholarship often has skewed the text and is guilty as charged. But to recognize skewing presupposes that one has a sense of what an unskewed reading would look like. And this implies that one can understand the text correctly and compare one's correct understanding with the incorrect understanding of others.

Some kind of objectivity in interpretation is thus logically presupposed by the feminist case. That case—which I personally find generally convincing—depends on the reader's being able to make a judgment about what the texts

---

and *The Taming of the Shrew* are obvious cases where these issues arise. See, on the "misogynistic" interpretation, Lisa Jardine, *Still Harping on Daughters: Women and Drama in the Age of Shakespeare* (London and New York: Harvester Wheatsheaf, 2nd ed., 1989); for the view that Shakespeare should be read as in favor of the liberation of women, see Karen Newman, "Renaissance Family Politics and Shakespeare's *The Taming of the Shrew*," in *Shakespeare's Comedies*, ed. G. Waller (Harlow: Longman 1986); Lisa Jardine, "Portia's Ring: Unruly Women and Structures of Exchange in *The Merchant of Venice*," in *The Merchant of Venice*, ed. M. Coyle, New Casebooks (Basingstoke: Macmillan, 1998).

mean, on the basis of which he or she can go on to criticize biblical scholars either for the moral failing of not dissociating themselves from a misogynistic Bible or for the exegetical failing (which is surely also a moral one) of reading misogynistic meanings into texts that lack them. What can surely not be said is that male scholars have been culpable in reading as misogynistic texts that have no determinate meaning anyway, only "meanings we choose."[41]

Anyone familiar with modern literary and hermeneutical theory will see at once that I am here taking a position on matters that are very hotly disputed at the moment and coming out in favor of the idea that "texts have meanings."[42] My point, however, is the logical one that feminist criticism, so far from denying determinate meaning to texts, actually requires it if it is to be coherent. The feminist case is that *the text will not support* the misogynistic use being made of it; it is not simply that misogyny is unacceptable, which is true but is not a point about biblical interpretation.

Now it seems to me that the same applies, mutatis mutandis, to other advocacy readings. The founders of liberation theology argued that the Bible expresses a preferential option for the poor, and they were prepared to argue for this by citing appropriate biblical passages and showing how the whole drift of many biblical narratives confirms the point. They were not arguing that the Bible can be read as expressing this option if one is already convinced that it is right, but on the contrary were trying to convince scholars who had not yet seen it that this exegesis was superior. This makes sense only on the basis that the question of the Bible's attitude to the poor is something that can be *discovered*, not imposed. Of course there was here a severe indictment of traditional Western scholarship, for having failed to see the challenge the Bible raises to those in power. Liberation theologians were saying that traditional critics had culpably failed to recognize the option for the poor. But they had failed to do

41. Cf. *The Meanings We Choose: Hermeneutical Ethics, Indeterminacy and the Conflict of Interpretations*, ed. Charles H. Cosgrove, Journal for the Study of the Old Testament: Supplement Series 411 (London: T. & T. Clark, 2004). As Cosgrove sees it, there is absolutely no determinate sense in texts, so that the question of what we should take them to mean depends wholly on what it is moral for us to believe ourselves—thus, for example, he writes: "Given the overwhelmingly patriarchal cast of biblical literature, Schüssler Fiorenza's discovery of a radically egalitarian way of construing the 'labourer' and 'coworker' language in Paul is very significant for the egalitarian cause in theology, and (for egalitarians) that is a powerful reason to embrace her interpretation theologically and not to treat the theological appropriation of its opposite as a neutral alternative to be celebrated under the banner of pluralism" (59). This confuses two things, the discovery of what Paul meant and its theological appropriation by us: this seems to me simply obvious. But it is not obvious at all to the authors of this collection—indeed, to them it is obviously mistaken.

42. Cf. Valentine Cunningham, *Reading after Theory*, 88: "You see, of course, that I assume there are things actually in a text."

so, it was urged, when it had been staring them in the face all the time in the biblical text. In other words, Western scholars were condemned, not for practicing biblical criticism, but for not practicing it well enough.

This means that the sense of passion shining through much writing of an advocacy kind is not misplaced, but its basis is not always being correctly understood. Criticizing the critics for failing to see what is in the text is not at all the expression of an anticritical spirit; it is saying, with Barth, that criticism has not been critical enough. Advocacy writers tend, however, to throw out the baby with the bathwater and to talk as though the failure of critics to perceive the truths that advocacy writers have perceived shows the bankruptcy of criticism. On the contrary, however, to say so undermines their own position, which depends utterly on there being an objective meaning in the Bible that supports the case they are arguing. No liberationist, surely, wants to argue that one should read the Bible as if it supported human liberation even though it doesn't, or even if it has no opinions of its own on anything. That would make it a matter of indifference which text one chose to read; one could tell people to read *Mein Kampf as if* it supported human liberation! The whole point is that the Bible is an effective weapon in the fight for liberation because even those who oppose such liberation can be brought to see that they have the Bible against them. And this presupposes that interpretation is a two-stage process: first, discover the meaning; then, evaluate or apply it.[43] E. D. Hirsch makes a telling point against such attempts to reduce the stages in reading to a single interpretative-cum-applicative one when he criticizes Gadamer (a classic case of this) by saying that "in the Gadamerian mode of interpretation, meaning is *made* to conform to the critic's view about what is true."[44] It is this danger that biblical criticism in its classic form seeks to avoid.

In insisting that exegetical proposals be tested against the text, then, critics are not being hostile to the Bible or trying to prevent anyone from taking its message to heart. They are simply trying to establish what that message is.

We can illustrate some of these points from a book whose stated aim is to

43. In postmodernist thinking, the idea of two stages here is strongly contested, since it is believed that the very perception of meaning is entirely determined by where one is standing. Indeed, this is true not just of reading but of every attempt to appropriate "external" reality. Cf. Elizabeth Freund: "The swerve to the reader assumes that our relationship to reality is not a positive knowledge but a hermeneutic construct, that all perception is already an act of interpretation, that the notion of a 'text-in-itself' is empty, that a poem cannot be understood in isolation from its effects, and that subject and object are indivisibly bound" (*The Return of the Reader: Reader-response Criticism*, ed. T. Hawkes, New Accents [London and New York: Methuen, 1987], 5).

44. E. D. Hirsch Jr., "Meaning and Significance Reinterpreted," *Critical Inquiry* 11 (1984): 202–25; quotation, 218.

give the Bible back to the church: Paul S. Minear's *The Bible and the Historian: Breaking the Silence about God in Biblical Studies*. The whole drift of Minear's argument, very much in line with *Reclaiming the Bible for the Church*, is that historical-critical study has worked to impose on the biblical text its own ideas of history and, indeed, of ontological reality, thereby blocking any appreciation of the saving gospel contained in the Bible. New Testament scholars, he argues, have been utterly reductionist in insisting that biblical history should conform to modern (post-Enlightenment) standards of truth. They have not been able to understand the New Testament in its own terms because they have methodically excluded the possibility of a real encounter with the transcendent God. Indeed, he maintains,

> I want . . . to argue that the deficiency in that [sc. the historical-critical] method extends beyond its metaphysical (or anti-metaphysical) presuppositions. It is deficient in accomplishing its historical objective, the recovery and description of past events in their original sequence and significance. When the historian succeeds, the story of the past remains in Fuchs's words "an incomplete obituary notice." This incompleteness condemns the method. The net used fails to catch the data that to early Christians constituted the significance of the events in which they shared, while the data that the historian does recapture would have been to them of only secondary importance.[45]

Minear goes on to illustrate his point by detailed studies of, in particular, the eschatological frame of reference of many New Testament writers and their communities. He presents a study of Revelation, which, he says, contains a conception of time wholly unlike "ours" and which modern biblical interpretation has therefore been unable to deal with adequately. "It is inevitable that historical science should reflect the cosmological presuppositions of the historian's own age. Among these presuppositions, the most pervasive and influential in our time are basal attitudes toward space and time."[46] These presuppositions have, he suggests, so conditioned scholars working on Revelation that they have failed to understand its remarkable picture of space and time. At the end of the chapter, he shows that John's conception cannot be adequately grasped through various "hermeneutical procedures": it does not conform to a gnostic celestial astronomy or to millennial speculations, nor can it be grasped through a contrast between biblical and Hellenistic thought. It is, he concludes, "wrong for a non-prophetic writer to classify the prophet John according to a scheme that gives to the

---

45. *The Bible and the Historian*, 48.
46. Ibid., 156.

scholar's presuppositions regarding space and time genuinely arbitrary prece-
dence over the prophet's own presuppositions."[47]

Now if modern students have been guilty of thus imposing their own attitudes on the New Testament, then Minear is no doubt right to criticize them.
The basis on which he does so, however, is his belief that his reading of Revelation is truer to the meaning of the text than theirs. What is this, if not an
exercise in biblical criticism? What is wrong with those attacked by Minear is
not that they have been historical-critical, surely, but that they have not been
historical-critical enough. They have failed to respect the otherness of the text
and have made it conform to their own preconceptions. Is it not precisely to
avoid this kind of thing that biblical criticism was developed? Minear's reading, if it is persuasive, is an example of historical criticism carried out more
successfully than that of those he opposes. He has been able, by clearing his
mind of modern presuppositions, to enter into the thought world of the text
of Revelation, while others have seen it through the distorting lens of their
own ideas. That is precisely the kind of thing I would understand biblical criticism to amount to. Instead of reading what we expect or would like to find,
we try to read the text on its own terms; only then do we go on to compare it
with the way we ourselves think.

Thus Minear is an unwilling witness against his own cause, precisely by
being such an excellent biblical critic. What he argues for and exemplifies is
good biblical criticism; what he attacks is bad biblical criticism. The ability to
recognize what the text is saying when that is *not* what we would say ourselves
is one of the pivots on which the whole critical operation turns.

THEOLOGICAL READING

It will by now seem unsurprising that I think a similar argument can be
deployed against those who talk of reclaiming the Bible for the church. Their
greatest charge against biblical criticism is that it brackets out questions of theological truth when studying the Bible and that to do so is evidence of an essentially secular or faithless attitude. If one begins with such an attitude, it is asked,
how will one ever be able to reconnect the Bible with faith? Yet the problem
will be of one's own making. It seems to me, on the contrary, that this bracketing out is methodologically essential. One cannot establish what the Bible
means if one insists on reading it as necessarily conforming to what one already
believes to be true—which is what a theological reading amounts to.

47. Ibid., 164.

This does not at all mean that readers of the Bible should be uninterested in its theology, or that biblical critics have been. The majority of biblical critics in modern times have been Christian believers, and it is implausible to think that they read the Bible with indifference to its theology. Nearly all the Old Testament scholars surveyed by Rudolf Smend in his *Deutsche Alttestamentler in drei Jahrhunderten* understood themselves as theologians and were at ease in theological faculties. What they did, however, was to engage in precisely the two-stage process described above. They did not permit their religious convictions to tell them what the biblical text meant; instead, they tried to discover what the Bible meant, and only then went on to ask how it fitted (or did not fit) with the religious convictions they already had. This produced results of which many modern readers disapprove. In Julius Wellhausen, for example, it resulted in a denigration of the theology of the priestly writer (the P source of the Pentateuch) as legalistic because of its concentration on matters of cult, a denigration that most scholars nowadays think unfairly dismissive and perhaps potentially or even actually anti-Semitic, as many Jews did at the time. But the point is that Wellhausen began by trying to establish what the priestly writer was actually saying; the value judgment was separate from the description, and we may accept one while rejecting the other. (Very few scholars would want to deny that P is massively concerned with the cult—indeed, this is one of the things many now find so satisfactory about it.) Wellhausen did not "read" P *as if* it expressed the sentiments he himself would have espoused (roughly those of liberal Protestantism), but recognized that what it taught was at variance from this. He felt free (as more recent scholarship tends to have been shy of feeling) to go on to pass judgment on its teachings. But he did not misread the text as if it said what he would have preferred it to say—quite the reverse, in fact.

It is on the whole those who believe in "moving beyond" criticism who are most prone to read their own theological systems into the scriptural text, and this is just what we should expect. Walter Eichrodt's attempt to move beyond mere historical criticism resulted in an Old Testament theology marked by exactly the kind of covenant theology one might have predicted on the basis of his Calvinism, mediated through Karl Barth.[48] Gerhard von Rad ostensibly described the theological system to be found in the Old Testament, but the result is strikingly Lutheran in its emphases, as pointed out trenchantly by Jon Levenson in commenting on the essay "Faith Reckoned as Righteousness," written in 1951:

48. See David G. Spriggs, *Two Old Testament Theologies: A Comparative Evaluation of the Contribution of Eichrodt and von Rad to Our Understanding of the Nature of Old Testament Theology* (London: SCM, 1974).

This brief sketch [in Levenson's preceding few paragraphs] of the premodern exegesis of Gen 15:6 enables us to locate von Rad's reading within the Pauline-Lutheran line of interpretation. His assumption that "only faith . . . brings man into a right relationship" implies an exclusion that is not to be found in the Hebrew Bible and certainly not in the J document, the pentateuchal source responsible for this verse. . . . Within the limited context of theological interpretation informed by historical criticism—the context von Rad intended—his essay must be judged unsuccessful. Within another limited context, however—the confessional elucidation of Scripture for purposes of Lutheran reaffirmation—it is an impressive success.[49]

This is a backhanded compliment von Rad would hardly have savored.[50] Compare James Barr:

Far from it being the case that biblical criticism introduced and encouraged an orgy of anticonfessional libertinism, critical scholars have been much more worthy of blame for being excessively governed and guided by the ruling trends of their own confessional tradition. Bultmann is an obvious example: for surely his entire theological position can be plausibly read as deriving from a profound and extreme application of the Lutheran understanding of justification by faith. If he thought that faith should not be built upon the reliability of historical reports about the life of Christ, this was not (as Anglo-Saxon critics have often supposed) a result of "historical scepticism," but because faith itself would be in danger of destruction if it relied upon such a support.[51]

Similarly, it is no surprise to find that Brevard Childs's *Biblical Theology of the Old and New Testaments* traces a theological system in the whole Bible that can be summarized under headings that could come from a Reformed textbook on Christian doctrine:

The Identity of God
God the Creator
Covenant, Election, People of God

49. Jon Levenson, "Why Jews Are Not Interested in Biblical Theology," in *Judaic Perspectives on Ancient Israel*, ed. J. Neusner, B. A. Levine, and E. S. Frerichs (Philadelphia: Fortress, 1987), 281–307; quotation, 303-4.

50. One might make a similar point about Walther Zimmerli. His great Ezekiel commentary (*Ezekiel: A Commentary on the Book of the Prophet Ezekiel* [Philadelphia: Fortress, 1979–83]) stresses the possibility of the conversion of non-Israelites to a degree that perhaps expresses more his own Christian hope than the natural horizons of the book itself.

51. Barr, *Holy Scripture: Canon, Authority, Criticism* (Oxford: Oxford University Press, 1983), 108–9.

Christ the Lord
Reconciliation with God
Law and Gospel
Humanity: Old and New
Biblical Faith
God's Kingdom and Rule
The Shape of the Obedient Life: Ethics

No doubt it is possible that the Bible and Reformed systematics really do coincide to this extent, but most interpreters would surely think that there are at least some points of variance. It looks as though there is an element of "reading in" at work.

IS BIBLICAL SCHOLARSHIP TOO THEOLOGICAL?

There is, in fact, an opposite case to be made: that much biblical scholarship has been altogether too theologically motivated and for that reason has often distorted the plain meaning of the biblical text. Such a case is made by David Clines[52] and Philip Davies.[53] They point out how seldom critics have been willing to recognize in the biblical text ideas that genuinely challenge their prior religious convictions, and argue that what is needed is not at all more theologically committed interpretation, but far less. For them, the currently prevailing idea that criticism has taken the Bible away from the churches is a complete straw man, which helps pious critics to delude themselves into thinking that they have been quite daring in their interpretations, when in fact they have been firmly in the grip of a theology (or ideology, as Clines and Davies would probably call it). They would, I think, agree in substance with what I wrote in the festschrift for Ronald Clements in 1999:

> On the one hand, most historical critics probably thought their historical conclusions were in themselves of religious importance. Since the God Christians believed in was continuous with the God worshipped as Yahweh in Old Testament times, what was then believed about him, as it could be reconstructed through historical criticism, could not be a matter of indifference to the modern believer. Paradoxically, the suggestion that the Christian God is not continuous with Yahweh, who is simply an ancient Near Eastern god of a fairly standard type, has come to be made only in the same period that has

52. David J. A. Clines, *Interested Parties: The Ideology of Writers and Readers of the Hebrew Bible* (Sheffield: Sheffield Academic Press, 1995).
53. Philip R. Davies, *Whose Bible Is It Anyway?* (Sheffield: Sheffield Academic Press, 1995).

witnessed the rise of such movements as canonical criticism. It would not have occurred to most of the scholars who taught me that one should use a small 'g' in referring to this god, since he was, after all, the same as the God and Father of our Lord Jesus Christ. And many scholars quite untouched by postcritical movements continue happily in this tradition. Whether or not it is ultimately compatible with a historical-critical approach, it was certainly perceived as being so. The idea that historical criticism emptied out the enduring religious value of the Old Testament is now common, but it was generally not a conscious part of the self-understanding of actual historical critics. It would be easier to construct a case against them as having been too pious, than to show them up as radically untheological and irreligious. Historical-critical questions were being asked of texts which were *taken for granted* as sacred texts: most historical critics were far from seeing themselves as iconoclasts.[54]

Many people *think* that biblical scholars are alienated from the life of the churches, but if that is so at all, it is a very recent development. In England, where there is a markedly anti-intellectual attitude among many church people, the mere fact that biblical scholarship is a technical operation inclines many to think it must be useless for faith; but such is seldom the intention of its practitioners, who are frequently deeply involved in a pastoral and preaching ministry. Parish clergy sometimes think biblical scholars—like all theologians—are useless; but scholars themselves do not in most cases see *themselves* as hostile to Christian faith; rather, they very often have a deep desire to support and uphold it. Whether or not this is a good thing, it makes them quite prone to being influenced in their exegetical judgments by questions about applicability and *Ergiebigkeit*. The possibility, for example, of judging that a biblical book simply has nothing to say to us today is almost never seriously envisaged. I do not necessarily say that it should be, though one might well maintain that actual relevance is possible only if irrelevance is also possible (questions to which one can only answer yes tend to be pseudoquestions); but I would suggest that the absence of the question gives the lie to the picture of the biblical scholar as a detached and untheological figure, and suggests that it is proreligious bias rather than indifference to faith that we should most be on our guard against. The guild of biblical studies does not seem to me to have given Clines and Davies the hearing they deserve, but has been content to see them in this respect (of course they

54. John Barton, "Canon and Old Testament Interpretation," in *In Search of True Wisdom: Essays in Old Testament Interpretation in Honour of Ronald E. Clements*, ed. E. Ball, Journal for the Study of the Old Testament: Supplement Series 300 (Sheffield: Sheffield Academic Press, 1999), 37–52; quotation, 40.

are widely respected for their scholarship in other spheres) as troublemak-ers—revealing in itself.[55]

The suggestion that biblical criticism has often been *too* theological comes also from one very unexpected source, Fernando Segovia's *Decolonizing Biblical Studies*. Segovia argues in much the same way as many other opponents of the historical-critical method that is has been too focused on history ("the text was to be read and analyzed from within its own historical context and regarded as a direct means for reconstructing the historical situation that it presupposed, reflected, and addressed"[56]), and that it has had positivistic tendencies ("the model had a strong positivistic foundation and orientation. . . . The proper methodology, scientific in nature, was [to be] rigorously applied"[57]), but then he goes on, astonishingly, to claim that "the model was profoundly theological in orientation. . . . It pursued a decidedly idealistic approach to [the texts] with a strong emphasis on biblical theology and on the theological positions, conflicts, and developments of the early Christian movement."[58] One can only admire a method that manages to be positivistic and idealistic at the same time! But if the reader has been persuaded by me that the standard attack on historical criticism as positivistic and history-orientated is misplaced, he or she may perhaps be open to Segovia's argument—which surely goes against his own interests—that it has indeed been heavily theological in much of its practice. Segovia is a witness Clines and Davies could well call in support of their position, arguing that even someone who is hostile to biblical criticism can see how religious its concerns have often been.

A recent article by Jacques Berlinerblau illustrates the present theme very clearly:

55. Cf. Barr, *Holy Scripture*, 45–46: "One must wonder whether the great question as posed by twentieth-century biblical hermeneutics was not wrongly conceived. It was often said that, given our knowledge of the original historical meaning of texts, the great hermeneutical task was to enable us to move from there to the meaning for today, to show how in some sense this could be meaningful and relevant for the life of the church today, how it could be seen also as an effective Word of God. Was this not an immense straining to accomplish something that was actually there all the time? Was not the special status of scripture both given and accepted throughout, in spite of the new angles introduced by modern criticism? Was not the real question this: not, given the historical meaning, how do we move from it to the meaning as Word of God for today, but, given the church's readiness to hear the scripture as Word of God for today, how is that hearing to be modified, refined, and clarified through our knowledge of the actual character of the biblical text, as mediated through critical, historical, and other sorts of knowledge?" For a spirited defense of "neutral" biblical criticism, see also the excellent introductory section in Lester L. Grabbe, *Ezra and Nehemiah*, Old Testament Readings (London: Routledge, 1998).
56. Segovia, *Decolonizing Biblical Studies*, 12.
57. Ibid., 13.
58. Ibid., 14.

The unspeakable that I allude to in my title concerns what we might label the demographic peculiarities of the academic discipline of biblical scholarship. Addressing this very issue thirty years ago, M. H. Goshen-Gottstein observed: "However we try to ignore it, practically all of us are in it because we are either Christians or Jews."[59] In the intervening decades, very little has changed. Biblicists continue to be professing (or once-professing) Christians and Jews. They continue to ignore the fact that the relation between their own religious commitments and their scholarly subject matter is wont to generate every imaginable conflict of intellectual interest. Too, they still seem oblivious to how strange this state of affairs strikes their colleagues in the humanities and social sciences.[60]

He continues by pointing out how far the study of not only the Bible but of religion in general tends to be in the hands of believers:

To their credit . . . faith-based scholars are often cognizant that they are engaged in a confessional enterprise. It is another category of Biblicist that, to my mind, is far more problematic. It is comprised of researchers who in every facet of their private lives are practicing Jews or Christians, but who "somehow" deny that this may influence their professional scholarly work (which just happens to concern those documents that are the fount of Judaism and Christianity!). This category extends to researchers in ancient Near Eastern Studies, who, anecdotally, are often very conservative in their religious views. It also applies, with some sectarian modifications, to many members of the American Academy of Religion. I am always amused to hear how some higher-ups in the latter society complain about the religious conservatism of the SBL, as if the AAR embodies the blasphemous spirit of Jean-Paul Sartre, Chairman Mao, and the Oakland Raiders of the 70s.[61]

Consequently,

To the non-believing undergraduate who tells me that he or she wants to go into biblical studies, I respond (with Dante and Weber) *lasciate ogni speranza* [abandon hope]. This is not so much because they will encounter discrimination. They might, but if my experiences are representative, they will more frequently be the beneficiaries of the kindness of pious strangers. There is a much more mundane reason for prospective non-theist Biblicists to abandon hope: there are no jobs for them.[62]

59. The reference is to M. H. Goshen-Gottstein, "Christianity, Judaism, and Modern Bible Study," Supplements to Vetus Testamentum 28 (1975): 68–88; quotation, 83.
60. Jacques Berlinerblau, "The Unspeakable in Biblical Scholarship," SBL Forum, March 2006.
61. Ibid.
62. Ibid.

Now this is no doubt an exaggeration: there are nonbelieving biblical scholars, and their work is taken seriously by others. Nevertheless, as a picture of the realities on the ground, Berlinerblau's sardonic sketch seems to me more accurate than the view propagated by conservatives, according to which biblical studies is a deeply skeptical and irreligious discipline. I am in no position to complain about the dominance of Christians and Jews of a believing or observant orientation in the biblical studies field, since I fit that description myself. But I do think it is much more likely that the field is skewed by religious commitment than by hostility or indifference to religion. How many biblical commentaries, for example, seriously countenance the possibility that the text they are commenting on may be mistaken, distorted, or just plain wrong? Wellhausen and others of his generation sometimes criticized (in the everyday sense of the word) the texts they studied; how many scholars ever do so today? Hardly any.

BRACKETING OUT

The case I am trying to make argues, as I put it above, that there are two stages involved in understanding a text. One must establish what it means; one may then ask whether what it means is true. This is an elementary point, which in reading texts other than the Bible almost everyone takes for granted. It does not depend on any subtle points in literary theory, nor is it the application of Enlightenment values to the text. The bracketing out of the question of truth while one tries to make sense of the text is not the result of some kind of skepticism or unwillingness to believe that the text is right; it is simply a procedure without which we have no meaning whose truth value we can even begin to assess. In many cases, especially with very simple texts, the logical distinction between the two stages may not result in a more than split-second temporal one. If we hear on the weather forecast, "It is raining at the moment," and we happen to be looking out of the window at the time, our recognition of the meaning of the utterance and our empirical checking against observable data are more or less simultaneous. But from the fact that we can see it is raining, we cannot deduce that that must be what the forecaster is saying, even if what we hear is, "The sun is shining at the moment." This is not, as people say, rocket science, nor is it advanced hermeneutics. It is, indeed, no more than a truism. Yet it is bitterly contested in the discussion of how we should read the Bible. Why is this so?

In this as in so many matters, Wellhausen hit the nail on the head. He wrote, as already quoted in chapter 4 above, that "the secret root of the manifest preference long shown by historical-critical theology for Gen. i appears to lie in this, that scholars felt themselves responsible for what the Bible says, and therefore liked it to come as little as possible in conflict with general culture."[63] A prior conviction that anything that is in the Bible must be true (in some sense or other) blocks the normal way of reading a text and convinces people that reading is a one-stage process in which meaning is understood and truth assessed in a single, undifferentiated act. They then come to regard those who do not follow such a route as in the grip of rationalism, skepticism, "the Enlightenment project,"[64] or some other piece of modern unbelief. But this is surely an overreaction.

We see from this that proponents of theological reading are, as they say, committed to the view that the Bible has a special status, which renders it unlike any other collection of texts. Most Bible readers who are Christian believers share the sense of something special about the Bible. But they would hardly conclude from this that the way it conveys meaning is wholly different from that of any other book. Why, for example, do very conservative scholars still think it necessary to learn biblical languages and to study the text in such detail, if they think that the meaning can be deduced from the fact that the text teaches a true message? The most conservative reader still believes that truth is to be *discovered* in the pages of the Bible, not imputed to them. Proponents of a theological hermeneutic clearly feel they are honoring the Bible, just as they think the critics dishonor it, but is this a kind of honor from which the Bible really benefits? Do we not, by insulating the Bible to this extent, also make it ultimately vacuous? As Richard Hooker put it:

> Whatsoever is spoken of God, or of things appertaining to God, otherwise than as the truth is, though it seem an honour, it is an injury. And as incredible praises given unto men do often abate and impair the credit of their deserved commendation, so we must likewise take great heed, lest, in attributing unto Scripture more than it can have, the incredibility of that do cause even those things which indeed it hath most abundantly, to be less reverently esteemed.[65]

---

63. Wellhausen, *Prolegomena*, 307–8; see p. 95 above. "Prior conviction" is a phrase particularly disliked by Francis Watson, but I do not think there is any alternative.

64. The phrase "the Enlightenment project" appears to have been coined by Alasdair MacIntyre in his *After Virtue* (London: Duckworth, 1981), 58–59. See the discussion in *The Future of Liberal Theology*, ed. Mark D. Chapman (Aldershot: Ashgate, 2002), 6.

65. Hooker, *Of the Laws of Ecclesiastical Polity*, 2:8. I already quoted this passage in my *People of the Book?* 90.

COMMITMENT AND NEUTRALITY

If reading the Bible critically implies separating out meaning from truth (as Spinoza argued), does that confirm the suspicion that critics are opposed to the Bible and the religions it serves? It is surely important to distinguish the personal and psychological commitment of the critic from the procedural task involved in understanding texts. Historically, rather few critics have been opposed either to the Bible or to religion, or have even been neutral about them. Until very recently, as we have just seen, most people who studied the Bible were religious believers; those who were not did not on the whole take any particular interest in the Bible anyway, unless they were serious atheists who thought it worth debunking the Bible. But this is not the same as saying that they felt, or should have felt, that their understanding of the text ought to be driven by their religious convictions. Biblical criticism is certainly, to use the current terms, a *nonconfessional*[66] approach to the meaning of the biblical texts. The proponents of a "committed" reading are right to see it as an enemy of their position, because it requires one to put one's own beliefs on hold while examining the meaning of the Bible. Now the meaning of a text cannot usually be established by someone who lacks empathy with it or who approaches it with reductionist assumptions, trying to make its meaning facile or trivial. But empathy is not the same thing as religious commitment. The attitude that thinks the text must be read as saying something one personally already believes to be true is quite fatal to the critical endeavor, as canonical critics, in my view, correctly perceive. On their own premises they are therefore entirely right to regard criticism as a movement that should be abandoned; and I am not even sure that Childs's commendations of it as "true so far as it goes" are correct. Surely a committed reading should have very little time for biblical criticism at all? In this the somewhat more strident claims of Seitz or Watson seem to me probably also more appropriate—given their particular starting point.

Perhaps an analogy from music may help. Few people would bother to spend time analyzing a symphony if they found it in performance trivial or vacuous. Once they have decided that it is worth attending to, however, their analysis needs procedurally to be separate from their evaluation. They must attend neutrally to the fact that a given movement is in 4/4 or 3/4 time, that the harmonies work in a certain way, that the structure is as it is. Quite

66. Walter Moberly prefers the terms "confessing" and "non-confessing," to distinguish the notion of religious commitment as such from the suggestion that may be present in "confessional" and "non-confessional" of allegiance to a particular Christian "confession"—Catholicism, Calvinism, Anglicanism, etc. This is a good point, though "confessional" seems likely to continue to be used despite its regrettable ambiguity.

possibly wonder at the musical skill of the work will be registered at the same moment as recognition of the technical devices employed, but the two remain conceptually distinct. Wonder cannot have the effect of making the analyst expect to find—and therefore actually to find—3/4 if the movement is in fact in 4/4.[67]

In this, biblical criticism is like musical analysis: it seeks to pinpoint what is there to be found. In some types of postmodernism—musical as well as literary or theological—there are theories that deny there is anything objective to be found at all. But canonical critics, like advocacy readers, do not go down that road. They claim that they are identifying the meaning of the biblical text, not creating it. And when they insist that this must be done from a confessional or committed viewpoint, they are plainly in opposition to the values that criticism stands for. As I said in the opening chapter, my primary aim in this book is to describe rather than to prescribe; and even though my preference for a critical over a confessional reading is obvious, my immediate purpose is simply to map the field and to point out that such readings are, precisely as they claim, in opposition to biblical criticism. Criticism is a "cool" rather than a "warm" procedure. Warmth toward the text may well be the reason for undertaking it, but one must turn down the heat in order to do the criticism. Coolness is not, however, the same as hostility; hostility has its own warmth and misleads just as much as its opposite. But in other fields we recognize the need for procedural neutrality alongside personal commitment without finding it problematic, as I hope my musical example suggests. Why it should be a particular problem for the study of the Bible seems rather mystifying.

The answer, I suppose, is that neutral criticism is felt to be nonproductive, not *ergiebig*: it does not yield anything for the religious believer. I hope to have shown that this is not so at all. The theological yield of biblical criticism in fact has been enormous. But even if this were not true, the procedural point would remain. Few would deny that music criticism has contributed hugely,

---

67. In the literary sphere David Lodge points to an interesting case of "wishful reading" in *Author, Author* (London: Secker & Warburg, 2004), his novel about Henry James: "Leon Edel, who made himself the world's greatest authority on the life and works of Henry James, summarizes the essay ["Is There a Life after Death?"], in his monumental biography, as follows: 'If one meant physical life, he believed there was none. Death was absolute. What lived beyond life was what the creative consciousness had found and made and only if enshrined in enduring form.' Actually, that was not quite what Henry James said. It was what you might expect him to say on the subject; it was what you might hope he would say, if you were a convinced materialist; but it is not what he in fact said." We make this kind of distinction all the time when we read; why do we find it hard to do so when it is the Bible we are reading?

not simply to the formal analysis, but to the actual appreciation and enjoyment of music. But equally few would say that it should give up its claims to illuminate musical works if people do not find it helpful. It has its own intellectual integrity.

To me it seems that proponents of confessing readings of the Bible risk requiring the interpreter to live inside a religious community that has closed boundaries and in which it is taken for granted that the believer has privileged access to the meaning of biblical texts. But there is no such privileged access, and it is essentially on this that biblical criticism insists. It is not hostile to faith, but it rests on the premise that truth is open to all comers, not the preserve of those "in the know." In this I agree strongly with Gerd Theissen:

> Historical criticism is addressed to anyone capable of understanding it, and not just to a privileged group handing on a particular tradition. By its very nature, historical criticism is concerned to make particular traditions generally accessible. Here it pursues quite different aims from those "theological" interpretations which begin with the premise that only Christians can legitimately deal with the biblical tradition and anything contrary to Christian views stems from an inappropriate understanding of the tradition. To hold such a view would be as nonsensical as to assert that only Hindus can interpret the Vedas properly, that only Marxists can understand Marx properly, and that only Rilke devotees are called on to interpret his poetry. There is no privileged knowledge in scientific investigation of traditions. Anyone who argues to the contrary betrays the ethos of critical interpretation, which is *ipso facto* concerned with universal communication. It is concerned with understanding, and therefore with breaking down the barriers between people with different cultural backgrounds, different religions or different views of the world. There is no doubt that some people find it easier than others to come to grips with a particular tradition. It is undeniable that Christians and Jews are at an advantage when it comes to understanding the biblical traditions. However, to make this affinity into a norm and to declare that there can be only one legitimate basis for understanding is a very suspicious procedure. Scientific investigation of the traditions of Christianity involves interpreting the Bible in such a way that virtually anyone can understand it, even if he or she is not a Christian. Only an attitude of this kind can command unconditional respect from members of any tradition, and *to seek such unconditional respect is hardly an un-Christian concern.*[68]

---

68. Gerd Theissen, *On Having a Critical Faith* (London: SCM, 1979), 2–3; trans. from *Argumente für einen kritischen Glauben* (Munich: Kaiser Verlag, 1978), my italics.

THE TERM "INTERPRETATION"

Another way of putting the argument I have been deploying is to point to a fatal ambiguity in the term "interpretation," which is so ubiquitous in the discussion of biblical studies. In the terms traditional in theoretical hermeneutics since the work of Ernesti, and as developed by Schleiermacher, there are three stages in the work of interpreting or understanding a text: the *subtilitas intelligendi*, the *subtilitas explicandi*, and the *subtilitas applicandi*. Understanding and explication both belong to what I have referred to as establishing the meaning of the text, though, more precisely, they already represent two (sub)stages. One begins by understanding a text oneself; in explaining it to someone else, one is already in effect producing another text, which is then subject to the same two stages—one reason why the exegesis of texts is never complete, since it requires attention to the recipient of the exegesis as well as to the text.[69] But both these stages—first, one in which the meaning of the text is established, and then, one in which it is explained to others—are distinct from the work of application, which includes both the attempt to show the reader how the text can be *ergiebig* and the act of deciding whether what the text asserts is true.

In the language traditionally used in biblical studies, the first two stages belong to exegesis and the third to interpretation. But there is also another usage, in which "interpretation" is used to cover all three stages, and it is just here that, in my view, the discussion easily becomes muddled. A "theological interpretation" of the Bible may mean (a) that the exegesis of the text attends to the fact that the content is theological: very little biblical criticism has ignored this fact. It may, however, mean (b) that once the exegesis is complete,

---

69. Thus Schleiermacher says that hermeneutics is "only the art of *understanding*, not also the art of *expounding* one's understanding. This latter would be a special part of the art of speaking and writing, which could depend only on general principles" ("nur Kunst des *Verstehens*, nicht auch *Darlegung* des Verständnisses. Dies wäre nur ein spezieller Teil von der Kunst zu reden und zu schreiben, der nur von allgemeinen Prinzipien abhängen könnte") (Frank, *Schleiermachers Hermeneutik und Kritik*, 75). Frank cites Lücke's note on this, which explains that Schleiermacher differs from Ernesti on this point: "Gegen die herrschende Definition seit Ernesti Instit. Interpret. N.T. ed. Ammon p. 7 et 8: Est autem interpretatio facultas *docendi*, quae cujusque orationi sententia subjecta sit, seu, efficiendi, ut alter cogitat eadem cum scriptore quoque. – Interpretatio igitur omnis duabus rebus continetur, sententiarum (idearum) verbis subjectarum intellectu, earumque idonea *explicatione*. Unde in bono interpreti esse debet, subtilitas intelligendi et subtilitas explicandi" (from Lücke's edition of Schleiermacher, 99). This explains that, according to the view prevalent since Ernesti, interpretation is essentially a form of teaching, of enabling someone else to understand what the author meant, and thus includes both understanding and explication: hence the good interpreter needs both the capacity to understand (*subtilitas intelligendi*) and the capacity to explain (*subtilitas explicandi*). Schleiermacher essentially contests this point, making a much sharper distinction between the two arts.

the interpreter then goes on to ask about the text's theological truth or false-hood, or to show how the text can be theologically productive. This has hap-pened patchily, but still to a significant extent, in biblical studies. But, thirdly, it may mean (c) that the exegesis itself is controlled by a theological or religious vision, so that the meaning found in the text in the course of exegesis is deter-mined by prior theological commitments. It is the third sense that is usually present in the current calls for theological (postcritical, committed) interpreta-tion, and I have tried to suggest reasons why this is a flawed understanding. In terms of the technical vocabulary just introduced, it is a confusion of the *sub-tilitas explicandi* with the *subtilitas applicandi*. But this does not at all rule out the other two possible senses of theological interpretation. Proponents of theo-logical interpretation in the third sense seem often to overlook the other two possibilities, with the result that they portray traditional biblical criticism as much more positivistic and theologically unconcerned than in fact it is.

That the act of understanding and the act of evaluating or applying a text cannot be collapsed into a single operation seems to me evident, and the attempt to combine these tasks undermines most of the approaches surveyed in this chapter. But when we have said that the first operation is to establish the meaning, we have of course stated a problem rather than solved one. It seems to me vital to hold that understanding a text is not the same as accept-ing it for true and that the two processes must be held apart; but this is far from implying that either process is a simple one. The nature of textual meaning is one of the most fraught topics in modern discussion, not only in biblical but also in literary studies. What I have tried to establish in this chapter is simply that biblical critics have been concerned to discern meaning, not to attack or to undervalue the biblical text. This discernment has required a stance that is methodologically detached. But that is a logical necessity, not an expression of hostility: it can coexist with an ultimate commitment to the Bible in which meaning is discerned just as well as with skepticism about it.

BELIEVING AFTER CRITICISM

After criticism, can we still believe? That is how the "problem" of biblical crit-icism presents itself to many students of biblical studies, who experience crit-icism as a negative force, challenging their religious convictions insofar as these rest on a positive attitude toward the Bible.

The reaction of many scholars to this question has been to begin by accept-ing the implication of negativity and then trying to find ways of negotiating it. Sometimes this is done by showing some of the positive benefits that particu-lar examples of criticism have brought. For example, on questions such as church order, a critical reading of the New Testament can break down old prejudices and divisions and recast our questions—though it can hardly be said that in practice the churches have grown any closer together on this issue, despite the labors of biblical critics. More often it is suggested that we should accept the findings of biblical critics but seek ways of moving beyond them. This is in effect the agenda of much that can be called biblical theology, which accepts the (as it is felt) fissiparous character of biblical criticism in dissecting and showing the differences between biblical texts, but then looks for a higher synthesis at the theological level. Biblical theologies, at least of the kind that synthesize the whole Bible (or at any rate the whole of one testament), may be called postcritical, not in the sense that they reject criticism, but in the sense that they seek to move on from it. The general tenor of much that is written on the Bible by critical scholars seeks to be reassuring to the religious reader, by showing that critical study is, perhaps surprisingly, productive (*ergiebig*) for religious faith. That, for example, is inherent in the very design of a series such as the Biblischer Kommentar or Hermeneia commentaries, and it is implicit in many other series such as the Anchor Bible; application is seldom neglected, even though critical principles are emphasized.

An alternative way of negotiating the alleged problem posed by biblical criticism is to argue that criticism has run into the sand and that we should move beyond it in the stronger sense of leaving it behind and treating the biblical text in a different manner altogether. This has been the burden of the canonical approach. As propounded by Brevard Childs, the canonical approach is not overtly hostile to biblical criticism but regards it as a necessary stage in the study of the Bible that has yielded many useful insights, but from which it is now time to move on. In the writings of other scholars inspired by Childs's work, however, it has acquired a somewhat sharper edge, as I have tried to show. These scholars tend to think that biblical criticism did indeed produce some worthwhile insights, but that taken as a whole it has been a diversion from the task of a properly theological reading of the Bible as the church's book. They argue that the negativity of traditional criticism is so great that we would now be better off without it. Even if it once represented a necessary and salutary emancipation from ecclesiastical authority, the boot is now very much on the other foot, and it has turned into a blight on the church's appropriation of the Bible. We should become self-consciously postcritical—indeed, in the process we should rediscover and repristinate what biblical critics are apt to call precritical exegesis, the exegesis of the Fathers of the church and the Reformers, who had a lively sense of the Bible as God's word spoken to humanity.

My own presentation of biblical criticism begins, as should be clear by now, in a different place. Rather than seeing criticism as an attack on the text, as reductionist, positivistic, or skeptical, so that, though we may have reluctantly to accept it, we should aspire to move on from it, I have tried to show that the essence of criticism is an attempt to understand the text by means of semantic inquiry, genre recognition, and the bracketing out of the question of truth. Bracketing out does not imply hostility but procedural neutrality, and it is quite compatible with a further stage at which the question of the truth of the now understood text returns and requires an answer. What I have been resisting is the imposition of a special biblical hermeneutic, arguing that biblical criticism requires the adoption of the same general hermeneutic for reading the Bible as for any other text. But perhaps we shall find (like Jowett) that when the Bible is read "like any other book," it may turn out to be unlike any other book—though indeed all texts are unlike all other texts, and discovering that is one of the pleasures of textual study.

What I have called bracketing out is perhaps more than merely procedural, in this sense: it proceeds from a conviction that texts have to be allowed the right to answer their own questions, and that only when we have seen them in their own light can we begin to use them to answer ours. The distance between ourselves and the text we are reading is essential to our understanding it; it is not a problem but the very precondition of our dialogue with the text. The best analogy for this is our relationship with other people, which similarly depends upon our recognition of the gap between them and ourselves. Only when we avoid making the other person in our own image can we truly enter into a dialogue, rather than conducting a monologue.[70] Recognizing the alien quality of the text is essential if we are not to fall into a solipsistic reading, as happens, I would argue, in much reader-response criticism. There is a danger of the same kind in canonical approaches that insist on reading the Bible as "our book," belonging to the church's internal structures.

This, I would argue, is the very opposite of consigning the Bible to the past, as though we were treating it as merely a historical artifact with no present relevance. What is relevant is the actual meaning (the plain sense) of the biblical text, which is determined by the context in which it came to be but is not therefore limited to that context. Modern literary critics are correct when they argue that texts have an afterlife, in which their meaning comes to expression in ever-new situations. Biblical criticism has sometimes been presented as hostile to the reapplication of the biblical text in new contexts, but it is not of its nature to be so; such hostility is a misunderstanding of the essence of criticism. Following Hirsch, I have stressed the distinction between meaning and significance, but this does not mean that significance does not matter. In reading the Bible critically, we recognize a discussion partner, a text that

---

70. Cf. John Barton, "Theology and Other Sciences," *Theology* 99 (1996): 52–58.

we did not create ourselves and that can therefore surprise us, but that sometimes for this very reason can throw a sudden shaft of light on to our questions and problems. Gerd Theissen sums it up very acutely:

> The Bible comes alive where authentic religious experience coincides with texts which are themselves testimony to an authentic religious experience: the past strikes a spark off the present or the present off the past, and both are illuminated. The chief reason why religious texts from the past are so difficult to understand is that modern man has become uncertain of his own religious experience. He mistrusts it, and expects his encounter with the past to supply information which he will obtain only if he is truly concerned with religious questions and experiences. . . . Only one conclusion can be drawn from the problem as we have described it: it is important to be aware of one's present religious experiences and to articulate the degree of independence which they have from the past; or, to put it in academic terms, it is important to work out a theory of religion so that it then becomes possible to enter into a dialogue with the past which is no longer expected to meet the impossible demand that the present should be legitimated by the past. Such a dialogue would be open to the past. And again and again we shall have the pleasant surprise of finding unexpected allies there, indeed a better way of expressing things, which can give a new stimulus to religious life in the present.[71]

71. Theissen, *On Having a Critical Faith*, 82. Compare these words of Lionel Trilling: "It is only if we are aware of the reality of the past that we can feel it as active and present. If, for example, we try to make Shakespeare literally contemporaneous, we make him monstrous. He is contemporaneous only if we know how much a man of his own age he was; he is relevant to us only if we see his distance from us. Or to take a poet closer to us in actual time, Wordsworth's Immortality Ode is acceptable to us only when it is understood to have been written at a certain past moment; if it had appeared much later than it did, if it were offered to us as a contemporary work, we would not admire it. . . . In the pastness of these works lies the assurance of their validity and relevance"; see Lionel Trilling, *The Liberal Imagination* (New York: Viking Press, 1950), quoted in David Daiches, *Critical Approaches to Literature* (London and New York: Longman, 2nd ed., 1981), 320–21. Or, again, this passage from Gerhard Ebeling's essay on the "critical historical method": "Everything depends on the critical historical method being freed from this mistaken curtailment to a mere technical tool and being understood in such a way as to include in itself the whole of the hermeneutic process. That does not imply the slightest prejudice to the stringent methods of historical research and their technical application. On the contrary, the very process of taking the historical source in all its historicity (and that means in its distance from the present) and making it luminous by means of a critical examination that penetrates to the uttermost limits of its explicability, and thereby at the same time also critically correcting the prejudices of the expositor himself and making clear to him the historical conditionedness of his own preconceptions—that very process creates the necessary basis for a genuine encounter with the text, and thereby also the possibility of having it speak to us" (Gerhard Ebeling, "The Significance of the Critical Historical Method for Church and Theology in Protestantism," 49).

Sparks can fly between past and present only if the past is really past, and one major function of biblical criticism is to ensure (as nearly as is humanly possible) that it is the real text from the past we are reading, not a modern imitation of it. But Theissen is right to stress also that the present must be really present. We need to know our own (modern) mind and not to be unreflective about it, so that the text does not simply take us over. To me it seems that the relation of the modern reader to the Bible is parallel to that of modern systematic theologians to theologians of the past. Most theologians would agree that in interrogating their predecessors it is important to establish what those predecessors actually said, not to engage in reader-response criticism of them. At the same time, it is important to enter into dialogue with them from a position of one's own, not simply to parrot their words in another time and place. By rejecting a special hermeneutic for the Bible, I am in effect proposing that this parallel is a good one. The Bible is a text from the past. Recognizing this does not mean that it is therefore an irrelevant text. We are in the present. Recognizing this does not mean that we have nothing to learn from the Bible. But without acknowledged distance, there can be no dialogue.

Of course all this raises difficulties, of exactly the same kind as meet us in our study of past theologians: how can we be sure that our own concerns and preoccupations are not contaminating our reading of past texts? We cannot, but we can try. An ideal of absolute objectivity is naturally unattainable, but that does not mean, at the other extreme, that anything goes. As Valentine Cunningham puts it, "There is something there in the text."

It is easy to contrast this approach unfavorably with a more committed, confessional, theological reading of the biblical text, regarding it as secularizing and religiously minimalist. But I would want to go on the offensive here and argue not simply that what I am proposing is no less religious than approaches such as the canonical one, but that it is actually more so. The essence of a religious approach to the world, it seems to me, is to be found, not in the imposition of theological dogma, but in the recognition of what is actually there. Before theological interpretation comes the recognition of simple givenness, the appreciation of reality. This has its analogue in the world of the text and of reading texts in the desire to be silent in the face of what confronts us, before we turn to consider how we can make it part of our own system. Prayer begins in attention to what is there, and then reflects on that thereness in the light of religious convictions. But attention comes first. To me it seems that biblical criticism is an admirable example of an approach to the reality of texts that similarly begins in contemplation of a given and does not seek to distort that given into something we can make something of. Biblical critics may, of course, not be religious, and that is a continuing offense to people who wish to insist on confessing readings. But the attitude to the text that the biblical critic has is, it seems to me, fully compatible with a religious commitment, indeed an attitude without which the proper religious study of the Bible cannot get underway. A critical faith, in Theissen's sense, seems to me actually a deeper faith than an uncritical one. This means that the religiously committed critic should not be trying, as a desperate salvage operation, to rescue something from the wreck caused by biblical criticism, but rather should affirm that a critical approach is inherent in a religious commitment in the first place. To try to discover what the biblical text actually means, rather than to impose on it our own theological categories, is to honor the text as part of the givenness of a world we did not make.

As Lothar Perlitt well observes, this was what Wellhausen was trying to do in his study of the Old Testament, from which he derived a "profane" version of the history of Israel.[72] It was at variance with the history the Bible tells, but it was to be found by minute examination of the biblical text in its givenness. Wellhausen was uncovering clues that were really there in the text and thereby was doing the text honor. And by reading it on its own terms he succeeded in showing much better than his noncritical opponents just how much it had to contribute to modern concerns, as is expressed in the following comment of Christof von Weizsäcker:

> In principle it is only since Wellhausen that the Old Testament has been rediscovered in its incredible fullness and density, and in its relevance for our own decisions—that is, since Old Testament scholarship has made it possible to see the cultural and social presuppositions that existed in Israel three thousand years ago, and into which the old texts fit, without any christological reinterpretation, in the most vivid way.[73]

Biblical criticism is the necessary precondition of the Bible's coming alive in this way, and as such it is a profoundly religious activity.

Such an idea has been developed by Paul Ricoeur. We saw above that Ricoeur adopted Karl Barth's idea of a second naiveté, which follows biblical criticism, just as the first naiveté is found in people who have not yet faced the critical challenge. At first glance one might think that Ricoeur, like Barth, is using the expression in order to call biblical criticism into question, and this

---

72. See above, p. 53.
73. "Das Alte Testament ist im Grunde erst seit Wellhausen in seiner unglaublichen Fülle und Dichte und seiner Relevanz für unsere eigenen Entscheidungen wiederentdeckt worden, d.h. seit die alttestamentliche Wissenschaft die kulturellen und sozialen Voraussetzungen sehen gelehrt hat, die vor dreitausend Jahren in Israel bestanden und auf welche die alten Texte ohne jede christologische Umdeutung in direkster Lebendigkeit passen" (C. F. von Weizsäcker, *Der Garten des Menschlichen*, 9th ed. [Munich: Hanser, 1984], 461; quoted in Smend, *Deutsche Alttestamentler in drei Jahrhunderten*, 99).

looks like a plausible reading of Ricoeur's famous maxim, "Beyond the desert of criticism, we wish to be called again"—as though criticism were a wholly sterile operation which we need to leave behind us if we are to be "called," that is, confronted and challenged, by the Bible and its message.[74] But this is to misunderstand Ricoeur. For him criticism is a desert in the sense that it is the wilderness, an austere experience, which is the necessary preparation for entry into the Promised Land—not a negative factor that needs to be avoided if possible. As Lewis Mudge puts it, "To participate in the history of testimony we must [according to Ricoeur] convert our naïve faith through criticism into the register of hope."[75] The true, second naiveté is available only to those who have passed through the "desert of criticism," and it is not a matter of simply reverting to a precritical naiveté. It depends on a critical interpretation of the text:

> [In *The Symbolism of Evil*, Ricoeur] proposes a philosophical analysis of symbolic and metaphoric language intended to help us reach a 'second naïveté' before such texts. The latter phrase, which Ricoeur has made famous, suggests that the 'first naïveté', an unquestioned dwelling in a world of symbol, which presumably came naturally to men and women in one-possibility cultures to which the symbols in question were indigenous, *is no longer possible for us*. But we may approximate that state—*of course with a difference.*
>
>> For the second immediacy that we seek and the second naïveté that we await are no longer accessible to us anywhere else than in a hermeneutics; we can believe only by interpreting. It is the 'modern' mode of belief in symbols, an expression of the distress of modernity and a remedy for that distress.[76]

And most clearly of all:

> Thus, as Ricoeur develops the importance of *critical explanation* of the text, it is not to destroy faith but to open the way for it. If one of the motives of the nineteenth-century historical-critical scholars was to free the Bible from dogmatic ecclesiastical interpretations, Ricoeur in turn seeks to free the Bible from culture-bound, subjectivizing interpretations as well as from fundamentalist, objectivizing interpretations by asking us to listen carefully to what biblical discourse testifies. We have no alternative to working through criticism toward

74. The maxim is taken from *The Symbolism of Evil* (Boston: Beacon Press, 1969), 349; trans. of *La Symbolique du mal* (Paris: Aubier, 1960).

75. Lewis Mudge, "Paul Ricoeur on Biblical Interpretation," in Paul Ricoeur, *Essays on Biblical Interpretation*, edited with an introduction by Lewis S. Mudge (London: SPCK, 1981), 28.

76. Ibid., 6. The indented paragraph is from Ricoeur, *The Symbolism of Evil*, 352; italics throughout are mine.

a second naïveté because the first naïveté available to us in our culture is deeply idolatrous.[77]

Criticism is not the enemy of a contemporary religious appropriation of the biblical text but its necessary precondition. Attempts to put back the clock and act as though criticism had never been are in vain; this promised land cannot be reached except through the desert, in which we learn to read, not what we should like to be in the Bible, but what is actually there. Thus criticism is, as argued above, a religious activity.

But what kind of religious activity is it? Should we, for example, refer to biblical criticism as "liberal"? This is normally done by those who are opposed to it. For example, students of a biblically conservative persuasion will complain that the critical scholars who are recommended by their lecturers are "all liberals," and will sometimes demand that noncritical works be included in book lists for the sake of balance. But the task of deciding whether or not biblical criticism should be called a liberal activity is bedeviled by the equal problem of knowing what, in theology, should in any case count as liberal. If we build into the definition the insistence that theological claims have to be checked against intellectual standards shared with the secular world, then there is an obvious affinity with the bracketing out I have been defending in biblical criticism. Establishing the meaning of a text is understood by biblical critics to be an operation belief does not enter into, from which indeed it should be kept distinct. And this may be felt to have analogies with the desire of liberal theologians to stand back from theological assertions and test them against general intellectual norms, rather than beginning from a fideistic or confessional standpoint. To that extent it seems to me that it is reasonable to call biblical criticism liberal.

On the other hand, the equation does not necessarily work all that well, once we attend to the biographies of biblical critics and of liberal theologians. Many biblical critics are not in practice interested in or attracted by liberal theology. It would be odd, for example, to describe Gerhard von Rad as a liberal theologian; he was a pretty traditional Lutheran. There are many biblical scholars today whose work is unimpeachably critical, but who in their own religious practice are traditional Catholics or Protestants and who have few affinities with a liberal agenda. Conversely, a good many liberal theologians are not particularly interested in biblical criticism or indeed in the Bible at all. To make biblical criticism out to be liberal, therefore, one will have to appeal to its internal structure and logic, rather than to empirical observation of correlations with actual liberal theology.

77. Mudge, "Paul Ricoeur on Biblical Interpretation," 23.

I would rather characterize the kind of theology that is associated with biblical criticism as *critical theology*, just as Theissen does in speaking of a "critical faith."[78] This shares certain features with liberal theology: notably the belief that faith must subject itself to scrutiny by reason. But the result of this scrutiny may not be anything that would usually be described as liberal theology. It is convenient for opponents of criticism to bundle it up with liberalism, since in some circles that damns it in advance. But the conservative/liberal polarization does not really correspond usefully to anything in the world of biblical criticism, whose parameters are set by quite different criteria. There is nothing specially liberal about investigations of genre and semantics, and no guarantee that such investigations will produce conclusions congenial to liberal theology any more than to conservative theology. The whole point of biblical criticism is that what conclusions it will produce is an open question, not predetermined by the theological stance of the investigator. That is why ecclesiastical authorities in the past so often distrusted it and why in our own day too it is under suspicion from those who already "know" which theology is the correct one. Criticism needs to be procedurally indifferent to its own theological implications; that is the respect in which it can properly be called scientific. Most biblical critics are in practice far from indifferent, because, as we have seen, very many of them are religious believers. But they have to keep their minds open to the meaning of the text without claiming to know in advance what that will be. In that sense criticism has always represented, and continues to represent, the claims of intellectual freedom. Insofar as that is what liberalism means, the label is appropriate. But if it is taken to identify a raft of nonconservative prior commitments, then it is just as inimical to criticism as conservatism itself.

CONCLUSION

There is a battle going on at the moment between those who believe that biblical criticism is too much in the grip of a secular and skeptical spirit and those who think it has still not managed to escape the hand of ecclesiastical and religious authority. My sympathies lie on the whole more with the second group. Far from biblical criticism's having subverted faith, it seems to me that for most people it has not even begun to make an impression on it. That criticism has taken the Bible away from the church is largely an illusion, though

---

78. Cf. Ebeling, "The Significance of the Critical Historical Method," 60: "Critical theology is not identical with liberal theology. It is, however, the indispensable means of reminding the church of the freedom rooted in the *justificatio impii*."

a widely held one. But my purpose in this chapter has been primarily to defend biblical criticism as a way of taking the Bible seriously on its own terms, really listening to what the text is saying before making up one's mind about its claims. I have argued that this attitude can itself be characterized as religious, if by that we mean not the acceptance of particular doctrines but an attitude of receptiveness to a reality we did not ourselves create. This may be felt as an attempt to capture the high ground from proponents of "committed" reading, and in many ways it is just that. I believe it is high time for biblical critics to stop arguing defensively that their work does, after all, little real damage to faith, and to start claiming firmly that a faith uninformed by it is, at this point in the history of Christian thought, simply an ostrich. But it is also an attempt—as is the rest of this book—to identify more closely just what is the essence of biblical criticism and to show that it is not best defined in terms of a religious/antireligious dichotomy but has its own independent integrity.

7

Conclusion

At the end of this inquiry into the nature of biblical criticism, I would refer the reader back to the ten theses put forward in the introductory chapter. I hope that it has become clear how they are to be understood, and that I have succeeded in making them plausible. Rather than working through them in detail with references back to the argument of individual chapters, I should like in this concluding chapter to concentrate on just three points.

First, I have defended what has traditionally been called biblical criticism, but I have also defined it in ways that will not commend themselves to everyone. In particular, I have proposed that it contains within itself much that is commonly seen as lying outside its purview or even as being alternative to it. What I have in mind here is chiefly what is nowadays usually called "literary" study of the Bible. A great rift has opened between those who read the Bible in a "literary" way and traditional "historical critics," each party on the whole regarding the other as largely worthless. My own position will perhaps seem nearer to historical criticism, but I would stress that my dislike of this term is seriously meant, and arises precisely from a sense that biblical criticism has always had a literary component, without which it has no point. Biblical criticism is first and foremost a literary procedure, which tries to construe and understand the biblical texts in their context. The idea that this can be satisfactorily done in a purely "synchronic" way misunderstands the nature of textual meaning, but the picture of biblical critics as interested only in the "diachronic" dimension is a caricature. In reading a text, one needs a sense of its anchorage in a particular period, but also some understanding of what sense it makes as part of the total literary "system" of that period. In the case of important and classic texts such as most of those in the Bible, it is also natural to be interested in possible contemporary relevance and use.

All this represents a constant crisscrossing of synchronic and diachronic dimensions and suggests to me that the use of these two terms as polar opposites has been far from helpful in biblical studies. Thus I would include much that is now called a literary approach—and seen as inimical to traditional criticism—*within* biblical criticism itself and would argue that it is rare for biblical scholars to be indifferent to it. There are some highly "positivistic" students of the Bible who have no ear for the text's resonance and applicability; but they are comparatively few. Biblical criticism has always been a "broad church," interested in any insight into the text from whatever quarter it comes. I hope that a more inclusive vision of the discipline may help toward some reconciliation between scholars who currently tend to see themselves as necessarily at loggerheads, or even as justified in feeling scornful of each other's work.

Secondly, I have tried to stress that biblical criticism has no inherent hostility toward what is traditionally called application. Most people go to the Bible because they think it will illuminate human life, and biblical criticism has no vested interest in denying this. What it does set up is a procedural distinction, between discovering what texts mean and evaluating or using them. Without this distinction, I have argued, things get hopelessly muddled. "Advocacy" interpretation in particular often denies that we can understand the text without first establishing a hermeneutical framework based on a sound theological or human principle, such as respect for the poor, a proper regard for the position of women, or a commitment to a religious vision. My argument has *not* been that such interpretations are wrong—far from it—but that so far from undermining the traditionally "objective" aim of biblical criticism, they actually require it if they are to carry conviction. It must be possible to establish what texts mean, regardless of one's own convictions. If they then turn out to support those convictions, that is a great gain; whereas if one takes the convictions as part of one's presuppositions in reading the text, there is always the danger of simply seeing one's own face at the bottom of the well. A realistic measure of objectivity in interpretation, which biblical critics have always insisted on, is the friend rather than the enemy of advocacy interpretation. Conversely, hermeneutical theories based on too heavy an emphasis on *Vorverständnis* are dangerous allies. Until we know what a text means, it makes no sense to think it can be used for any purpose at all, unless as mere ornament. And we shall never find out what it means if we approach it with the belief that we already know. This is the very simple basis of my problem with "confessing" readings: that however sophisticated they may be, they never avoid the risk of what is widely called eisegesis. Only certain readings are permissible, and what these are can be known in advance. This is simple, indeed obvious—except that there are very many people to whom it does not seem obvious at all.

Thirdly, I have tried to make some adjustments to the traditional understanding of where the intellectual and religious roots of biblical criticism lie.
It has become so common to talk of the historical-critical method as a child of
the Enlightenment that other possibilities are scarcely considered. Personally
I do not share the disdain for the Enlightenment felt by many in the theological world, and it would not greatly worry me if it could be shown that the
Enlightenment was indeed the source of biblical criticism. It seems to me,
however, that such a theory is seriously flawed. To deny that biblical criticism
came on by leaps and bounds from about the eighteenth century onward would
be foolish, but it is the working out of possibilities that had been discovered
somewhat earlier—in some cases in the early church or in early Judaism, in
other cases at the Renaissance and during the Reformation. German-speaking
scholars have long tended to be more sensitive to the Reformation roots of
criticism than Anglophone ones. While agreeing with this Germanic tradition
that the sense of freedom from external authority in the interpretation of the
Bible is indeed rightly linked to Reformation insights, I have also suggested
that criticism has still earlier sources in a philological tradition that can be
found in the ancient world as well. If this is accepted, then biblical criticism
does not fall under a blanket condemnation of the spirit of modernity, and its
use of reason in handling the biblical text cannot simply be put down to
Enlightenment rationalism.

This makes me wary of the expression "precritical," and I have proposed that
biblical study should be distinguished as "critical" or "noncritical," avoiding the
chronological emphasis of the common terminology. There is early criticism
that is definitely noncritical, as in the harmonizing attempts by Augustine and
others surveyed in chapter 2, but there is also plenty of noncritical study going
on today; conversely, there are ancient as well as modern examples of the application of critical intelligence to the biblical text. The Antiochenes emerged as
important here, not in their traditional role as proponents of literal interpretation (which we saw to be partial at best), but as showing a concern for genre
and *Duktus* that is comparable to much criticism in our own day.

Critical reading of the Bible, as of any other text, represents insights that,
once encountered, cannot be suppressed. It is possible, certainly, to be postcritical in the sense that one seeks to use critical conclusions as a key to a rich
and profound reading of the Bible: Paul Ricoeur is an example of how this may
be done. But the call to be postcritical seems to me in most quarters to be an
attempt to become noncritical again, and this is to be resisted. Underlying it
is often a sense that critical study has yielded no great understanding of the
Bible, but is concerned with small, nit-picking investigations of technical
details of the text. On the contrary, critical study has utterly transformed how
we read the Bible. In the Old Testament world, the critical work of a giant such

as Wellhausen produced a totally new way of seeing the whole development of religious thought in ancient Israel (let alone of Israel's history) that cannot be bypassed in any attempt to do justice to the Old Testament's theological meaning. Critical study of the Gospels and of Paul similarly transform our entire understanding of Jesus and the early church. It is commonly said that the findings of critical scholarship are of no value in communicating the Christian gospel to ordinary people. My own conviction is that this is because hardly anyone has ever tried. Biblical criticism as I conceive it is a rich and profound way of taking the Bible seriously, which ordinary Christians ought not be kept in ignorance of. When the penny drops, the Bible suddenly becomes three-dimensional rather than a flat, uniform surface. Most biblical scholars can remember the moment when the penny dropped for them. It would be a great thing if they tried to communicate this to others, rather than looking for ways of bypassing criticism and returning to a monocular vision.

This is what I want to do.

Bibliography

Abrams, M. H. *The Mirror and the Lamp: Romantic Theory and the Critical Tradition.* New York: Oxford University Press, 1953.

Alter, Robert. *The Art of Biblical Narrative.* London: George Allen & Unwin, 1981.

Astruc, Jean. *Conjectures sur les mémoires originaux dont il paroit que Moyse s'est servi pour composer le livre de la Genèse.* Brussels, 1753.

Baarda, Tjitze. *Essays on the Diatessaron.* Kampen: Kok Pharos, 1994.

———. "Factors in the Harmonization of the Gospels, Especially in the Diatessaron of Tatian." In *Gospel Traditions in the Second Century: Origins, Recensions, Text, and Transmission,* ed. W. L. Petersen, 133–56. Christianity and Judaism in Antiquity 3. London and Notre Dame: University of Notre Dame Press, 1989.

Bainton, R. H. "The Bible in the Reformation." In *Cambridge History of the Bible,* 3:1–37. Cambridge: Cambridge University Press, 1963.

Baird, W. "New Testament Criticism." In *Anchor Bible Dictionary,* ed. David Noel Freedman, 1:730–36. New York and London: Doubleday, 1992.

Barr, James. "Bibelkritik als theologische Aufklärung." In *Glaube und Toleranz: Das theologische Erbe der Aufklärung,* ed. T. Rendtorff, 30–42. Gütersloh: Mohn, 1982.

———. *The Garden of Eden and the Hope of Immortality: The Read-Tuckwell Lectures for 1990.* London: SCM, 1992.

———. *Holy Scripture: Canon, Authority, Criticism.* Oxford: Oxford University Press, 1983.

———. "Is God a Liar? (Genesis 2–3)—and Related Matters." *Journal of Theological Studies* 57 (2006): 1–22.

———. "Jowett and the 'Original Meaning' of Scripture." *Religious Studies* 18:433–37.

———. "Jowett and the Reading of the Bible 'Like Any Other Book.'" *Horizons in Biblical Theology: An International Dialogue* 4 (1982): 1–44.

———. "The Literal, the Allegorical, and Modern Biblical Scholarship." *Journal for the Study of the Old Testament* 44 (1989): 3–17.

Barth, H., and O. H. Steck. *Exegese des Alten Testaments: Leitfaden der Methodik (Ein Arbeitsbuch für Proseminare, Seminare und Vorlesungen).* Neukirchen-Vluyn: Neukirchener Verlag, 1971, 9th edition 1980.

Barth, Karl. *Die Kirchliche Dogmatik I: Die Lehre vom Worte Gottes,* 2. Zollikon-Zurich: Evangelischer Verlag, 1932. Translated as *Church Dogmatics* I/2. Edinburgh: T. & T. Clark, 1956.

———. *Römerbrief.* Zurich: Theologischer Verlag, 1919. Translated as *The Epistle to the Romans.* 2nd edition, London: Oxford University Press, 1933, from 6th German edition.

———. *Das Wort Gottes und die Theologie.* Munich: Kaiser Verlag, 1925.

Barthes, Roland. "The Death of the Author." In *Modern Criticism and Theory: A Reader*, ed. David Lodge with Nigel Wood, 146–50. 2nd edition, Harlow: Longman, 2000.

———. "Textual Analysis: Poe's 'Valdemar.'" In *Modern Criticism and Theory: A Reader*, ed. David Lodge with Nigel Wood, 151–72. 2nd edition, Harlow: Longman, 2000.

Barton, John. "Canon and Old Testament Interpretation." In *In Search of True Wisdom: Essays in Old Testament Interpretation in Honour of Ronald E. Clements*, ed. E. Ball, 37–52. Journal for the Study of the Old Testament: Supplement Series 300. Sheffield: Sheffield Academic Press, 1999.

———. "Classifying Biblical Criticism." *Journal for the Study of the Old Testament* 29 (1984): 19–35.

———. *The Future of Old Testament Study*. Oxford: Clarendon Press, 1993.

———. "Historical-critical Approaches." In *The Cambridge Companion to Biblical Interpretation*, ed. John Barton, 9–20. Cambridge: Cambridge University Press, 1998.

———. *People of the Book? The Authority of the Bible in Christianity*. London: SPCK, 1988; 2nd edition 1993.

———. "Reading the Bible as Literature: Two Questions for Biblical Critics." *Journal of Theology and Literature* 1 (1987): 135–53.

———. *Reading the Old Testament: Method in Biblical Study*. London: Darton, Longman & Todd, 1984; 2nd edition 1996.

———. "Theology and Other Sciences." *Theology* 99 (1996): 52–58.

———. "Unity and Diversity in the Biblical Canon." In *Die Einheit der Schrift und die Vielfalt des Kanons/The Unity of Scripture and the Diversity of the Canon*, ed. J. Barton and M. Wolter, 11–26. Beihefte zur Zeitschrift für die neutestamentliche Wissenschaft 118. Berlin: W. de Gruyter, 2003.

———. "What Is a Book? Modern Exegesis and the Literary Conventions of Ancient Israel." In *Intertextuality in Ugarit and Israel: Papers Read at the Tenth Joint Meeting of the Society for Old Testament Study and Het Oudtestamentische Werkgezelschap in Nederland en België, Held at Oxford, 1997*, ed. J. C. de Moor, 1–14. Oudtestamentische Studiën 40. Leiden: Brill, 1998.

Bauckham, Richard. *James: Wisdom of James, Disciple of Jesus the Sage*. New York: Routledge, 1999.

Berger, Benjamin L. "Qoheleth and the Exigencies of the Absurd." *Biblical Interpretation* 9 (2001): 141–79.

Berger, Klaus. *Hermeneutik des Neuen Testaments*. Gütersloh: Mohn, 1988.

Berlinerblau, Jacques. "The Unspeakable in Biblical Scholarship." SBL Forum, March 2006.

Borges, Jorge L. "Pierre Menard, Author of the Quixote." In *Labyrinths: Selected Stories and Other Writings*, 62–71. Harmondsworth: Penguin, 1970.

Bouyer, Louis. "Erasmus in Relation to the Medieval Biblical Tradition." In *Cambridge History of the Bible*, vol. 2. Cambridge: Cambridge University Press, 1963.

Braaten, Carl E., and Robert W. Jenson. "Introduction: Gospel, Church, and Scripture." In *Reclaiming the Bible for the Church*, ix–xii. Grand Rapids: Eerdmans, 1995; Edinburgh: T. & T. Clark, 1996.

———, eds. *Reclaiming the Bible for the Church*. Grand Rapids: Eerdmans, 1995; Edinburgh: T. & T. Clark, 1996.

Breen, Quirinius. *John Calvin: A Study in French Humanism*. Grand Rapids: Eerdmans, 1931.

Bright, John. *A History of Israel*. London: SCM, 1960; 3rd edition 1981.

Bultmann, Rudolf. *Die Exegese des Theodor von Mopsuestia.* Stuttgart: Kohlhammer, 1984.

Burger, Christoph, August den Hollander, and Ulrich Schmid. *Evangelienharmonien des Mittelalters.* Assen: Royal Van Gorcum, 2004.

Burridge, Richard A. *What Are the Gospels? A Comparison with Graeco-Roman Biography.* Cambridge: Cambridge University Press, 1992.

Burrow, J. A. *Medieval Writers and Their Work: Middle English Literature and Its Background 1100–1500.* Oxford: Oxford University Press, 1982.

Carr, David. "Reading for Unity in Isaiah." *Journal for the Study of the Old Testament* 57 (1993): 61–80.

Carroll, Robert. "Poststructuralist Approaches." In *The Cambridge Companion to Biblical Interpretation,* ed. John Barton, 50–66. Cambridge: Cambridge University Press, 1998.

Cassuto, Umberto. *The Documentary Hypothesis and the Composition of the Pentateuch.* Jerusalem: Magnes Press, 1961; (Hebrew original; Jerusalem: Hebrew University, 1941).

Catechesis Ecclesiarum Polonicarum (1609). Irenopoli, 1659.

Chapman, Mark D., ed. *The Future of Liberal Theology.* Aldershot: Ashgate, 2002.

Cheyne, T. K. *Founders of Old Testament Criticism.* London: Methuen, 1893.

Childs, Brevard S. *Biblical Theology in Crisis.* Philadelphia: Fortress Press, 1970.

———. "Interpretation in Faith: The Theological Responsibility of an Old Testament Commentary." *Interpretation* 18 (1964): 432–49.

———. *Introduction to the Old Testament as Scripture.* Philadelphia: Fortress Press; London: SCM, 1979.

———. "The Sensus Literalis of Scripture: An Ancient and Modern Problem." In *Beiträge zur Alttestamentlichen Theologie: Festschrift für Walther Zimmerli zum 70. Geburtstag,* ed. H. Donner, R. Hanhart, and R. Smend, 80–95. Göttingen: Vandenhoeck & Ruprecht, 1977.

———. *The Struggle to Understand Isaiah as Christian Scripture.* Grand Rapids: Eerdmans, 2004.

Clines, David J. A. *Interested Parties: The Ideology of Writers and Readers of the Hebrew Bible.* Sheffield: Sheffield Academic Press, 1995.

Coleman, Christopher B. *The Treatise of Lorenzo Valla on the Donation of Constantine.* Toronto: University of Toronto Press, in association with the Renaissance Society of America Press, 1993.

Conrad, Edgar W. *Reading Isaiah.* Overtures to Biblical Theology 27. Minneapolis: Fortress Press, 1991.

———. *Reading the Latter Prophets: Toward a New Canonical Criticism.* Journal for the Study of the Old Testament: Supplement Series 376. London: T. & T. Clark International, 2003.

Cosgrove, Charles H., ed. *The Meanings We Choose: Hermeneutical Ethics, Indeterminacy and the Conflict of Interpretations.* Journal for the Study of the Old Testament: Supplement Series 411. London: T. & T. Clark, 2004.

Cunningham, Valentine. *Reading after Theory.* Oxford: Blackwell, 2002.

Dahl, Niels A. "'Widersprüche in der Bibel, ein altes hermeneutisches Problem." *Studia Theologica* 25 (1971): 1–19.

Dahood, Mitchell. *Psalms II—51–100.* Anchor Bible. New York: Doubleday, 1968.

Daiches, David. *Critical Approaches to Literature.* London and New York: Longman, 2nd edition, 1981.

Daniel, O. E. *A Harmony of the Four Gospels.* Grand Rapids: Baker Book House, 2nd edition, 1996.

Davies, Philip R. *In Search of "Ancient Israel."* Journal for the Study of the Old Testament: Supplement Series 148. Sheffield: JSOT Press, 1992.

———. *Whose Bible Is It Anyway?* Sheffield: Sheffield Academic Press, 1995.

Diestel, Ludwig. *Geschichte des Alten Testaments in der christlichen Kirche.* Jena: Hermann Dufft, 1869.

Dilthey, Wilhelm. *Gesammelte Schriften.* Stuttgart: Teubner, 1961.

———. *Selected Writings.* Edited, translated, and introduced by H. P. Rickman. Cambridge: Cambridge University Press, 1976.

Dobbs-Allsop, F. W. "Rethinking Historical Criticism." *Biblical Interpretation* 7 (1999): 235–71.

Donfried, Karl P. "Alien Hermeneutics and the Misappropriation of Scripture." In *Reclaiming the Bible for the Church*, ed. Carl E. Braaten and Robert W. Jenson, 19–45. Grand Rapids: Eerdmans, 1995; Edinburgh: T. & T. Clark, 1996.

Ebach, Jürgen. *Ursprung und Ziel: Erinnerte Zukunft und erhoffte Vergangenheit. Exegesen, Reflexionen, Geschichten.* Neukirchen-Vluyn: Neukirchener Verlag, 1986.

Ebeling, G. "Bedeutung der historisch-kritischen Methode." *Zeitschrift für Theologie und Kirche* 47 (1950): 1–19. Translated as "The Significance of the Critical Historical Method for Church and Theology in Protestantism." In his *Word and Faith*, 17–61. London: SCM, 1963. *Word and Faith* is a translation of *Wort und Glaube* (Tübingen: Mohr Siebeck, 1960).

———. "The Bible as a Document of the University." In *The Bible as a Document of the University*, ed. Hans Dieter Betz, 5–23. Chico, CA: Scholars Press, 1981.

———. "Wort Gottes und Hermeneutik." *Zeitschrift für Theologie und Kirche* 56 (1959): 224–51.

Eco, Umberto. *Lector in fabula: La cooperazione interpretativa nei testi narrativi.* Milan: Tascabilli Bompiani, 1979.

———. *The Limits of Interpretation.* Bloomington and Indianapolis: Indiana University Press, 1990.

———. *The Open Work.* Cambridge, MA: Harvard University Press, 1989. Translation of *Opera aperta*, 1962.

———. *The Role of the Reader: Explorations in the Semiotics of Texts.* London: Hutchinson, 1981.

Eco, Umberto, with Richard Rorty, Jonathan Culler, Christine Brooke-Rose, ed. Stefan Collini. *Interpretation and Overinterpretation.* Cambridge: Cambridge University Press, 1992.

Eichrodt, Walter. *Theologie des Alten Testaments.* Stuttgart: E. Klotz, vol. 1, 1933; vol. 2, 1935; vol. 3, 1939. Translated as *Theology of the Old Testament.* London: SCM, vol. 1, 1960 (from 6th edition of the German, 1959); vol. 2, 1967 (from 5th edition of the German of vols. 2 and 3 in one volume, 1964).

Fischer, Rainer. *Die Kunst des Bibellesens: Theologische Ästhetik am Beispiel des Schriftverständnisses.* Frankfurt am Main: Peter Lang, 1996.

Flacius Illyricus, Matthias. *De ratione cognoscendi sacras littera*s. Edited by L. Geldsetzer. Düsseldorf: Stern Verlag, 1968.

Frank, Manfred. *Schleiermachers Hermeneutik und Kritik.* Frankfurt am Main: Suhrkamp, 1977.

Freund, Elizabeth. *The Return of the Reader: Reader-response Criticism.* New Accents, edited by T. Hawkes. London and New York: Methuen, 1987.

Frye, Northrop. *Anatomy of Criticism.* Princeton, NJ: Princeton University Press, 1957.

Gadamer, Hans-Georg. *Wahrheit und Methode: Grundzüge einer philosophischen Hermeneutik.* Tübingen: Mohr, 4th edition, 1975. Translated as *Truth and Method.* New York: Crossroad, 1975.

Garfinkel, Stephen. "Clearing *Peshat* and *Derash.*" In *Hebrew Bible/Old Testament: The History of Its Interpretation,* ed. M. Sæbø, I/2:129–34. Göttingen: Vandenhoeck & Ruprecht, 1996.

Gore, Charles, ed. *Lux Mundi: A Series of Studies in the Religion of the Incarnation.* London: John Murray, 1889.

Goshen-Gottstein, M. H. "Christianity, Judaism, and Modern Bible Study." Supplements to Vetus Testamentum 28 (1975): 68–88.

Grabbe, Lester L. *Ezra and Nehemiah.* Old Testament Readings. London: Routledge, 1998.

Grant, Robert M., with David Tracy. *A Short History of the Interpretation of the Bible.* London: SCM, 1984.

Greene-McCreight, K. E. *Ad Litteram: How Augustine, Calvin and Barth Read the "Plain Sense" of Genesis 1–3.* Issues in Systematic Theology 5. New York: Peter Lang, 1999.

Greer, Rowan A. *Theodore of Mopsuestia: Exegete and Theologian.* London: Faith Press, 1961.

Halivni, David Weiss. *Peshat and Derash: Plain and Applied Meaning in Rabbinic Exegesis.* New York and Oxford: Oxford University Press, 1991.

———. *Revelation Restored: Divine Writ and Critical Responses.* Radical Traditions: Theology in a Postcritical Key. London: SCM, 2001.

Hartlich, Christian. "Historisch-kritische Methode in ihrer Anwendung auf Geschehensaussagen der Hl. Schrift." *Zeitschrift für Theologie und Kirche* 75 (1978): 467–84.

Harvey, Van A. *The Historian and the Believer: The Morality of Historical Knowledge and Christian Belief.* London: SCM, 1967.

Hathaway, Baxter. *The Age of Criticism: The Late Renaissance in Italy.* Ithaca, NY: Cornell University Press, 1962.

Hill, Robert C. *Reading the Old Testament in Antioch.* The Bible in Ancient Christianity 3. Leiden: Brill, 2005.

Hirsch, E. D., Jr. *The Aims of Interpretation.* Chicago and London: University of Chicago Press, 1976.

———. "Meaning and Significance Reinterpreted." *Critical Inquiry* 11 (1984): 202–25.

———. "Past Intentions and Present Meanings" (The F. W. Bateson Memorial Lecture). *Essays in Criticism* 33 (1984): 79–98.

———. *Validity in Interpretation.* New Haven and London: Yale University Press, 1967.

Hornig, Gottfried. *Die Anfänge der historisch-kritischen Theologie: J. S. Semlers Schriftverständnis und seine Stellung zu Luther.* Forschungen zur systematischen Theologie und Religionsphilosophie 8. Göttingen: Vandenhoeck & Ruprecht, 1961.

Jardine, Lisa. "Portia's Ring: Unruly Women and Structures of Exchange in *The Merchant of Venice.*" In *The Merchant of Venice,* ed. M. Coyle. New Casebooks. Basingstoke: Macmillan, 1998.

———. *Still Harping on Daughters: Women and Drama in the Age of Shakespeare.* London and New York: Harvester Wheatsheaf, 2nd edition, 1989.

Jowett, Benjamin. "On the Interpretation of Scripture." In *Essays and Reviews.* London: Longman, Green, Longman, & Roberts, 6th edition, 1861.

Kidner, Derek. *Psalms 73–150: A Commentary on Books III–V of the Psalms.* Leicester: Inter-Varsity Press, 1975.

Kimmerle, H. "Hermeneutical Theory or Ontological Hermeneutics." *Journal for Theology and the Church* 4 (1968): 107–21.

Kingsmill, Edmée. *The Song of Songs and the Eros of God.* Oxford: Oxford University Press, forthcoming.

Kinney, A. F. *Continental Humanist Poetics: Studies in Erasmus, Castiglione, Marguerite de Navarre, Rabelais, and Cervantes.* Amherst: University of Massachusetts Press, 1989.

Kitchen, Kenneth A. *On The Reliability of the Old Testament.* Grand Rapids: Eerdmans, 2003.

Kosellek, Reinhart. *Critique and Crisis: Enlightenment and the Pathogenesis of Modern Society.* Oxford, New York, and Hamburg: Berg, 1988. Translation of *Kritik und Krise. Eine Studie zur Pathogenese der bürgerlichen Welt.* Freiburg and Munich: Karl Alber, 1959.

Kraeling, Emil G. *The Old Testament since the Reformation.* London: Lutterworth, 1955.

Kraus, Hans-Joachim. *Geschichte der historisch-kritischen Erforschung des Alten Testaments von der Reformation bis zur Gegenwart.* Neukirchen Kreis Moers: Verlag der Buchhandlung des Erziehungsvereins, 1956; 3rd edition, Neukirchen-Vluyn: Neukirchener Verlag, 1982.

Kugel, James L., and Rowan A. Greer. *Early Biblical Interpretation.* Philadelphia: Westminster Press, 1986.

Kuhrt, Amélie. "Israelite and Near Eastern Historiography." In *Congress Volume Oslo 1998,* ed. A. Lemaire and M. Sæbø, 257–79. Supplements to Vetus Testamentum 80. Leiden: Brill, 2000.

Kümmel, Werner G. *Das Neue Testament: Geschichte der Erforschung seiner Probleme.* Freiburg: Alber, 1958, 1970. Translated as *The New Testament: The History of the Investigation of Its Problems.* London: SCM, 1973.

Lambe, Patrick J. "Biblical Criticism and Censorship in Ancien Régime France: The Case of Richard Simon." *Harvard Theological Review* 78 (1985): 149–77.

———. "Critics and Skeptics in the Seventeenth-Century Republic of Letters." *Harvard Theological Review* 81 (1988): 271–96.

Leavis, F. R. "Literary Criticism and Philosophy: A Reply." *Scrutiny* 6:1 (1937): 59–70.

Lehmann, K. "Der hermeneutische Horizont der historisch-kritischen Exegese." In *Einführung in die Methoden der biblischen Exegese,* ed. J. Schreiner. Würzburg: Echter Verlag, 1971.

Levenson, Jon. "Why Jews Are Not Interested in Biblical Theology." In *Judaic Perspectives on Ancient Israel,* ed. J. Neusner, B. A. Levine, and E. S. Frerichs, 281–307. Philadelphia: Fortress Press, 1987.

Liebing, H. "Historisch-kritische Theologie: Zum 100. Todestag F. C. Baurs am 2.12.1960." *Zeitschrift für Theologie und Kirche* 57 (1960): 70–93.

Lindbeck, George. *The Nature of Doctrine: Religion and Theology in a Postliberal Age.* London: SPCK, 1984.

Lindo, E. H. *The Conciliator of R. Manasseh ben Israel; A Reconcilement of the Apparent Contradictions in Holy Scripture,* 2 vols. London, 1842.

Lodge, David. *Author, Author.* London: Secker & Warburg, 2004.

Loewe, Ralph. "The 'Plain' Meaning of Scripture in Early Jewish Exegesis." In *Papers of the Institute of Jewish Studies,* ed. J. G. Weiss, 1:140–85. Jerusalem: Magnes Press, 1964.

Louth, Andrew. *Discerning the Mystery: An Essay on the Nature of Theology.* Oxford: Clarendon Press, 1983.

Lowth, Robert. *On the Sacred Poetry of the Hebrews.* London: Routledge/Thoemmes Press, 1997.

Luther, Martin. *Luther's Works*. Edited by Jaroslav Pelikan. Philadelphia: Fortress Press, 1955–86.

MacIntyre, Alasdair. *After Virtue*. London: Duckworth, 1981.

McEvoy, Sean. *Shakespeare: The Basics*. London and New York: Routledge, 2000.

Metzger, Bruce M. *The Canon of the New Testament: Its Origin, Development, and Significance*. Oxford: Clarendon Press, 1987.

Metzger, Paul. *Katechon: II Thess 2.1–12 im Horizont apokalyptischen Denkens*. Berlin: W. de Gruyter, 2005.

Minear, Paul S. *The Bible and the Historian: Breaking the Silence about God in Biblical Studies*. Nashville: Abingdon Press, 2002.

Minnis, A. J. *Medieval Theory of Authorship: Scholastic Literary Attitudes in the Later Middle Ages*. London: Scolar Press, 1984.

Moberly, R. W. L. *The Bible, Theology, and Faith: A Study of Abraham and Jesus*. Cambridge: Cambridge University Press, 2000.

Montrose, Louis A. "Professing the Renaissance: The Poetics and Politics of Culture." In *The New Historicism*, ed. H. Aram Veeser. New York and London: Routledge, 1989.

———. "'Shaping Fantasies': Figurations of Gender and Power in Elizabethan Culture." In *A Midsummer Night's Dream*, ed. R. Dutton. New Casebooks. Basingstoke: Macmillan, 1983.

Morgan, Robert, with John Barton. *Biblical Interpretation*. The Oxford Bible. Oxford: Oxford University Press, 1988.

Mowinckel, Sigmund. *The Psalms in Israel's Worship*. Oxford: Blackwell, 1962. Translation of *Offersang og Sangoffer*. Oslo: Aschehoug, 1951.

Newman, Karen. "Renaissance Family Politics and Shakespeare's *The Taming of the Shrew*." In *Shakespeare's Comedies*, ed. G. Waller. Harlow: Longman, 1986.

North, C. R. "The Pentateuch." In *The Old Testament and Modern Study: A Generation of Discovery and Research*, ed. H. H. Rowley, 48–83. Oxford: Clarendon Press, 1951.

Noth, Martin. *Überlieferungsgeschichte des Pentateuch*. Stuttgart: Kohlhammer, 1948. Translated as *A History of Pentateuchal Traditions*. Englewood Cliffs, NJ: Prentice-Hall, 1972.

———. *Überlieferungsgeschichtliche Studien I*. Schriften der Königsberger Gelehrten Gesellschaft 18. Halle: Niemeyer Verlag, 1943. 2nd edition, Tübingen: Niemeyer Verlag, 1957. Translated as *The Deuteronomistic History*. Journal for the Study of the Old Testament: Supplement Series 15. Sheffield: JSOT Press, 1981.

Oeming, Manfred. *Gesamtbiblische Theologien der Gegenwart*. Stuttgart: Kohlhammer, 1985.

———. "'Man kann nur verstehen, was man liebt': Erwägungen zum Verhältnis von Glauben und Verstehen als einem Problem alttestamentlicher Hermeneutik." In *Altes Testament und christliche Verkündigung: Festschrift für Antonius H. J. Gunneweg zum 65. Gerburtstag*, ed. Manfred Oeming and Axel Graupner. Stuttgart: Kohlhammer, 1987.

O'Neill, J. C. "Biblical Criticism." In *Anchor Bible Dictionary*, ed. David Noel Freedman, 1:725–30. New York and London: Doubleday, 1992.

Origen. *La lettre à Africanus sur l'histoire de Suzanne*. Sources Chrétiennes 302. Paris: Éditions du Cerf, 1983.

Pannenberg, Wolfhart. "The Crisis of the Scripture Principle." In *Basic Questions in Theology*, 1:1–14. London: SCM, 1970. Translation of *Grundfragen systematischer Theologie*. Göttingen: Vandenhoeck & Ruprecht, 1967.

Parker, David C. *The Living Text of the Gospels*. Cambridge: Cambridge University Press, 1997.

Patterson, S. J. "Harmony of the Gospels." In *Anchor Bible Dictionary*, ed. David Noel Freedman. New York: Doubleday, 1992, vol. 3.

Perlitt, Lothar. *Vatke und Wellhausen. Geschichtsphilosophische Voraussetzungen und historiographische Motive für die Darstellung der Religion und Geschichte Israels durch Wilhelm Vatke und Julius Wellhausen*. Beihefte zur Zeitschrift für die alttestamentliche Wissenschaft 94. Berlin: W. de Gruyter, 1965.

Pesch, C. "Über Evangelienharmonien." *Zeitschrift für Theologie und Kirche* 10 (1886): 225–44 and 454–80.

Petersen, W. L. *Tatian's Diatessaron: Its Creation, Dissemination, Significance, and History in Scholarship. Vigiliae Christianae* Supplement 25. Leiden: Brill, 1994.

Pontifical Biblical Institute. *The Interpretation of the Bible in the Church*. Rome: Libreria editrice vaticana, 1993.

The Postmodern Bible. By the Bible and Culture Collective. New Haven and London: Yale University Press, 1995.

Rad, Gerhard von. *Genesis: A Commentary*. London: SCM, 1961; 2nd edition 1972. Translated from *Das Erste Buch Mose, Genesis*. Göttingen: Vandenhoeck & Ruprecht, 1956.

———. *Die Priesterschrift im Hexateuch literarisch untersucht und theologisch gewertet*. Stuttgart and Berlin: Kohlhammer, 1934.

———. "The Theological Problem of the Old Testament Doctrine of Creation." In *The Problem of the Hexateuch and Other Essays*, 131–43. Edinburgh and London: Oliver & Boyd, 1966. Translated from *Gesammelte Studien zum Alten Testament*. Munich: Kaiser Verlag, 1936.

Radford, Colin, and Sally Minogue. *The Nature of Criticism*. Brighton: Harvester Press, 1981.

Rashi's Commentary on Psalms, with English Translation, Introduction and Notes by Mayer I. Gruber. Atlanta: Scholars Press, 1998.

Reimarus, H. S. *Fragments*. Philadelphia: Fortress Press, 1970.

Reventlow, H. Graf. *Bibelautorität und Geist der Moderne: Die Bedeutung des Bibelverständnisses für die geistesgeschichtliche und politische Entwicklung in England von der Reformation bis zur Aufklärung*. Göttingen: Vandenhoeck & Ruprecht, 1980. Translated as *The Authority of the Bible and the Rise of the Modern World*. London: SCM, 1984.

———. *Epochen der Bibelauslegung IV: Von der Aufklärung bis zum 20. Jahrhundert*. Munich: C. H. Beck, 2001.

Ricoeur, Paul. *Essays on Biblical Interpretation*. Edited with an Introduction by Lewis S. Mudge. London: SPCK, 1981.

———. *The Symbolism of Evil*. Boston: Beacon Press, 1969. Translated from *La Symbolique du mal*. Paris: Aubier, 1960.

Rogerson, John W., ed. *Beginning Old Testament Study*. London: SPCK, 1983.

———. *Old Testament Criticism in the Nineteenth Century: England and Germany*. London: SPCK, 1984.

———. *W. M. L. de Wette, Founder of Modern Biblical Criticism: An Intellectual Biography*. Sheffield: JSOT Press, 1992.

Sanders, E. P. *The Historical Figure of Jesus*. London: Allen Lane, Penguin Press, 1993.

———. *Paul and Palestinian Judaism: A Comparison of Patterns of Religion*. London: SCM, 1977.

Schleiermacher, Friedrich. *Schleiermacher: Hermeneutik und Kritik*. Edited by F. Lücke. Berlin, 1838.

Schmidt, Werner H. "Grenzen und Vorzüge historisch-kritischer Exegese." "Zugänge zur Bibel," *Evangelische Theologie* 45 (1985): 469–82.

Scholder, Klaus. *Ursprünge und Probleme der Bibelkritik im 17. Jahrhundert (Ein Beitrag zur Entstehung der historisch-kritischen Theologie)*. Forschungen zur Geschichte und Lehre des Protestantismus 10:33, Munich: Kaiser Verlag, 1966. Translated as *The Birth of Modern Critical Theology*. London: SCM; Philadelphia: Trinity Press International, 1990.

Schüssler Fiorenza, Elisabeth. "Biblical Interpretation and Critical Commitment." *Studia Theologica* 43 (1989): 5–18.

Schwöbel, C., ed. *Karl Barth—Martin Rade, Ein Briefwechsel*. Gütersloh: Mohn, 1981.

Segovia, Fernando F. *Decolonizing Biblical Studies: A View from the Margins*. Maryknoll, NY: Orbis Books, 2000.

Seitz, Christopher R. *Word without End: The Old Testament as Abiding Theological Witness*. Grand Rapids: Eerdmans, 1998.

Sharp, Carolyn J. "Ironic Representation, Authorial Voice, and Meaning in Qohelet." *Biblical Interpretation* 12 (2004): 37–68.

Sherwin-White, A. N. *Roman Society and Roman Law in the New Testament*. Oxford: Clarendon Press, 1963.

Sherwood, Yvonne. *A Biblical Text and Its Afterlives: The Survival of Jonah in Western Culture*. Cambridge: Cambridge University Press, 2000.

Sidney, Philip. *Selected Writings*. Edited by Richard Dutton. Manchester: Carcanet Press, 1987.

Smalley, Beryl. *The Study of the Bible in the Middle Ages*. Oxford: Basil Blackwell, 1941.

Smend, Rudolf. *Deutsche Alttestamentler in drei Jahrhunderten*. Göttingen: Vandenhoeck & Ruprecht, 1989.

———. *Julius Wellhausen: Ein Bahnbrecher in drei Disziplinen*. Munich: Carl Friedrich von Siemens Stiftung, 2006.

———. "Karl Barth als Ausleger der Heiligen Schrift." In *Theologie als Christologie: Zum Werk und Leben Karl Barths. Ein Symposium*, ed. H. Köckert and W. Krötke. Berlin: Evangelische Verlagsanstalt, 1988.

———. "Nachkritische Schriftauslegung." In *Parrhesia. Karl Barth zum 80. Geburtstag*, ed. E. Busch, J. Fangmeier, and M. Geiger, 215–37. Zurich: EVZ-Verlag, 1966. Also in Smend, *Die Mitte des Alten Testaments*, 212–32. Munich: Kaiser Verlag, 1986. Also in Smend, *Bibel und Wissenschaft*, 230–50. Tübingen: Mohr Siebeck, 2004.

———. "Theologie im Alten Testament." In *Verifikationen. Festschrift für Gerhard Ebeling zum 70. Geburtstag*, ed. E. Jüngel, J. Wallmann, and W. Werbeck, 11–26. Tübingen: J. C. B. Mohr (Paul Siebeck), 1982. Reprinted in R. Smend, *Die Mitte des Alten Testaments*, 104–17. Munich: Kaiser Verlag, 1986.

Sommer, Benjamin. "Inner-biblical Interpretation." In *The Jewish Study Bible*, ed. Adele Berlin and Mark Z. Brettler. New York: Oxford University Press, 2004.

———. "The Scroll of Isaiah as Jewish Scripture, or, Why Jews Don't Read Books." In *SBL Seminar Papers: 132nd Annual Meeting*, 225–42. Atlanta: Scholars Press, 1996.

Soulen, R. Kendall. *The God of Israel and Christian Theology*. Minneapolis: Fortress Press, 1996.

Spangenberg, Izak J. J. "Irony in the Book of Qoheleth." *Journal for the Study of the Old Testament* 72 (1996): 57–69.

Spinoza, Baruch. *Tractatus theologico-politicus*. New York: E. J. Brill, 1989.

Spriggs, David G. *Two Old Testament Theologies: A Comparative Evaluation of the Contribution of Eichrodt and von Rad to Our Understanding of the Nature of Old Testament Theology*. London: SCM, 1974.

Staerk, Willy. "Willy Staerk." In *Die Religion der Gegenwart in Selbstdarstellungen*, ed. Erich Stange, 5:159–206. Leipzig: F. Meiner, 1929.

Steinmann, Jean. *Biblical Criticism*. London: Burns & Oates, 1959.

Stendahl, Krister. "The Bible as a Classic and the Bible as Holy Scripture." *Journal of Biblical Literature* 103 (1984): 3–10.

———. "Biblical Theology, Contemporary." In *The Interpreter's Dictionary of the Bible*, 1:418–32. Nashville: Abingdon Press, 1962. Reprinted in *Reading the Bible in the Global Village: Helsinki*, ed. Heikki Räisänen et al., 67–106. Atlanta: Society of Biblical Literature, 2000.

———. "Dethroning Biblical Imperialism in Theology." In *Reading the Bible in the Global Village: Helsinki*, ed. Heikki Räisänen et al., 61–66. Atlanta: Society of Biblical Literature, 2000.

Strauss, David Friedrich. *Das Leben Jesu*. Tübingen, 1835. Translated as *The Life of Jesus Critically Examined*. London: SCM, 1973.

Strauss, Leo. *Die Religionskritik Spinozas als Grundlage seiner Bibelwissenschaft: Untersuchungen zu Spinozas theologisch-politischem Traktat*. Berlin: Akademie-Verlag, 1930.

Stuhlmacher, Peter. *Schriftauslegung auf dem Wege zur biblischen Theologie*. Göttingen: Vandenhoeck & Ruprecht, 1975. Translated as *Historical Criticism and Theological Interpretation of Scripture: Toward a Hermeneutic of Consent*. Philadelphia: Fortress, 1977.

Sugirtharajah, R. S. "Critics, Tools, and the Global Arena." In *Reading the Bible in the Global Village: Helsinki*, ed. Heikki Räisänen et al., 49–60. Atlanta: Society of Biblical Literature, 2000.

Swift, Jonathan. *A Modest Proposal and Other Sceptical Works*. New York: Dover, 1995.

Tanner, Kathryn. "Theology and the Plain Sense." In *Scriptural Authority and Narrative Interpretation*, ed. G. Green, 59–78. Philadelphia: Fortress Press, 1987.

Tate, Marvin E. *Psalms 51–100*. Word Bible Commentary. Dallas: Word Books, 1990.

Theissen, Gerd. *Argumente für einen kritischen Glauben*. Theologische Existenz heute 202. Munich: Kaiser Verlag, 1978. Translated as *On Having a Critical Faith*. London: SCM, 1979.

Theissen, Gerd, and Dagmar Winter. *The Quest for the Plausible Jesus: The Question of Criteria*. Louisville, KY, and London: Westminster John Knox, 2002.

Theodoret of Cyrus. *Commentary on the Psalms, Psalms 1–72*. Fathers of the Church 101. Washington, DC: Catholic University of America Press, 2000.

Thiselton, Anthony C. "The New Hermeneutic." In *New Testament Interpretation*, ed. I. H. Marshall, 308–33. Carlisle: Paternoster, 1977.

———. *New Horizons in Hermeneutics: The Theory and Practice of Transforming Biblical Reading*. London: HarperCollins, 1992.

Tillyard, E. M. W., and C. S. Lewis. *The Personal Heresy: A Controversy*. London: Oxford University Press, 1939.

Tolkien, J. R. R. *Beowulf: The Monster and the Critics (The Sir Israel Gollancz Lecture for 1936)*. Oxford: Oxford University Press, 1958.

Trible, Phyllis. *God and the Rhetoric of Sexuality*. Philadelphia: Fortress Press, 1978.

Trilling, Lionel. *The Liberal Imagination*. New York: Viking Press, 1950.

Troeltsch, Ernst. *Gesammelte Schriften*. Tübingen: J. C. B. Mohr, 1913.

———. "Historiography." In *Encyclopedia of Religion and Ethics*, ed. James Hastings, 6: 716–23. New York: Charles Scribner's Sons, 1914.

Vanhoozer, Kevin J. *Is there a Meaning in This Text?* Leicester: Apollos, 1998.

Van Seters, John. *The Edited Bible*. Winona Lake, IN: Eisenbrauns, 2006.

Vermes, Geza. *Jesus the Jew: A Historian's Reading of the Gospels*. London: Collins, 1973.

Vosté, J.-M. "Le commentaire de Théodore de Mopsueste sur Saint Jean, d'après la version syriaque." *Revue biblique* 32 (1923): 244–45.

Watson, Francis. *Text and Truth: Redefining Biblical Theology*. Edinburgh: T. & T. Clark, 1997.

———. *Text, Church and World: Biblical Interpretation in Theological Perspective*. Edinburgh: T. & T. Clark, 1994.

Weiser, Artur. *The Psalms: A Commentary*. London: SCM, 1962.

Weizsäcker, C. F. von. *Der Garten des Menschlichen*. Munich: Hanser, 9th edition, 1984.

Wellhausen, Julius. *Geschichte Israels I*. Berlin: G. Reimer, 1878. 2nd edition, 1883 as *Prolegomena zur Geschichte Israels*. Translated as *Prolegomena to the History of Israel*. Edinburgh: A. & C. Black, 1885.

Westermann, Claus. *Genesis 1–11: A Commentary*. London: SPCK, 1984.

Wette, W. M. L. de. *Beiträge zur Einleitung in das Alte Testament*, 2 vols. Halle: Schimmelpfennig, 1806–7.

Williamson, Hugh G. M. *The Book Called Isaiah: Deutero-Isaiah's Role in Composition and Redaction*. Oxford: Clarendon Press, 1994.

Wink, Walter. *The Bible in Human Transformation*. Philadelphia: Fortress Press, 1973.

Wünsch, Dieter. "Evangelienharmonie." In *Theologische Realenzyklopedie*, 1:626–36. Berlin: W. de Gruyter, 1982.

Yarchin, William. *History of Biblical Interpretation: A Reader*. Peabody, MA: Hendrickson, 2004.

Young, Frances M. *Biblical Exegesis and the Formation of Christian Culture*. Cambridge: Cambridge University Press, 1997.

———. "The Rhetorical Schools and Their Influence on Patristic Exegesis." In *The Making of Orthodoxy: Essays in Honour of Henry Chadwick*, ed. Rowan Williams, 182–99. Cambridge: Cambridge University Press, 1989.

Zaharopoulos, Dimitri Z. *Theodore of Mopsuestia on the Bible: A Study of His Old Testament Exegesis*. New York: Paulist Press, 1989.

Zimmerli, Walther. *Ezekiel: A Commentary on the Book of the Prophet Ezekiel*. Philadelphia: Fortress Press, 1979–83.

Index of Authors